Dramatic Spaces

For literary scholars, plays are texts; for scenographers, plays are performances. Yet clearly a drama is *both* text and performance. *Dramatic Spaces* examines period-specific stage-spaces in order to assess how design shaped the thematic and experiential dimensions of plays. This book highlights the stakes of the debate about spatiality and the role of the spectator in the auditorium—if audience members are co-creators of the drama, how do they contribute?

The book investigates:

- Roman comedy and Shakespearean dramas in which the stage-space itself constituted the primary scenographic element and actors' bodies shaped the playing space more than did sets or props
- the use of paid applauders in nineteenth-century Parisian theaters and how this practice reconfigured theatrical space
- transactions between stage designers and spectators, including work by László Moholy-Nagy, William Ritman, and Eiko Ishioka.

Dramatic Spaces does for stage design what reader-response criticism has done for the literary text, with specific case studies on *Coriolanus*, *The Comedy of Errors*, *Romeo and Juliet*, *Tales of Hoffmann*, *M. Butterfly*, and *Tiny Alice* exploring the audience's contribution to the construction of meaning.

Jennifer A. Low is Associate Professor of English at Florida Atlantic University.

Dramatic Spaces

Scenography and Spectatorial Perceptions

Jennifer A. Low

Routledge
Taylor & Francis Group

LONDON AND NEW YORK

First published 2016
by Routledge
2 Park Square, Milton Park, Abingdon, Oxon OX14 4RN

and by Routledge
711 Third Avenue, New York, NY 10017

Routledge is an imprint of the Taylor & Francis Group, an informa business

British Library Cataloguing-in-Publication Data
A catalogue record for this book is available from the British Library

Library of Congress Cataloging in Publication Data
Low, Jennifer A., 1962–
Dramatic spaces : scenography and spectatorial perceptions / Jennifer A. Low.
pages cm
1. Theater audiences. 2. Drama–History and criticism. 3. Theaters–Stage-setting and scenery. 4. Theater–History. I. Title.
PN1590.A9L69 2015
792–dc23
2015003887

ISBN: 978-1-138-85248-8 (hbk)
ISBN: 978-1-315-72345-7 (ebk)

Typeset in Sabon
by Taylor & Francis Books

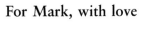

Contents

List of figures

Acknowledgments

In the course of writing this book, I have received support from many quarters; it is my pleasure now to acknowledge those debts.

I would not have been able to complete this project without visits to several libraries and archives, including the Bibliothèque Nationale, the Performing Arts Library at Lincoln Center, and the archive of the Comèdie-Française. My thanks go to the staffs of these institutions.

A sabbatical granted by Florida Atlantic University enabled me to do the research for chapter 4 and revise most of the other chapters. I appreciate the institutional support, as well as the personal support I have received from my department chairs and the deans of my college.

I am grateful for the comments I received on an early version of chapter 6 from members of the research group "Imagining Scenography and Design Theory as a Discipline" at the ASTR conference in 2007. Chapter 2 reached its final form thanks to comments from members of the SAA seminars "Form and Desire on the Early Modern Stage" (Victoria, BC, 2003) and "Ecologies of the Early Modern Body" (New Orleans, 2004). Chapter 1 benefitted from the comments of SAA members in the seminars "Representing Space on the Stage" (San Diego, 2007) and "Theatrical Conventions and Conventions of Theater History" (Dallas, 2008). Brigitte Shull of Palgrave-Macmillan Press helped develop an earlier version of the piece for publication in the essay collection that Nova Myhill and I coedited, *Imagining the Audience in Early Modern Drama, 1558–1642*.

Melissa Evans gave her time and expertise generously, providing much of the foundation of my work on chapter 4 with her skillful translations. Dorothea Trotter also gave invaluable aid, translating several much-needed—and much-valued!—items from German to English. I am grateful for the hours I spent on French texts with several MA students in the Florida Atlantic French department—Alexandre Dufaur, Stephanie Sense, and, most of all, Laurine Ferreira.

Marcella Munson, my wonderful colleague, provided invaluable help in planning and developing chapter 3. Richard Shusterman, Adam Bradford, and Paula Wilson gave me the opportunity to present my work to various groups at Florida Atlantic University.

A number of scholars near and far have suggested sources, discussed my ideas, and read various chapters. The foremost among these is my dear husband, Mark Scroggins. Among the others are my cousin Christopher Long and my friends Marcella Munson, Nova Myhill, Martha Hollander, Wenying Xu, and Stephen Di Benedetto. Matthew Ostrowski read several chapters and offered thoughtful, cogent comments that made the book much better. Judith Haber and Matthew Wilson Smith inspired me with germs of ideas that grew into sturdy plants over the course of several years. Without the aid and encouragement of Shira Malkin and Noel Peacock, I might not have discovered the materials I found in Paris archives. A number of other scholars also generously gave time and thought to questions I put to them. I would like to thank Douglas Cardwell, Virginia Scott, Rachel Brownstein, Arthur Saxon, Susan McCready, Lenard Berlanstein, Rebecca Houze, and Lloyd Engelbrecht here.

The Harvard Theatre Collection at Houghton Library, Harvard University; the Moholy-Nagy Foundation; and Stuart Ostrow, Tracy Roberts, and Eiko Design, Inc. allowed me to reproduce material in their holdings. I am touched by their generosity, and very grateful.

Finally, I would like to acknowledge a special debt to my mother, Stephanie Low, who cultivated my enthusiasm for the theater by sharing her own. Her willingness to take a small child to the theater has given me treasured memories of Peter Brook's *A Midsummer Night's Dream*, Andrei Serban's *Fragments of a Trilogy*, and Hal Prince's 1974 revival of *Candide*, as well as other productions that used space in ways I was able to experience feelingly. I am very grateful that she opened these doors for me on so many occasions.

Publisher's acknowledgments

A version of chapter 1 appeared in *Imagining the Audience in Early Modern Drama, 1558–1642*, eds. Jennifer A. Low and Nova Myhill (New York: Palgrave, 2011), 71–91. A version of chapter 2 appeared in *Comparative Drama* 39.1 (Spring 2005): 1–29.

Introduction

> Any stage is an instrument: some are very complex in what they can offer and what they demand; others are much simpler, but all require the creative input of a number of artists and artisans, skilled in different but related techniques, and all these practitioners need to learn to play the instrument that is the stage, just as a musician needs to learn to play his instrument.
>
> Gay McAuley, *Space in Performance*

> For the practice of theatre history, "What did audiences see?" is a far more productive question than "What did playwrights create?"
>
> Stephen Orgel, *From Script to Stage in Early Modern England*

This book is about the shaping force of performance spaces; it mediates between a literary approach that treats plays as texts and a theatrical approach that assumes a play is a performance. Bringing these perspectives together, this volume explores the role that theatrical design and architecture play in the creation of theatrical meaning. The transaction may occur anterior to the performance, as it does when a playwright's choices are affected by knowledge of a particular venue's parameters, or at the conclusion of the production's development, when the dramatic spectator responds to the interplay of words and performance.

A number of scholars and critics have discussed the mimetic places evoked onstage. Others have analyzed the significance of urban geography in the location of a theater or theaters, but few have turned their attention to the actual performance space to examine the experience of specific dramas.[1] This omission is strange: until the twentieth century, most playwrights in Western Europe could make reasonably accurate assumptions about the shape of the stage upon which their works would be enacted. Some may have seen their role as that of an artisan who provides the basic armature for an elaborate structure that will be finished by other craftsmen; other playwrights insisted that their writing represented an essential artwork that the producers of the performance should endeavor to reproduce. Whatever view they took of their contribution to a performance, they wrote works that exploited the possibilities of the stage they expected the producers to employ. They drew upon theatrical conventions derived from the possibilities of the stage on which plays were most commonly performed. The design of the stage shaped their dramas, regardless of whether that design should be ascribed to an active consciousness.

Few people who think about theater today would dispute that the shape of the stage shapes audience experience—that seeing a play in an intimate store-front theater differs from seeing a play in a Broadway house designed for the Shubert brothers. While there is a substantial body of literature on how actors have used the stage-space (or ought to use it), I focus on the experience of the drama as it is structured by its performance space. My purpose is not to prescribe particular stagings or discover a playwright's original intention. W. B. Worthen rightly notes that the text's efficacy in providing a strong theatrical experience is variable and, as he emphasizes, historical fidelity does not guarantee a production's theatrical vitality.[2] But despite what might be read as his negative perception of historical recovery, Worthen insightfully comments on the text's relation to theatrical conditions: "Dramatic performance is not determined by the text of the play: it strikes a much more interactive, *performative* relation between writing and the spaces, places, and behaviors that give it meaning, *force*, as theatrical action."[3] In this book I place the text in its experiential context in order to improve our understanding of how space shapes perceptions of a performance, and how performance might be shaped by space.

As David Wiles points out in his magisterial *Short History of Western Performance Space*, "Most works of theatre history present theatre spaces as immobile lifeless containers within which unfold the rich and fecund careers of authors and actors."[4] Space or, more properly, spatiality is the final element in "6 Axioms for Environmental Theatre," the well-known manifesto of director and performance studies doyen Richard Schechner, who characterizes "the theatrical event" as consisting of a set of transactions, the primary ones occurring

Among performers.
Among members of the audience.
Between performers and audience.[5]

The transactions he regards as secondary involve "production elements" and, finally, "the space in which it takes place."[6] I assert the primacy of spatiality, its centrality to the relation among performers and audience members, even shaping the choices of the playwright.

This volume consists of three parts. The first segment examines how play-wrights responded to the limitations imposed upon them by the theater spaces for which they wrote. This part of the volume investigates Roman comedy and early modern English drama because, at the times these traditions developed, the stage-space itself constituted the primary scenographic element. Actors' bodies shaped the playing space more than sets or props did, so I treat proxemic experience in this section as well. In the second section I examine two related elements: the social machinery of the commercial theater company and the reshaping of theatrical space engineered by the employment of the claque, paid applauders. This segment treats French theater of the nineteenth century, the period in which the claque became part of the theater industry and was on the payroll at state-sponsored theaters. In the final segment of the book, the focus is the stage designer's effect on audience experience. By the twentieth century, stage designers played a major role in creating a production, most frequently in a house with a proscenium arch (unless the company was engaged in active rebellion against what that stood for). Many designers began to theorize about how to break down the divide between performance and spectators; in their work they actively planned the shaping of space, often influenced more by modern artistic movements than by a desire to achieve illusion or imitation. The results engaged the audience in a new relation to what they were seeing. I investigate instances of interplay between designer intentions and audience response, dealing with a European production and two American productions. In this section I attempt to do for stage design what reader-response criticism has done for the literary text: outline the audience's contribution to the construction of meaning.

One purpose of this project is to show what can be achieved through historical comparisons of scenography, a key innovation of this work. Most scholars interested in these questions (almost exclusively scholars of theater and performance writing in the last thirty years) have focused on productions that they have seen. Few have considered original productions and have instead examined contemporary scenographic choices. Theater historians, however, collect information about past productions from a variety of sources and more recently have begun to work with the evidence to develop interpretive hypotheses. Like Gay McAuley, who broke new ground in her 1999 book *Space in Performance*, I examine audience perceptions in order to understand more fully "the space of interaction between performers and spectators, the energized space of the stage when it is occupied and rendered meaningful by the presence of performers, [and] the organization of stage and offstage."[7] Unlike McAuley, however, I work with productions as a literary/historical scholar: through archival and archeological evidence such as the structures themselves, photographs, documents, and the conclusions of other theater historians. This project's range of historical periods makes an eclectic methodology necessary; in different chapters I draw on such elements as semiotics, phenomenology, spatial theory, and Edward T. Hall's research on proxemics, as well as theater history, histories of stage design, and theories of visual perception in the arts. This methodological diversity coalesces around the interplay between spectacle and text in original performances. W. B. Worthen observes that, "as countless thrust-stage, blackbox, in-the-round, and otherwise 'experimental' productions have shown, the text gains different force in alternative regimes of performance."[8] Thus it is particularly important when considering a playwright's compositional process to bear in mind the theatrical conditions in which he or she expected the work to be produced. It is for this reason that this project concentrates on the conditions of original performances: because those productions occurred in the environments that the playwrights envisioned when they composed their plays.

McAuley resorts in her book to the strictures of the Marxist spatial theorist Henri Lefebvre, stating that the stage-space is "not an empty container but an active agent; it shapes what goes on within it, emits signals about it to the community at large, and is itself affected. The frame constituted by a particular building or venue is not something fixed and immutable but a dynamic and continually evolving social entity."[9] The stage is active because it is, in Lefebvre's terms, *social space*—more so than many designed spaces because it is constructed specifically for performance. Like a town hall or a courthouse, a theater is intended as a place for a narrowly defined set of ritualistic behaviors to be enacted. Though it may be adapted for purposes beyond or contrary to its original purpose, its use is planned before it is built, and its structure is based on the purpose to which it will be put. While many stages were (and are) indeed improvised, my purpose is to examine performances of plays written for a specific type of venue.

This project treats its subjects as agents as well as givens. In my examination of space, I treat the shape of the stage (a given for many pre-twentieth-century playwrights); staging and blocking (which grow out of convention and theatrical necessity); and set design (increasingly created by designers as theater developed). I show how playwrights' intentions were shaped by their assumptions about the stage-space, and how they shaped performance in order to affect theatergoers. Audiences too shape the theater, not least by filling it; they shape the playwright's decisions by their assumptions or demands, and they shape the performance by responding to it during and after it "takes place" (so to speak). While the interchange between theater design and theater audience is the basis upon which this project rests, my concern with agency made me decide that consideration of a playwright's literary production—*dramatic text*—must be part of the analysis I offer here.

Text versus performance: a debate

Michael Issacharoff insists (mistakenly, in my view) that the text exists anterior to performance, but he also more wisely asserts that "it is language that creates and focuses space in the theatre, or at least any functional stage-space."[10] While the playscript may structure how a given space is *used*, generally the space exists before the play is written. Its anterior existence is important: I contend that it structures the playwright's assumptions about theater's potential. Prior knowledge of the stage design shapes the way the playwright imagines the action and, consequently, the plot that he or she dramatizes. When a subsequent production takes place on a different kind of stage, the signifiers may shift. I analyze both how the standard stage-space of a particular period may have shaped the plots of that era, and how the staging of dramas may have affected audience experience. I consider how playwrights responded to the parameters resulting from different stage designs and developed thematic emphases that grew out of the shape of the stage. While this point is most evident in my first chapter, with its comparison of Plautine theater to Shakespeare's adaptation of it, the issue resurfaces throughout the book.

In treating the performative aspect of dramas as a phenomenon in its own right, I enter a debate that is over one hundred years old. As Marvin Carlson explains in his groundbreaking *Places of Performance* (1989), it is important to understand "how places of performance generate social and cultural meanings of their own which in turn help to structure the meaning of the entire theatre experience" because we now define that encounter in terms of "the experience of the audience assembled to share in the creation of the total event."[11] Carlson contextualizes his work by invoking the debate between Brander Matthews and Joel Spingarn, two Columbia professors of the early twentieth century. Spingarn was an important New Critic; Matthews, the first professor of dramatic literature in the United States. Spingarn, understandably, urged the preeminence of the text in understanding the drama; Matthews "insisted that a proper understanding of the plays of Shakespeare, Sophocles, Moliere, or Ibsen required a knowledge of what sort of physical stage each had in mind as he was creating his dramas."[12] This volume returns to the Matthews-Spingarn debate, building on the urban research developed by Carlson. With Matthews, I assert that dramas are shaped by the design of the theatrical spaces that playwrights envision as containers of the dramas they write. These assumptions may or may not be conscious, but they influence dramatic composition. The effect occurs at other moments of the theatrical transaction as well: a play's effect upon its spectators is shaped by their experience of its theater. Stage and theater design alter dramatic meaning and also condition the audience's experience. I analyze both how staging affects the dramatic possibilities of plot and how it alters the physical knowledge of the spectator.

Terminology of the stage

Terminology is a vexed question for scholars discussing theatrics and spatiality because we must inevitably define both a physical area and what that area *does*—how it functions in a specific context. While the classical drama scholar Lowell Edmunds distinguishes simply between the theater space (as architectural design) and the stage-space (stage and set design, costume, actors' bodies, etc.),[13] Gay McAuley discusses the merits of several different taxonomies of theatrical space (including those developed by Hollis Huston, Anne Ubersfeld, Patrice Pavis, and Hanna Scolnicov) before drawing on them to develop her own. Saying that we need at least three terms "to account for the relationship between physical space and fictional space as it operates in the theater," she offers the terms *stage space* ("the physical space of the stage"); *presentational space* ("the physical use made of this stage space in any given performance," and which includes the work of set designers, scenographers, and whoever is in charge of blocking); and *fictional place* (a term referring to "the place or places presented, represented, or evoked onstage and off").[14] I am principally concerned with McAuley's *stage space* (Edmunds's theater space) and her *presentational space* (Edmunds's stage-space). However, the design of the entire theater, most especially the audience area, is also significant since the layout of this part of the theater defines the nature of those who attend. The structure of the auditorium area also determines many aspects of the nature of the exchange between performers and attendees—most obviously, whether the attendees place more emphasis on what they hear or what they see.[15]

While Carlson's *Places of Performance* calls attention to specific performance venues and their designs, Carlson left the interpretation of their semiotic codes to others. My work draws upon semiotic theory when I examine the spatial cues that influence audience experience during a dramatic performance. Keir Elam points out that

> The drama is usually considered as a "given," offered to the spectator as a ready-structured whole through the mediation of the performance. The reality of the process is altogether different. The spectator is called upon ... to work hard and continuously at piecing together into a coherent structure the partial and scattered bits of dramatic information that he receives from different sources. The effective construction of the dramatic world and its events is the result of the spectator's ability to impose order upon a dramatic content whose expression is in fact discontinuous and incomplete.[16]

Though Elam does say that "[i]t should not be thought that a reader of dramatic texts constructs the dramatic world in the same way as a spectator," he emphasizes textual cues, giving little attention to the experience of the spectator or to phenomenological perception of a specific theatrical experience.[17] In his efforts to understand "the entire theatrical experience," Carlson provides a useful corrective to Elam's emphasis on what the spectator consciously assimilates. But Carlson seldom treats the spectator's or audience member's experience; his work emphasizes the physical conditions that affect experience.

Audience experience is shaped—almost literally so—by the physical layout of the stage.[18] However, the shape of the stage, like the playscript, is merely one component of the performance, which is directed at the audience. Ultimately, the final transaction is not what the production offered, but *what the audience received*.

The role of the audience

The role of the audience, or theater attendee, has been examined by many scholars.[19] Yet, as McAuley points out, we have no term that exactly describes this role: "The English language provides us with a collective noun *audience* but then rather confusingly tells us that an audience is made up of spectators, as though hearing were a communal act but seeing an individual one."[20] McAuley examines the implications offered by the words used to specify this concept in other languages, considering German, Italian, and French words, and points out that the French term *l'assistance* is a richer and perhaps more appropriate term: "it refers primarily to the spectators' physical presence, to the being there, but the secondary meaning of *assister* (to help) is also relevant and suggests that in the theatre the collective presence of the audience provides something more than mere listening."[21]

At one time, scholars and practitioners of the theater assumed that audiences not actively engaged with the action are passively absorbed in the act of watching. On this basis, Bertolt Brecht established the need for the *Verfremdungseffekt*, arguing in such essays as "Theater for Pleasure or Theater for Instruction" that audience passivity must be disrupted in order to ensure that the audience's intellectual faculties will not lie dormant during the performance. Following Brecht and his ilk, theater historians such as Arnold Aronson have argued that "frontal performance" creates a clearly defined boundary between performer and spectator, whereas environmental performance "places the spectator at the center of the event, often with no boundary between performer and spectator."[22] Similarly, Bert O. States, who initiated the turn toward phenomenology in theater studies, suggests that among the modes of acting, the "self-expressive mode" is opposed by the "collaborative mode," whose purpose is "to break down the distance between actor and audience and to give the spectator something more than a passive role in the theater exchange."[23] More recently, however, the theater semiotician Anne Ubersfeld has carefully examined the role of the spectator, flatly contradicting the idea that "the role of the spectator in the process of communication is passive":[24]

> In fact, the receiver-function of the audience is much more complex. First, because the spectators sort information, choose, and reject some of it, they push the actor in one direction, albeit through weak signs that the original sender can nonetheless clearly perceive as feedback. Second, there is no one spectator; rather there is a multiplicity of spectators who react to each other. ... [Finally] it is the spectators, much more than the director, who create the spectacle: they must reconstruct the totality of the performance, along both the vertical axis and the horizontal axis. Spectators are obliged not only to follow a story, a fabula (horizontal axis), but also to constantly reconstruct the total figure of all of the signs engaged concurrently in the performance. ... Probably there is no other activity requiring as much psychological and intellectual engagement.[25]

Similarly, the philosopher Jacques Rancière asserts, "Being a spectator is not some passive condition that we should transform into activity."[26] Rancière urges that freedom begins "when we challenge the opposition between viewing and acting."[27] Just as the reader of literature deserves critical study as the receiver of textual signs, surely theater attendees, *l'assistance*, deserve similar study as the receivers and therefore the makers—in Ubersfeld's terms—of theatrical meaning in performance.

Gay McAuley comments that the audience's relation to the actors depends on the performance necessarily being "embedded in a social event." But it is the physical presence of the audience at the theater that she perceives as the key element that particularizes the relationship between performers and spectators. The presence of the audience at the performance results in "an energy exchange among and between spectators and performers."[28] She stresses the importance of the minute signals that the audience gives and that experienced actors heed; she also discusses the "complex play of looks" of spectators upon actors (which may be avid, even voracious), of actors upon spectators (especially when old forms of lighting rendered each group equally visible), and of spectators upon spectators, a varied gaze that emphasizes the social nature of theater attendance. McAuley briefly discusses the nature of the space and its effect upon the audience as well, pointing out, for example, that the "[d]ivision of the auditorium into boxes provided personal and domestic space within the public arena" and that Tyrone Guthrie's thrust stage brought spectators into the visual picture, as did the transverse stage.[29]

Left behind: traces of the audience

In this study of theatrical space, the objects of study include three primary elements: the architecture of the stage-space, the set design, and the movement of bodies. At the same time, I emphasize *perception* as Maurice Merleau-Ponty uses the word—to refer to physical experience as well as intellectual perceptions. In each period I treat, the available evidence of theatrical practice is different. Scholars of classical history and drama examine contemporary documents, artistic representations, and artifacts.[30] Those who study early modern drama by Shakespeare and his contemporaries have found abundant information about theatrical practice in diaries, travelers' journals, acting manuals, prop lists, scripts, printed stage directions, illustrations from the period, and archeological digs.[31] While the evidence amassed calls for more interpretation than a photograph might, our understanding of the early modern theater has increased substantially in recent years. Later periods of the theater produced the same kinds of documentation with the addition of advertisements, posters, programs, and reviews. The advent of photography more than supplemented written descriptions with photographs of theaters, actors, sets, and performances. The closer one comes to the twentieth century, the more the sheer amount of evidence balloons.

As I study productions from the past, my process is different from that of McAuley, whose work is the result of observing and recording rehearsals and performances of particular productions. My historical research is sometimes necessarily more speculative than hers, as is that of all scholars who work with theatrical artifacts from the past; similarly, it is more closely tied to the text, and not merely because the playscript is often the most substantial document available for a particular performance. The text itself can be valuable for discovering the process of production, and while it does not provide overt information about audience experience, it provides rough evidence that theater history and a variety of methodological tools enable us to examine.

For the reasons I have stated, this analysis is text-based in that I discuss not merely theatrical effects overall but also those specific to particular moments in the dramatic work. This analysis is performance-based in that I endeavor to discover how assumptions about space and staging affect both playwrights and audience members. Though the subject of this book is the manipulation of the stage-space, I consider it through the lens of the observers and their relation to the stage. Moreover, the stage-space can be a dynamic force in shaping the audience's perceptions. McAuley ascribes agency to space when she comments, "My interest ... is not the place in itself but the ways in which space functions in practice in the performance experience and in the construction of meaning by spectators."[32] This ascription rests upon Lefebvre's assertion that all space is social. What he means is that space "is social morphology: it is to lived experience what form itself is to the living organism, and just as intimately bound up with function and structure."[33] Lefebvre warns against the assumption, derived from semiology, that "social space is the result merely of a *marking* of natural space, a leaving of traces upon it."[34] Instead, he argues, social space "'incorporates' social actions, the actions of subjects both individual and collective who are born and who die, who suffer and who act."[35] In other words, space is shaped by the needs and resulting actions of different societies; it is developed as a result of social practice that, according to Lefebvre, "is lived directly before it is conceptualized."[36] Space, then, is shaped by the formation of communities, which develop and define their ideologies only after shaping the space to suit the needs that have evolved.

We see this shaping of space in broad terms in the history of the drama. Students of theater learn that the phenomenon of Western drama was born in the religious festivals of the Great Dionysia; the location of the *theatron* was determined by civic and religious needs, while its design grew out of the structure of Athenian society. The shape of Burbage's Theater derived from both practical concerns and the Renaissance admiration for the rituals of the ancients, while the walls were Burbage's response to the commercial possibilities of a secular drama. Proscenium stages evolved across Europe for many different reasons, but the painted flats and two-dimensional stagings derive largely from the tradition of court performances for the aristocracy and the desire to present a perfect perspective to the monarch. It is easy enough to apply Lefebvre's ideas to the development of theater since the early modern period and, in a rough sense, Lefebvre's theories can explain why every theatrical production is so much imbued with the constructs of its own time. Yet the specifics of the history of theater go substantially beyond these potted theories, and these ideas merely carry me to the point where I would like to begin.

Script versus spectacle

While the dispute over the relative importance of words and visual effects was most famously showcased in the ongoing quarrels of the Jacobean playwright Ben Jonson and Inigo Jones, stage designer for Jonson's numerous court masques, their debates took little account of the technologies that shaped actual audience experience. Carlson points out that when theatrical performance left the open-air stage for indoor venues, elaborate scenic backgrounds became possible, but insufficient illumination kept performers in obscurity. The result was that it became necessary for actors to stand on the lip of the stage to declaim their lines. Carlson contends,

> From the start of the modern indoor theatre in the Renaissance until the beginning of the nineteenth century ... the stage space (although in fact dimensional) was from the audience's point of view, and the actors' use of this space was more like a painting or at best a bas-relief.[37]

Theatrical production became increasingly pictorial in nature, and theatergoers became spectators more than auditors.

The terms of the Jonson-Jones debate were refigured in the nineteenth century, as Carlson points out, when the theater theorists of the Romantic era sought the organizational principles of effective theater after having cast aside the Neo-classical rules from the drama of the previous century. With spectacle playing such a major role in theatrical production, literary theorists wondered whether the dramatic text was not more effectively realized in the mind of the reader and not onstage at all. Schlegel, Goethe, and Lamb all examined whether or not dramatic texts were "organic wholes, complete within themselves and with each part related to every other."[38] If this was indeed the case, then wasn't performance an excrescence, a parasitical growth attached to something already complete? If, on the contrary, "performance itself were regarded as an organic whole, must not every part of it be incomplete if considered by itself? How then could organic unity be claimed for the text, obviously a part of this larger whole?"[39] The result of this debate was that in the nineteenth century performance was viewed "as not merely a distraction, but an actual menace, in that it threatens always to corrupt the original vision by 'interpretation'—making it something other and ... necessarily inferior."[40] Onstage, spectacle continued to dominate throughout the nineteenth century; the list of great names in theater of that period includes Ludwig Tieck, Louis-Jacques Daguerre, James Robinson Planché, William Poel, and David Belasco, figures whose effects were often more memorable than the plays they produced.

However, a number of theater designers and directors since the late nine-teenth century have attempted to unify script and spectacle. André Antoine's 1891 production of Ibsen's *The Wild Duck* featured a set that correlated remarkably well with the themes of the play:

> Despite the solid box set, and electric light capable of revealing the physical authenticity of the props, the theme ... relates to the inner world of the cavern that opens up at the back of the stage. ... [T]he main box set represents at once the false façade of bourgeois society, and the front which an individual puts before the world, whilst perspectival depth reveals inner truth.[41]

As Oscar Brockett puts it, "Antoine helped to establish the principle that each play requires its own setting quite distinct from that of any other work."[42] Max

Reinhardt did the same. Technologies for illumination improved, and the actors' use of the full stage expanded. Carlson notes that the changes were articulated in theory by the early twentieth-century scenic designer Adolphe Appia, who "characterized the stage space not as an animated painting but as a cubic, three-dimensional space, with the living forms within it defined by light."[43] Appia also suggested that actors should be trained in eurhythmics (musical rhythm exercises) because "[t]he discipline of the rhythm will make [them] particularly sensitive to the dimensions of space."[44]

Yet, as Carlson points out, designers like Adolphe Appia and Gordon Craig tended to reject the dramatic text wholesale, accepting the implication that a play like *Hamlet* is complete in its textual form and "for us to add to it by gesture, scene, costume or dance, is to hint that it is incomplete and needs these additions."[45] To avoid the subordinate role of "illustrator," Craig urged that "theatre should reject the traditional texts, to which performance can add nothing significant, and develop its own independent art of color, light, rhythm, and abstract form."[46] In contrast, directors such as Ashley Dukes and Harley Granville-Barker, as well as the critic Brander Matthews, suggested that performance could be seen as *fulfillment* of the dramatic text.[47] The Canadian theater theorist Ric Knowles recently posited a model of performance analysis "in which conditions of production, the performance text itself, and the conditions for its reception, operate mutually constitutive poles."[48] His assertion offers a balanced view that has helped shape this project: building on Knowles's conception, I imagine a complex diagram of elements that affect and respond to one another, weaving a "mutually constitutive" web, a fabric thickened by the number of elements in even a single production that create the totality of theatrical experience.

Space in the theater: phenomenological concerns

Since at least the 1980s, scholars have grappled with these concerns by examining how the space of the theater affects the audience's experience of dramatic performance. Bert O. States initiated theater scholars' use of phenomenology, the philosophical study of physical consciousness gained through sensual perception and the subjective experience of the body.[49] States suggests that theater is not merely mimetic, nor should it be perceived as a series of signs. He attempts to valorize theater and performance over the written text on the basis that theater is its own art in which signs

> achieve their vitality—and in turn the vitality of theater—not simply by signifying the world but by being *of* it. In other words, the power of the sign ... is not necessarily exhausted either by its illusionary or its referential character.[50]

In States's view, the theatrical image only superficially resembles a sign; in fact, it effects a *"desymbolization of the world."*[51] Reading, States asserts, is "a transparent process" in which the eye is "little more than a window to the waiting consciousness on which a world of signification imprints itself. ... What the text loses in significative power in the theater [i.e. performance], it gains in corporeal presence."[52] Though States acknowledges that watching a performance engages the mind less fully than the "mental enactment" of reading a play, that engagement is not the point: the *bisociality* of reality and mimesis offers a unique experience that deserves consideration in its own right. States explores "the sensory basis of scenic illusion," focusing on the auditory and the optical.[53] He is interested in how every new theatrical age brings forth "a new relationship between perceived space and heard language."[54]

Stanton B. Garner, Jr. follows up States's concern with the sensory basis of theater in his volume *Bodied Spaces: Phenomenology and Performance in Contemporary Drama* (1994). Garner's phenomenology, inflected by Husserl, Heidegger, Merleau-Ponty, and Ricoeur, redirects attention

> from the world as it is conceived by the abstracting, "scientific" gaze (the objective world) to the world as it appears or discloses itself to the perceiving subject (the phenomenal world) ... [and] return[s] perception to the fullness of its encounter with its environment.[55]

Though his work analyzes text-based works of drama primarily, Garner emphasizes performative elements more than the interaction of text and performance. His volume examines both "spatiality, through which plays establish fields of visual and environmental relationship, and the human body, through which these fields receive their primary orientation."[56] These foci return the experience of theater to proprioception, the physical perception of the world. Garner most clearly states what phenomenology offers to the theater scholars who draw on this branch of philosophy: the opportunity to study the stage as both "scenic space, given as spectacle to be processed and consumed by the perceiving eye, objectified as field of vision for a spectator who aspires to the detachment inherent in the perceptual act" and yet, simultaneously, "environmental space, 'subjectified' ... by the physical actors who body forth the space they inhabit."[57] Building on Garner's work in her book *Space in Performance: Making Meaning in the Theatre* (1999), Gay McAuley suggests that theater's uniqueness as an art does not depend on the dramatic element that theater shares with film and television, but on "the interaction between performers and spectators in a given space."[58] McAuley nonetheless examines text-based works of theater, though she analyzes them in terms of live performance (indeed, she cites the specific productions that she examines). Like Ric Knowles, she emphasizes the interaction among the different components that contribute to a theatrical performance. Her chapter-length treatment of such elements as objects in performance and bodies onstage is the most detailed of any scholar working on theater and spatiality today.

In *Reading the Material Theatre* (2004), Ric Knowles develops a mode of performance analysis in order to better understand what it is that theater companies produce. I follow the model Knowles provides in his consideration of conditions "both cultural and theatrical, in and through which theatrical performances are produced, on the one hand, and received, on the other."[59] However, Knowles tends to elide the contribution of the playwright, an element that I try to emphasize. Part of my goal, as I have said, is to call attention to the text's importance in the creation of theatrical moments—my case studies are individual plays. Knowles, significantly, takes a case study approach to his subject as well, but his individual cases are theater companies: the Stratford Festival, the Tarragon Theatre, the Wooster Group, and the English Shakespeare Company.

Theorizing the spectator

Scholarly interest in the theater audience has burgeoned since 1990 when Susan Bennett commented that "despite the extensive debate on the ideological gaze of the cinema audience, we lack any detailed picture of the theatre audience and, in particular, their role(s) in the production-reception relationship."[60] However, some theater professionals in the early twentieth century did try to define the role of the audience in theatrical performance. One of the most significant of these is the Russian theater director and theorist Vsevolod Meyerhold (1874–1940). Meyerhold perceived two methods of interaction between director and actor. When the spectator comprehends the work of the author and actor solely through the creation of the director, said Meyerhold, the actor and even the spectator are deprived of creative freedom. Consequently, he advocates a different mode of interaction in which creative input is increased incrementally as it is passed from one contributor to another. The first to contribute (chronologically) is the playwright. This creativity is assimilated by the director, who in turn offers what he can to the actor; the actor, finally, offers his creative efforts to the spectator, who himself responds with his own creative assimilation of the previous efforts. In the first instance, the director prescribes everything to the actor; in the second, each contributor can offer his contribution freely; in sum, "the spectator is made to comprehend the author and the director through the prism of the actor's art."[61] Meyerhold further characterized the relationship, emphasizing the spectator's role, in a 1907 document:

> The director erects a bridge between actor and spectator. He depicts friends, enemies or lovers in accordance with the author's instructions, yet by means of movement and poses he must present a picture which enables the spectator not only to hear the spoken dialogue but to penetrate through to the *inner* dialogue. ... He will suggest plastic movements to the actor which will help the spectator to perceive the inner dialogue as the actors and he, himself, understand it. ... [T]here must be a *pattern of movement* on the stage to transform the spectator into a vigilant observer, to furnish him with ... the material which helps him grasp the true feelings of the characters. Words catch the ear, plasticity—the eye.[62]

Meyerhold perceived the performance as a spectacle; he was heavily influenced by the proscenium theaters he was working in at the time. His ideas about the significance of the tableau are evident in other documents he wrote during this period.

Another theater professional, the set designer and theorist Frederick Kiesler, characterized the proscenium stage as "the peep-show stage," arguing that it "functions as relief, not as space." He argued that designs for a three-dimensional stage were necessary because spectators could not experience space within the proscenium stage. In Kiesler's words, "The public's shaft of vision pushes the stage space back towards the rear. As is always true of rigid space, it is projected onto the surface of the back-drop."[63] A number of directors and designers besides these figures altered the parameters of performance with some consideration of spectatorial experience, among them Max Reinhardt, Erwin Piscator, and Norman Bel Geddes. Interest in altering the relation between performers and spectators also occurred within avant-garde theater; many theater manifestos written by figures within the Dadaist, Surrealist, and Futurist movements address this concern. Later figures in avant-garde theater, from Brecht and Artaud to Brook and Schechner, have written influential treatises touching on this subject.

More recently, theater scholars have returned to the question of spectatorial experience, as I have noted. Stanton B. Garner, Jr., draws on phenomenology to characterize spectatorial experience:

> At the point at which I insert myself as the lone spectator in the auditorium, this field is immediately focalized through a scientific perspective. ... [P]heno-menological space is *oriented* space. The stage and its elements are now situated in terms of such variables as frontality, angle, and depth. ... As I add more spectators (and remind myself of the director, designers, and other collaborators in the theatrical event who have left their signatures on this mise-en-scene), I introduce variables of intersubjectivity and multi-perspectivity as these impinge on my own situation within the audience, and as these constitute a perceptual field that is both private (*Lebenswelt*) and shared (*Umwelt*).[64]

Bridget Escolme treats audience experience in the context of discussing actors' aims as theatrical performers. Escolme—director, performer, dramaturge, and theater scholar—bridges the perceptions of the theater professional and the more disengaged perspective of the scholar. In her examination of con-temporary productions of Shakespeare plays, Escolme considers "how far the meaning produced by the shifting distance between performer and audience might be constitutive of the ways in which the plays produce meaning."[65] Her work integrates current scholarly theories of the postmodern theater with a theater professional's knowledge of viable staging practice.

A balance of agencies

My own project crosses period boundaries in order to see how the stage-space shapes text, how theatrical performance shapes space, and how space, performance, *and* text shape the experience of the theatergoer. These inter-connected elements are the common denominators of the project. In the earliest productions I treat, the design of the stage is itself an important factor; in later productions, the stage design is reshaped through the intervention of set designers and, in some cases, spectators. All these elements impinge on spectatorial experience. I have chosen to present a series of case studies that investigates the interaction of these elements in some depth rather than a survey of stage designs. Given my emphasis on authorial input, I have considered it important to focus on dramas that provide evidence of an authorial mind at work.

In my case studies, close readings demonstrate the fluidity of spatiality, how the text indicates changes in spatial definition from scene to scene or even from sentence to sentence. Each chapter of this volume examines a different balance of agencies, recognizing that the space may be manipulated by a variety of theater professionals—playwrights, actors, directors, and designers—but can have no active agency itself. I focus primarily on dramatic works in which text (and therefore the playwright's agency) is a significant and relatively stable component; on original performances; and on works conceived by the playwright for per-formance in traditional theaters of the time. The purpose in these decisions is largely to investigate the choices playwrights made in accommodating their work to the theater settings in which, as they wrote, they imagined their work; a multiplicity of meanings derives from the spatial parameters that playwrights expected. While most of my predecessors have focused on visual spectacle and seldom incorporated consideration of the text, this volume focuses on the dramatic text in order to examine how staging and the stage-space modify, alter, and engage in dialectical tension with particular dramatic texts. The interaction of script and staging is always mediated by audience experience, for it is the audience members who perceive the tension between visual fields and images on one hand, and verbal signs on the other.

Despite the importance of theatrical spectacle, however, it is an under-standing of space and phenomenological experience in the theater that I wish to provide. As Wiles notes,

> Cartesian space is an ocular space. The invisible *ego* not only views the action but also quells the actors with the controlling power of its gaze. It does not submit to any embodied immersion in space—space as appre-hended through kinetics, smell, sonic vibrations or an osmosis running through packed shoulders.[66]

Wiles emphasizes the value of challenging what he calls "the Cartesian theatrical dichotomy: the split between stage and auditorium, between the performance as object and the spectator as disembodied subject."[67] Rather than moving metho-dically through the different stages of theater design according to the history of European dramatic performance, this project is organized around the different entities involved in theatrical production. The first chapter is concerned with the author; it analyzes the effects of theater design upon two playwrights who respond in their dramas to the shape of their stages. The second chapter examines the actor-audience relationship: it discusses blocking as a means of shaping the open stage and examines how audiences experience such stage shaping through physical perception. This emphasis continues in the third chapter, which considers instances in which the audience members shape the stage or engage in a responsive performance that shapes the actors' experience. When spectators themselves have a role, the theater is no longer clearly divided into stage and auditorium; these two spaces become mutually constitutive stages from which each performing body responds to the other. The fourth chapter focuses on the potential of set design, showing how a designer's vision for an opera revival modified the work's original themes and brought its concerns to the attention of a national audience. The final chapters continue the focus on set design, examining how two designers responded to playtexts in the creation of sets that brought out the spectators' metatheatrical role.

A variety of theatrical traditions are examined here: Roman comedy, early modern English theater, and French Romantic theater; the twentieth century is represented by an avant-garde German production of 1929 as well as two post-war experimental productions working against the constraints of Broadway's proscenium stage. As the book moves forward in time, the analysis shifts to different aspects of theatrical space. The first two chapters are concerned with theater architecture, stage blocking, and proxemics. The third examines audience performance in the auditorium; the fourth chapter shows modern scenographers reshaping the stage-space through sculptural means, while the fifth and sixth look at scenographers doing something similar through the manipulation of metatheatricality.

***

As I have said, in considering spatiality in the theater I also wish to reexamine the role of the spectator and make a case for the audience's constitutive force. The presence of the audience shapes the theatrical space in basic ways, and the audience's perceptions are crucial in defining theatrical success. The spectator may be active through physical experience (phenomenologically), intellectual experience (interpretively), or participatory response. In defining reader-response criticism, Stanley Fish proposed "a method of analysis which takes the reader, as an actively mediating presence, fully into account."[68] Part of the purpose of the approach was to call attention to the transaction between the text and the reader, as well as to acknowledge the illusory nature of "the objectivity of the text." Dramatic theorists have suggested that just as the reader's experience merits attention, so does that of the audience member.

The conclusions that I reach about each production cannot be generalized to all the productions of their era, but arguments about the potential effect of specific staging elements may well carry beyond these plays. In Fish's words, "I am not here making a claim beyond that made for the works I discuss, but, on the other hand, I will be pleased if others find this study helpful to their consideration of more modern (or, for that matter, more ancient) documents."[69] This project is intended to reveal possibility; its primary argument is that the dimensions of theatrical performance must be included in the study of drama, as should be the role of the audience in the hermeneutic process. To state conclusions, as such, would be to foreclose on those possibilities.

Notes

1 For critics who discuss mimetic place in drama or dramas, see among others Una Chaudhuri, *Staging Place: The Geography of Modern Drama* (Ann Arbor: University of Michigan Press, 1997); Anne Lancashire, "The Emblematic Castle in Shakespeare and Middleton," in *Mirror Up to Shakespeare: Essays in Honour of G. R. Hibbard*, ed. J. C. Gray (Toronto: University of Toronto Press, 1984), 223–41; and Michele Marrapodi, ed., *Shakespeare's Italy: Functions of Italian Locations in Renaissance Drama* (Manchester: Manchester University Press, 1993). For critics who have considered the effects of urban geography on theater and theater location, see Steven Mullaney, *The Place of the Stage: License, Play, and Power in Renaissance England* (Chicago: University of Chicago Press, 1988) and Marvin Carlson, *Places of Performance: The Semiotics of Theatre Architecture* (Ithaca: Cornell University Press, 1989).
2 Two of the most influential figures who have written against masterpieces are Antonin Artaud, whose writings are collected in *The Theater and Its Double*, trans. Mary Caroline Richards (New York: Grove, 1958) and Peter Brook, *The Empty Space: A Book about the Theatre* (New York: Touchstone, 1968).
3 W. B. Worthen, *Shakespeare and the Force of Modern Performance* (Cambridge: Cambridge University Press, 2003), 12.
4 David Wiles, *A Short History of Western Performance Space* (Cambridge: Cambridge University Press, 2003), 7.
5 Richard Schechner, "6 Axioms for Environmental Theatre" *TDR: The Drama Review* 12, no. 3 (Spring 1968): 44.
6 Ibid., 45.
7 Gay McAuley, *Space in Performance: Making Meaning in the Theatre* (Ann Arbor: University of Michigan Press, 1999), 7.
8 Worthen, *Shakespeare*, 8. Similarly, William Faricy Condee recalls Richard Foreman pointing out that "when the spectator hears 'To be or not to be,' he or she is experiencing that phrase in Lincoln Center, or the Comédie Française, or wherever," and he quotes Foreman as saying, "'The weight of that phrase has a different meaning depending upon what's surrounding it, what it's bouncing off of'" (*Theatrical Space: A Guide for Directors and Designers* [Lanham, MD: Scarecrow, 1995], 15.
9 McAuley, *Space in Performance*, 41.
10 Michael Issacharoff, *Discourse as Performance* (Stanford: Stanford University Press, 1989), 57, qtd in McAuley, *Space in Performance*, 27.
11 Carlson, *Places of Performance*, 2.
12 Ibid., 1.
13 Lowell Edmunds, *Theatrical Space and Historical Place in Sophocles'* Oedipus at Colonus (New York: Rowman and Littlefield, 1996), 24–25.
14 McAuley, *Space in Performance*, 29.
15 Condee points out that the relation between the performance area and the audience area changes according to whether the theater's architecture designates these as one unified space or two separate spaces. Proscenium theaters and arena, thrust, and transverse theaters all create different relationships between performers and watchers (Condee, *Theatrical Space*, vii–x).
16 Keir Elam, *The Semiotics of Theatre and Drama* (London: Routledge, 1991), 98–99.

17 Ibid., 99.
18 What I call "the shape of the stage" is only to some degree its literal shape (rectangular, fan-shaped, and circular being a few possible shapes among many). See Condee's Introduction to *Theatrical Space*, vii–xi.
19 Cf. Herbert Blau, *The Audience* (Baltimore: Johns Hopkins University Press, 1990); Susan Bennett, *Theatre Audiences: A Theory of Production and Reception* (New York: Routledge, 1990); Natalie Crohn Schmitt, *Actors and Onlookers: Theater and Twentieth-Century Views of Nature* (Evanston, IL: Northwestern University Press, 1990); Anne Ubersfeld, *Lire le Théâtre* (Paris: Editions Sociales, 1977), reprinted in English as *Reading Theatre*, trans. Frank Collins, eds. Paul Perron and Patrick Debbèche (Toronto: University of Toronto Press, 1999); Barbara Freedman, *Staging the Gaze: Postmodernism, Psychoanalysis, and Shakespearean Comedy* (Ithaca: Cornell University Press, 1991); Bert O. States, *Great Reckonings in Little Rooms: On the Phenomenology of Theater* (Berkeley: University of California Press, 1985); Bridget Escolme, *Talking to the Audience: Shakespeare, Performance, Self* (Routledge: London, 2005), Anthony B. Dawson and Paul Yachnin, *The Culture of Playgoing in Shakespeare's England: A Collaborative Debate* (Cambridge: Cambridge University Press, 2001); Jeremy Lopez, *Theatrical Convention and Audience Response in Early Modern Drama* (Cambridge: Cambridge University Press, 2003); Jacques Rancière, *The Emancipated Spectator*, trans. Gregory Elliott (London: Verso, 2009), 1–23; Jennifer A. Low and Nova Myhill, *Imagining the Audience in Early Modern Drama, 1558–1642* (New York: Palgrave, 2011); among others.
20 McAuley, *Space in Performance*, 251.
21 Ibid., 251; see also John Russell Brown, *Effective Theatre* (New York: Heinemann, 1969).
22 Arnold Aronson, *The History and Theory of Environmental Scenography* (Ann Arbor: UMI Research Press, 1981), 13.
23 States, *Great Reckonings*, 170. Originally published in *Theatre Journal*, Oct 1983.
24 Ubersfeld, *Reading Theatre*, 22–23.
25 Ibid., 23.
26 Rancière, *Emancipated*, 17.
27 Ibid., 13.
28 McAuley, *Space in Performance*, 245.
29 Ibid., 267, 268.
30 Anthony Corbeill cites Bourdieu as saying that every social and economic group "can be characterized by a particular set of external characteristics he calls the *habitus*" in *Nature Embodied: Gesture in Ancient Rome* (Princeton: Princeton University Press, 2004), 109. Other classical scholars who have engaged in similar projects include Eleanor Winsor Leach, *The Rhetoric of Space: Literary and Artistic Representations of Landscape in Republican and Augustan Rome* (Princeton: Princeton University Press, 1988); Maud W. Gleason, *Making Men: Sophists and Self-Presentation in Ancient Rome* (Princeton: Princeton University Press, 1985); Alan L. Boegehold, *When a Gesture Was Expected: A Selection of Examples from Archaic and Classical Greek Literature* (Princeton: Princeton University Press, 1999); Matthew B. Roller, *Dining Posture in Ancient Rome: Bodies, Values, and Status* (Princeton: Princeton University Press, 2006); Florence Dupont, *Daily Life in Ancient Rome*, trans. Christopher Woodall (Oxford: Blackwell, 1992); Ray Laurence, *Roman Pompeii: Space and Society* (London: Routledge, 1994); and Kathleen McCarthy, *Slaves, Masters, and the Art of Authority in Plautine Comedy* (Princeton: Princeton University Press, 2000).
31 It would be impossible to begin to cite all the scholars engaged in this kind of investigation; I will cite some classic works and a few innovative studies that build on the earlier projects. For early modern theater history, see E. K. Chambers, *The Elizabethan Stage*, 4 vols. (Oxford: Clarendon, 1923); Glynne Wickham, *Early English Stages, 1300–1600*,

3 vols. (London: Routledge and Kegan Paul, 1963); J. L. Styan, *Shakespeare's Stagecraft* (Cambridge: Cambridge University Press, 1967); Andrew Gurr, *The Shakespearean Stage, 1574–1642* (Cambridge: Cambridge University Press, 1992); and John H. Asting-ton, *Actors and Acting in Shakespeare's Time: The Art of Stage Playing* (Cambridge: Cambridge University Press, 2010). For studies built upon a foundation of theater history, see Joseph R. Roach, *The Player's Passion: Studies in the Science of Acting* (Cranbury, NJ: Associated University Presses, 1985); Mullaney, *The Place of the Stage*; Andrew Sofer, *The Stage Life of Props* (Ann Arbor: University of Michigan Press, 2003); Henry S. Turner, *The English Renaissance Stage: Geometry, Poetics, and the Practical Spatial Arts, 1580–1630* (Oxford: Oxford University Press, 2006); and Simon Palfrey and Tiffany Stern, *Shakespeare in Parts* (Oxford: Oxford University Press, 2007).

32 McAuley, *Space in Performance*, 8.

33 Henri Lefebvre, *The Production of Space*, trans. Donald Nicholson-Smith (Oxford: Blackwell, 1991), 94.

34 Ibid., 141.

35 Ibid., 33.

36 Ibid., 34.

37 Marvin Carlson, "Space and Theatre History," in *Representing the Past: Essays in Performance Historiography*, eds. Charlotte M. Canning and Thomas Postlewait (Iowa City: University of Iowa Press, 2010), 200.

38 Marvin Carlson, "Theatrical Performance: Illustration, Translation, Fulfillment, or Supplement?" *Theater Journal* 37, no. 1 (1985): 5–6.

39 Ibid., 6.

40 Ibid., 6.

41 Wiles, *Performance Space*, 231.

42 Oscar Brockett, *History of the Theatre*, 7th ed. (Needham Heights, MA: Allyn and Bacon, 1995), 433.

43 Carlson, "Space and Theatre History," 200.

44 Adolphe Appia, "Eurhythmics and the Theatre," in *Adolphe Appia: Essays, Scenarios, and Designs*, ed. and trans. Walter R. Volbach (Ann Arbor: UMI Research Press, 1989), 136.

45 Gordon Craig, *On the Art of the Theatre* (Chicago: Browne's, 1911), 143–44; qtd. in Carlson, "Theatrical Performance," 7.

46 Ibid., 7.

47 Ibid., 8.

48 Ric Knowles, *Reading the Material Theatre* (Cambridge: Cambridge University Press, 2004), 19.

49 For most phenomenologically oriented theater scholars, foundational philosophers include Edmund Husserl, Paul Ricoeur, and Maurice Merleau-Ponty.

50 States, *Great Reckonings*, 20.

51 Ibid., 23.

52 Ibid., 29.

53 Ibid., 50.

54 Ibid., 61.

55 Stanton B. Garner, Jr., *Bodied Spaces: Phenomenology and Performance in Contemporary Drama* (Ithaca: Cornell University Press, 1994), 2.

56 Ibid., 1.

57 Ibid., 3.

58 McAuley, *Space in Performance*, 5.

59 Knowles, *Material Theatre*, 3.

60 Bennett, *Audiences*, 92. Similarly, in 1999 McAuley stated, "[I]t is true to say that theatrical spectatorship is still relatively untheorized compared with film" (*Space in Performance*, 236).

61 Edward Braun, trans. and ed., *Meyerhold on Theatre* (New York: Hill and Wang, 1969), 50–52; 52–53.

62 Ibid., 56.

63 Frederick Kiesler, "Debacle of the Modern Theatre," *The Little Review* 11 (Winter 1926). In fact, so many theater people have responded negatively to the divide created by the proscenium arch that, as Condee recounts, the physical comedian Bill Irwin once created a performance piece called *The Regard of Flight* that satirizes "this idea of mistrust for the proscenium." In it, Irwin battles against the tug of the proscenium, which eventually pulls him offstage (Condee, *Theatrical Space*, 28–29).

64 Garner, *Bodied Spaces*, 46.

65 Escolme, *Talking*, 18.

66 Wiles, *Performance Space*, 7.

67 Ibid., 11.

68 Stanley Fish, "Literature in the Reader: Affective Stylistics," *New Literary History* 2, no. 1 (Autumn 1970): 123.

69 Stanley Fish, *Self-Consuming Artifacts: The Experience of Seventeenth-Century Literature* (Berkeley: University of California Press, 1972), xiii.

1 Inside the theater

Audience experience at *The Menaechmi* and *The Comedy of Errors*

When comparing *The Comedy of Errors* to its Plautine source, some critics have suggested that the primary difference between the two plays is their genre.[1] I assert that the difference between the plays is more organic—that it depends upon the design of the stage for which each playwright wrote. Theater design may alter a writer's sense of a plot's possibilities, and both of these may in turn affect the audience. Plautus and Shakespeare were each accustomed to a particular stage-space upon which, as they wrote, they imagined their plays being performed. As the playwrights wrote their farces, their assumptions about the stage-space shaped the way each plot made use of the audience and, consequently, the way that each audience experienced the dramatic action.[2] The picaresque tale of twins searching for one another after a lifetime of separation can be viewed in decidedly different ways, and the significance of the story in each drama developed from the way the playwright was using his theater. My argument is that the way the playwright positions the audience with regard to the action is shaped largely by the relation between the stage and the spectators' area, and by the way the playwright makes use of that relation. The analysis that follows builds on Stanton B. Garner, Jr.'s observation that theatrical space

> is "bodied" in the ... fundamental sense of "bodied forth," oriented in terms of a body that exists not just as the object of perception, but as its originating site, its zero-point. To stage this body in space before the witness of other bodies is to engage the complex positionality of theatrical watching.[3]

In the original production of *The Menaechmi*, the space in which the audience sat was clearly defined by characters within the drama. The spectators are implicitly the allies of the Syracusan brother; the space itself is Syracuse, the idealized heterotopia to which, at the play's end, the brothers return. In original productions of *The Comedy of Errors*, the dimension emphasized at the play's denouement was time, though time was represented largely in spatial terms. The amazing conclusion uses tricks of perspective to make the audience cognizant of time past through the play's emphasis on what might be glimpsed, Bob Barker fashion, behind curtain number three—in this case, the doorway of the priory.

The mimetic nature of dramatic performance itself suggests that the edge of the stage is a boundary between two different kinds of places—one that should not be crossed on a whim.[4] But, as several scholars have noted, Plautus's long, shallow stage encourages acting that acknowledges the audience as a presence. In *The Menaechmi* (more so even than in most other plays of the period), gesture and blocking reach outward toward the audience, transforming spectatorial space into dramatic space. In *The Comedy of Errors*, the use of Roman stage convention, specifically the three doorways, calls attention to the door of the priory, never used until the final act. The presence of the door to the priory creates a sense of expectancy gratified first when Antipholus takes refuge in the abbey and, more fully, when Aemilia comes out of it. Both the design and this use of it lends this door extra significance, which is heightened when Aemilia promises a resolution that can be achieved only when the characters pass through the door and leave the space of the stage.

The presentation of interior space in *The Comedy of Errors* has recently become a subject of critical concern. While critics like Mary Crane and Amanda Piesse have extensively discussed the scene in which Antipholus of Ephesus is locked out of his house while his wife dines inside with his brother, few have noted how thoroughly Aemilia's speeches evoke a space and the events to come within the priory.[5] The gestures and the staging implied by her words could be said to acknowledge the advances of Serlio and Scamozzi or to prefigure the perspective sets of Inigo Jones. Aemilia's priory provides a door into the past when she, a *dea ex machina*, steps forward to resolve the conflicts and relocate all the characters within the family circle. The play's use of that doorway, creating almost a visual tableau of the expression "Time reveals all things," promotes a sense of perspective and focus. Rather than opening out expansively, the narrow doorway finally represents an opportunity for the characters to go back in time, an emphasis that excludes the audience from the plot's conclusion and reinforces for us the thematic importance of temporality in the play.

***

At the end of *The Menaechmi*, the Epidamnian brother will be redeemed "through the agency of Tyche (Chance deified)."[6] But what he is going *to* is suggested by the staging, which characterizes offstage and the audience as two opposed worlds. The detachment of the Syracusan Menaechmus and his brother's deeper engagement with his community are reinforced by the play's staging, which was structured by the design of the Roman theater. Plautine comedies were performed on a narrow wooden stage (the *scaena*), perhaps sixty yards long, with a background of painted boards that generally represented two or three houses, depending on the demands of the play. Actors entered and exited both through the wings and through actual doors into the "houses" onstage. There is evidence from Vitruvius indicating common conventions: that one wing entrance commonly led from the forum while the other led from the harbor, where people arrived from foreign parts.[7] Certainly, playwrights like Plautus used the many entrances to localize the action, with each representing a particular place.

Figure 1.1 Photograph of the Roman theatre of Mérida, built in the Roman city of
    Emerita August (now Mérida, Spain) in the years 16 to 15 BCE. One can see here
    many of the traits that Duckworth and Beacham describe.
    Wikimedia Commons, https://en.wikipedia.org/wiki/Roman_Theatre_(Mérida)
    #mediaviewer/File:Merida_Roman_Theatre1.jpg.

The doors "were probably recessed to provide small vestibules" or porches, often
supported by columns.[8] Duckworth comments, "the length of the stage … made
the numerous soliloquies and asides, the instances of eavesdropping, and the
failure to see other characters on the stage, far more natural than is possible on
the modern stage."[9] Beacham cites *Amphitruo* in support of the possibility of a
roof strong enough to climb onto over at least one of the stage doors.[10] As for
the tableau of the whole, Beacham says that "[t]he area in front of the three
doors was thought of … as an open street which the characters normally refer
to as *platea*; less frequently as *via*."[11] The rest of the theater was notable for
special seats reserved for members of the Senate.[12]

In sum, Plautus's stage was long and narrow, and painted with mimetic effect
to depict a street—as Plautus himself says, often in Athens but, equally often,
"Greekish. Not Athensish, though."[13] The combination of these conventional
elements is, as Niall W. Slater has shown, a drama of frequent metatheater. As
Slater says,

> Plautus' remarkable achievement is to include self-conscious awareness of
> theatrical convention in a new concept of comic heroism, which I believe
> emerges most clearly in performance. A number of Plautus' characters …
> demonstrate a self-awareness of the play as play and through this aware-
> ness demonstrate their own ability to control other characters in the play.[14]

Slater also cites several key elements that define Plautine dramas as metatheatrical: "the monologue, the aside, eavesdropping, role-playing, and the
play-within-the-play."[15]

What interests me is twofold: first, how the place actually staged in *The
Menaechmi* defined itself in relation to the rest of the mimetic world of the

play, and second, how the mimetic world made use of the spectators. Like so many of Plautus's plays, *The Menaechmi* is set in a section of a street—clearly a mere segment of a microcosm. Commercial and civic life take place offstage and *not* on the street, for that is the liminal space on which the Menaechmi's drama unfolds. Their stage is merely a *part* of a community.

The way Plautus uses the twins extends the mimetic world of the Eastern Mediterranean into the spectator area. Plautus's alien twin, in contrast to Shakespeare's, keeps aloof from the community he is visiting, except for his presumably erotic tryst with Erotium. He almost never begins a conversation with Epidamnians, only speaking to them when he is accosted. Yet while he remains aloof from the citizens of Epidamnus, surprisingly, he solicits the views of the audience in frequent addresses. Eventually, he makes them his accomplices, amusing them with a show that is meant to confuse and confound the Epidamnians onstage. Unlike Shakespeare's Syracusan Antipholus, whose actions, body language, and dialogue demonstrate his willingness to be integrated into Ephesian society, the Syracusan Menaechmus, encouraged by Roman stage design, gradually forms a relationship with the audience instead. The partial nature of the staged community, completed for Menaechmus of Epidamnus by the world offstage, is completed for his twin by the audience members who sit watching his plight, themselves a cross-section of the Graeco-Roman society on which all the characters are based. For the alien twin, the audience, by virtue of its silence, merits his confidence. It is the only group whom he freely approaches.

To picture the process at work, we must consider Roman stage design once again, reverting to Duckworth's comment:

> the length of the stage (believed to be as much as sixty yards) made the numerous soliloquies and asides, the instances of eavesdropping, and the failure to see other characters on the stage, far more natural than is possible on the modern stage which is usually smaller and often represents indoor scenes.[16]

Like the parasite Peniculus, Menaechmus of Syracuse addresses the audience repeatedly, but unlike Peniculus, Menaechmus voluntarily addresses the audience almost exclusively: his servant Messenio is the only character with whom he initiates any extensive exchange. He clearly feels at ease with the audience: his comments to them range from the general, musing type—"Who's this woman talking to?"—to more pointed addresses that summarize his strategic exploitation of the Epidamnians' apparent mistaking of his identity from line 479 through line 485.[17] Gradually, he reaches the point where he asks questions that all but invite a response: when he sees Peniculus approaching, he inquires of the audience, "Who's this advancing on me?"[18] In contrast, neither one of Shakespeare's Antipholi soliloquizes often, and they never address the audience so directly. Such questions appear more often in the dramas of Shakespeare's contemporaries than in those of Shakespeare himself. When questions *do* figure as part of a Shakespearean soliloquy, the addressee tends to be ambiguous, as in Iago's query, "And what's he then that says I play the villain, / When this advice is free I give, and honest?" (2.3.336–37).[19] On the page, such a question can be taken either as rhetorical or as directed toward the spectator, or both. Onstage, the actor's interpretation would determine the addressee.

The unique role of the audience in *The Menaechmi* becomes evident after the Syracusan twin encounters his brother's parasite, who, confusing him with his brother, berates him for not including him at the meal he has just had with the native twin's mistress, Erotium. After an acid exchange, Peniculus (the parasite) exits. The Syracusan then turns to the audience and asks for an explanation of the parasite's bizarre behavior: "Everyone," he says, is making a fool of him.[20] But of course the audience is excluded from this "everyone"; they are the passive, receptive, yet approving friends to whom he turns to reveal his puzzlement and his resulting vulnerability. With them, he avoids the bellicosity that he has addressed to the parasite and will soon address to the Matrona. Believing that they can be trusted not to make aggressive demands, he seems to expect empathy and, perhaps, even an answer to the mystery from them.

Menaechmus of Syracuse soon reverts to the audience again, turning to them in mid-sentence as he concludes a brief conversation with Erotium's maid: "Say I'll take care of these things—(*aside, as maid leaves*) take care that they're sold as soon as possible for what they'll bring. ... Gone now, has she? Gone! She's shut the door."[21] The audience is played again as Menaechmus's accomplice, as if its members are telling him what is going on behind his back. He plays them off against the characters onstage, counting on them to let him know when he can no longer be observed by the other characters.

This sympathetic relationship is disrupted when Menaechmus of Syracuse stages an extraordinary charade to alienate his angry and mystified sister-in-law. Menaechmus resituates the stage as an arena for a fantasy, a mad scene that keeps the audience as well as his sister-in-law at bay. Simultaneously a scene of divine possession, a mad scene, a lie, a misunderstanding, a fantasy, and a performance, Menaechmus's acting literally makes him strange to all who watch him. He confounds watchers most when his behavior imitates that of an actor, one who pretends to be what he decidedly is not. But his acting skill is most hilarious when he shifts abruptly from confidences addressed to the audience to conjuring up an entirely self-contained world.

Act 5 begins with a confrontation between Menaechmus of Syracuse and his brother's wife; she repeatedly berates him for what his brother has done, while he responds with mystification that she takes as further provocation:

WIFE: Why, I'd rather live without a husband all my life than put up with the outrageous things you do.
MEN. S: And how does it concern me whether you can endure your married life, or leave your husband? Or is this the fashion here—to prattle to arriving strangers?

WIFE: Prattle? I will not put up with it any longer, I tell you. I'll get a divorce rather than tolerate your goings-on.

MEN. S: Lord, Lord! Get divorced, for all I care—and stay so as long as Jove reigns![22]

The joke here is that Menaechmus of Syracuse speaks the truth but his brother's wife assumes that he is acting. In the ensuing scene, Menaechmus speaks truthfully and confidentially to the audience about what he purposes next: "Seeing they declare I'm insane, what's better for me than to pretend I am insane, so as to frighten them off?"[23] To reinforce the old man's initial impression that he is deranged, the alien twin conjures up a complete world in order to fall in with the family's expectations: concession, he expects, may enable him to evade their wishes more effectively than flat denial. What renders his pretense even more complex is that he enacts madness by pretending to believe that he is possessed by Apollo. Madness has already been repeatedly invoked by both the Epidamnian and the Syracusan twin to explain the bizarre behavior that results from being mistaken for someone else. But madness is also a powerful trope for possession, poetic inspiration, and acting ability, sometimes even representing artistic ability more generally. The madness that Menaechmus of Syracuse impersonates complicates the character's relation to the audience, because it creates yet another world and resituates the audience in relation to it.

The madness of Menaechmus of Syracuse consists in seeming to be inspired by religious ecstasy—seeming to be visited by a god. Such behavior, his words suggest, is mad, because no one is really visited by gods. This implication is in accord with the essentially realistic nature of Plautine farce; yet such possession is common as a real event in Greek dramas that Plautus's audience might well have known. Thus, Menaechmus simultaneously invokes and discards the tradition of many classical myths in which such events actually occur. In Euripides's play *The Bacchae*, for example, Bacchus, himself in disguise as his own celebrant, executes spells invisible to his cousin Pentheus, who responds by thinking that he, Bacchus, is insane. Members of Roman society in Plautus's time could easily cite such precedents for occasions when possession was misinterpreted as madness because onlookers were understandably skeptical of a verbal exchange with an invisible interlocutor.

What was likely to have confused the audience is that Menaechmus's imitation of madness is so rich in its imagery, so vivid in its descriptions, that the satyrs and chariots he calls to are as real in mimetic terms as the world of Ephesus, as real as the marital relations he denies. The character of Menaechmus is hopelessly overburdened by multiple layers of mimesis, leaving bare the actor playing Menaechmus enacting yet another illusion.

Menaechmus of Syracuse no longer denies being known to the other characters onstage; instead, he merely performs the character as one who is possessed. He calls for Bacchus and his companions. Addressing them, he mixes the world of the god with the world of Epidamnus as he drolly comments, "I hear, but I cannot quit these regions, with that rabid bitch on watch there at my left, aye, and

there behind a bald-headed goat."[24] When his insults irritate the wife past
bearing, she and her father plan to carry him off for treatment with the help of
servants; he finds he must enact "some scheme, [or else] they'll be taking me off
to their house."[25] After dispatching the wife, he recreates a contest in an arena:

> Many are thy commands, Apollo. Now thou dost bid me take yoked steeds,
> unbroken, fiery, and mount a chariot that I may dash to earth this aged,
> stinking, toothless lion. ... Now am I in my car! Now do I hold the reins!
> Now have I goad in hand! On, steeds, on! Let the ring of your hoof-beats
> be heard! Let your fleetness of foot rush you rapidly on![26]

The extensive stage directions provided by every editor indicate how remarkably this scene conjures action and props out of thin air. If Apollo is not
necessarily imagined as physically present, the chariot and horses certainly are.
Given the world that Menaechmus draws in the air, why *shouldn't* the actor
playing his brother's father-in-law temporarily shift to playing the role of an
old lion?

To cap the scene, as soon as he has chased his father-in-law off the stage,
Menaechmus abruptly returns to the world of Epidamnus:

> For Heaven's sake, are they out of my sight now, those two that absolutely
> compelled me, sound though I am, to go insane? I'd better hurry off to the
> ship while I can do so safely. ... I beg you, all of you, if the old man comes
> back, don't tell him which way I bolted.[27]

His words open up a chasm—an ambiguity that suggests both that the act was
just that, a performance, but also that "his" wife and father-in-law literally drove
him insane. Once again, the audience are Menaechmus's accomplices, serving to
protect him from the residents of Epidamnus. With this direct address ("Don't
tell him which way I bolted"), the audience members become his supporters
once again, alien to Epidamnus and allied to him. They complete the scene,
filling out the incomplete world onstage with their judgments, their initiative.
They are part of his world, though not of the world of Epidamnus.

For the audience, the Syracusan twin's performance is a play-within-a-play;
yet the character provides such detail in his speeches that the world of gods and
men that he invokes is as real as that of Epidamnus. Whereas the audience are
aligned with Menaechmus of Syracuse for most of the play, for a short period
they lose their role; the venue of the theater is entirely changed—even reshaped—
during the Syracusan's mad scene. When he is engaged in transforming the
everyday world of Epidamnus into a world of myth, the audience ceases to exist
for him, and the mimetic world no longer includes the seating area but terminates
at the rim of the stage. In fact, Menaechmus of Syracuse's performance challenges
the status of the mimetic world. His acting is so complete a performance that it
almost equates him with the actor who plays the part. Menaechmus's involvement in the world of the gods is to all appearances deeper and more fully

committed than his involvement in the community of Epidamnus. Watching his fiction, the audience would have had no reason to think there was anything to prevent the world of Menaechmus's fake madness from becoming as real as the frame of the world of Epidamnus. His performance alters their relation to Epidamnus as well. For the other characters, the Syracusan twin must be disingenuous when he speaks honestly about his ignorance of the city; at that point, the audience (in contrast to the other characters) does know that he speaks the truth. In the mad scene, the audience knows that he is pretending, even as the other characters believe that he is speaking what he believes is the truth. Yet, to their eyes, staged possession and staged insanity are indistinguishable, and neither one can be distinguished from mimesis itself. All three are equally valid, and all three equally invalid.

This challenge to mimetic reality undermines the audience's sense of how they fit into the action. Were they Menaechmus's accomplices, or were they part of a fantasy world in his head? And if he was self-consciously creating that fantasy world, to what degree had he created the audience themselves? What *is* their relation to the drama enacted onstage? As Tweedledee says to Alice of the Red King's dream, "'[I]f he left off dreaming about you, where do you suppose you'd be? ... You'd be nowhere. Why, you're only a sort of thing in his dream.'"[28] This metatheatrical show is matched less fantastically by the play's conclusion, when the former slave Messenio enacts the role he will play in one week as auctioneer: "Auction ... of the effects of Menaechmus ... one week from today."[29] Both Nixon and Casson specify in their editions of the play that Messenio bawls out the news in an auctioneer's chant, as if he were opening the sale itself—which he will not do for a week. He performs an action that he will not engage in until later in the mimetic world: in doing so, he imitates a speech-act, thereby disrupting the relation between the performance of the auction and the immediacy that the performance supposedly communicates.

The audience's unique relation to Menaechmus of Syracuse is also challenged at the play's conclusion simply by the fact that brings the play to a close: the two brothers' discovery of one another. The two are overjoyed to find each other and agree to fulfill the *nostos* fantasy by returning to their own country, Syracuse. They pause only so that Menaechmus of Epidamnus can sell his possessions at auction: "In the meantime let's go inside for the present, brother."[30] They return to the Epidamnian's house "for the present," excluding both the Epidamnian community and the wider, possibly Syracusan, community of the audience. In retiring this way, they create for the first time a sense of possible intimacy, gesturing toward their ability to do without other society now that they have discovered each other. Unlike the Epidamnian Menaechmus, who was always caught up in a net of social relations, and the Syracusan Menaechmus, who preferred to be alone, the united pair enjoy each other's company and resolve their social difficulties by joining together. This conclusion leaves the audience's role open-ended: they could see themselves as the ones to welcome the twins back to Syracuse, or they might perceive their role as no longer necessary, as the twins were finally united. Plautus's text leaves this point undecided, and how the original audience felt at the end of the play must remain a matter of conjecture.

***

In his adaptation of Plautus's plot, Shakespeare treats his audience differently. Changes in the plot result in a more passive role for the audience until the play's conclusion, which differs markedly from that of *The Menaechmi*. In *The Menaechmi*, the two brothers return to Syracuse, leaving behind the wife, mistress, parasite, and responsibilities of the Epidamnian Menaechmus. In *The Comedy of Errors* the alien brother is integrated into Ephesus, the community represented onstage. As a result, the audience lacks the explicit role in the play that it had in the Roman version, where the audience served as the community—indeed, as the group of accomplices—of the Syracusan Menaechmus. Shakespeare diverges from Plautus as well in adding new elements to the dramatic structure, specifically a framing story that begins and ends with the father of the twins; he even surprises the audience with the last-minute introduction of their mother. (Neither parent is present or much dwelt on in *The Menaechmi*.) Many of the early modern play's thematic elements encourage the audience to enjoy the play passively, but Shakespeare's borrowings from Roman theater reshape the space at the close, creating a visual allegory and an emphasis on the visual perception of time, represented by a hint of three-point perspective (something absent from—and indeed irrelevant to—the Roman play). The staging demanded by *The Comedy of Errors* thrust the watchers away from experience of the action; the visual tableau nudged them toward the necessity of actively interpreting the play's connection between recountal and recovery of the past.

The play's emphasis on the semiotics of the visual does go contrary to ruling assumptions about staging in the public theater and may have resulted from unusual conditions in the play's original staging. In our own recent past, London's recreation of the Globe Theatre and the discovery of the remains of the Rose have driven certain basic assumptions about Shakespearean theater. Andrew Gurr, intimately involved with both projects, notes (along with Mariko Ichikawa) that the early modern theater audience's sense of where to place themselves was not structured primarily upon an expectation of tableaux:

> The modern use of the concept of a "front" to the stage reflects a basic change in audience thinking since 1601. ... Hearing is possible all around a speaker, and it is natural for an audience listening to a speech to group themselves all around him. Spectacle by contrast presupposes a frontal view, and spectators expect to group themselves in front of the picture. Modern audiences are more properly spectators. ... Elizabethans would not have positioned themselves anything like so readily at the "front" of the stage for a play.[31]

Gurr and Ichikawa suggest here that playgoers at early modern public theaters are more accurately defined as hearers, audience members, rather than watchers or spectators. Given the shape of the public theaters of early modern London, this comment makes perfect sense. We know that the thrust stage jutted out from the tiring-house into the yard where the groundlings stood; most were square, though the stage of the Rose was wider than it was long, thereby resembling the Roman stage.[32] The stage was about five feet above the yard level. Gurr and Ichikawa emphasize not only the spectators' proximity but also their field of vision:

> Wherever you stood or sat, you were never more than thirty-five feet from the stage platform, and most people were much closer, but from every position you could see most of the other gazers and gapers on the far side of the stage platform. It was a self-conscious grouping.[33]

In general, there was a clear difference between the Roman and the Elizabethan or Jacobean stage. Farce is a more natural development in Roman theater: not only does the frieze-like display make eavesdropping scenes more plausible (since those speaking would have been turned away from the eavesdroppers), the clear

Figure 1.2 Arnoldus Buchelius (1565–1641), after a drawing of the Swan Theatre by Johannes de Witt (1566–1622). Image from Nils Personne: Svenska Teatern VIII (1927), Wikimedia Commons, http://commons.wikimedia.org/wiki/File: 032_Swan_Theatre_Svenska_teatern_1.jpg.

binary division between stage and audience makes direct address to the audience a likely bit of stage business. In contrast, jigs and slapstick comedy would have been a more natural part of early modern English dramas because physical humor is more likely to be enjoyed from any perspective. However, *The Comedy of Errors* seems to have been constructed according to a different model of stagecraft. Whether or not the play was composed for the well-known Gray's Inn performance on December 28, 1594, is still debated.[34] Dorsch discusses possible stagings of the play at the Great Hall of Gray's Inn; should this production have been the original one, it would have influenced later productions on the public stage. But even if the play premiered on the public stage (a possibility currently undocumented), it would have been affected by Shakespeare's Roman borrowings. Shakespeare's use of Roman theatrical convention in *The Comedy of Errors* has led many critical commentators to emphasize similarities in the way *The Menaechmi* and *The Comedy of Errors* make use of space. *The Comedy of Errors* may be unique in Shakespeare's *oeuvre* in calling for three doorways on the rear wall of the stage, very likely a borrowing from the conventional setting of Roman comedy.[35] The effect would have rendered the frontal viewing of the stage more important than for most early modern dramatic productions on the public stage.[36] That full frontal view would probably have been the only view available at a Gray's Inn production. It would not have been the only perspective in the public theater; nonetheless, the demands of the play seem to call for it.

In shaping this stage-space to emphasize the pictorial, Shakespeare used a form of visual perspective to offer his audience a new way of seeing time, a concept more traditionally represented on the English stage by use of an allegorical character. Many plays of the period (including Shakespeare's late play *The Winter's Tale*) represented time onstage by an allegorical figure, often accoutred with his emblematic scythe, hourglass, and wings.[37] Such representations may be derived from medieval ways of thinking. The anthropologist Benjamin Whorf suggests that literacy has structured the currently more prevalent way of perceiving time:

> Our objectified time puts before imagination something like a ribbon or scroll marked off into equal blank spaces, suggesting that each be filled with an entry. Writing has no doubt helped toward our linguistic treatment of time, even as the linguistic treatment has guided the uses of writing.[38]

As the geographer Yi-fu Tuan points out,

> A characteristic of Indo-European languages is to spatialise time. Thus, time is "long" or "short," "thenafter" is "thereafter," and "alltimes" is "always." European languages lack special words to express duration, intensity, and tendency. They use explicit spatial metaphors of size, number (plurality), position, shape and motion. It is as though European speech tries to make time and feelings visible, to constrain them to possess spatial dimensions that can be pointed to.[39]

In this manner, the Antipholi characterize their experience in terms of movement, and though critics have often observed that Antipholus of Syracuse wanders as a manifestation of his sense of loss, we have seldom noted that the concept most frequently elided by the imagery is temporality—specifically, lost time. This theme emerges as a major concern in *The Comedy of Errors* in act 2, long before time and the possibility of its recovery is staged in the final scene.

Initially Antipholus of Syracuse characterizes his source of grief in explicitly spatial terms: "I to the world am like a drop of water, / That in the ocean seeks another drop, / Who, falling there to find his fellow forth / (Unseen, inquisitive), confounds himself. / So I, to find a mother and a brother, / In quest of them (unhappy), ah, lose myself" (2.2.35–40). Antipholus compares himself to a questing drop of water in order to describe two distinct parallels: between knowing one's family and knowing oneself, and between memory loss and loss of orientation.[40] This Antipholus searches for his family because he believes that knowing his origins will provide a point from which he can observe the world. He believes that this understanding of his origins will provide a foundation for locating himself within society, as a sense of where one is physically enables one to orient oneself. Thus, when he searches for mother and brother, as he says, he can lose his sense of lack in the physical experience of wandering aimlessly, focusing on his lack of physical orientation to the exclusion of his lack of psychological orientation.[41]

His precarious sense of self is soon undermined by the confusion that results from arriving in the town where the other Antipholus has established himself. The experience of being recognized by people unknown to him does not provoke his ire, as it does for the alien Menaechmus; it makes him question the validity of his experience of reality: "What, was I married to her in my dream? / Or sleep I now and think I hear all this? / What error drives our eyes and ears amiss?" (2.2.182–84). Through language, he elucidates the experience that the audience of *The Menaechmi* undergoes when the Syracusan Menaechmus feigns madness. He questions how he can be confident that he can correctly identify waking consciousness. Though Dromio initially alludes to magic as an explanation—"We talk with goblins, owls, and sprites" (2.2.190)—he soon combines the idea of magic with that of altered consciousness:

S. DROMIO: I am transformed, master, am [not I]?
S. ANTIPHOLUS: I think thou art in mind, and so am I.
S. DROMIO: Nay, master, both in mind and in my shape.

(2.2.195–97)

This notion of metamorphosis indicates his utter disorientation: finding himself known among the unknown, he no longer trusts his physical experience to indicate the familiar form of his body. Despite the joking, Dromio's characterization of his experience indicates his sense that boundaries are melting and he can no longer count upon his shape to remain solid. Antipholus too describes the experience as a "mist":

> Am I in earth, in heaven, or in hell?
> Sleeping or waking, mad or well-advis'd?
> Known unto these, and to myself disguis'd?
> I'll say as they say, and persever so,
> And in this mist at all adventures go.
>
> (2.2.212–16)

In this soliloquy, Antipholus uses the climatic term "mist" to describe the experience that prevents him from gaining clarity on his situation. Unlike the Syracusan Menaechmus, he does not or cannot hew to his own perceptions. Antipholus is willing to accept Adriana's knowledge of him as accurate; what troubles him is that he has no memory, no sense of self that can corroborate what she tells him.[42]

While the Antipholi tend to perceive their problems in terms of spatial diffi-culties, the Dromios consistently allude to temporality instead. The Ephesian Dromio urges timeliness to a master concerned with concreteness: ""'Tis dinner-time,' quoth I: 'My gold!' quoth he. / 'Your meat doth burn,' quoth I. 'My gold!' quoth he. / 'Will you come?' quoth I: 'My gold!' quoth he" (2.1.62–64). As Gamini Salgado comments, "the series of pictures of disrupted time ... are the first words uttered by E. Dromio."[43] Ironically, time *has* drawn the Syracusan Antipholus to travel across the seas; Egeon comments, "My youngest boy, and yet my eldest care, / At eighteen years became inquisitive / After his brother; and importun'd me / That his attendant ... / Might bear him company in the quest of him" (1.1.124–29). Yet in Ephesus this same Antipholus is unmoved by the demands of time. The power of time is stressed by the Syracusan Dromio again when he argues wittily that "There's no time for a man to recover his hair that grows bald by nature" (2.2.72–73). Time cannot be commanded or manipulated, and the best response to the changes that time brings is acknowledgment of Time's power. The Syracusan Antipholus is also correct, however, when he says, "there's a time for all things" (2.2.65). This play is built on the Syracusans' desire to restore lost time and to recapture the lost years when twins and parents were divided from one another. To do so, however, Egeon's family need to recognize that their task is that of recovering time.

Time's capacity to steal from men is most clearly delineated in the Syracusan Dromio's comic turn late in the play, which I will quote in full:

S. DROMIO: No, no, the bell, 'tis time that I were gone:
            It was two ere I left him, and now the clock strikes one.
ADRIANA: The hours come back! That did I never hear.
S. DROMIO: O yes, if any hour meet a sergeant, 'a turns back for very fear.
ADRIANA: As if Time were in debt! How fondly dost thou reason!

S. DROMIO: Time is a very bankrout and owes more than he's worth to season.
Nay, he's a thief too: have you not heard men say,
That Time comes stealing on by night and day?
If 'a be in debt and theft, and a sergeant in the way,
Hath he not reason to turn back an hour in a day?

(4.2.53–62)

One point he makes is that time can reverse itself, a foolish assertion that
becomes metaphorically true in Aemilia's terms. The other point is that time is
a thief and a bankrupt: a thief because he creeps forward and steals opportunity
away from people. And a bankrupt? Because time is both static and progressive.
The word "time" can refer either to the moment or to the passage of time, the
flow of temporality. As Merleau-Ponty argues,

> If we separate the objective world from the finite perspectives which open
> upon it … we find everywhere in it only so many instances of "now."
> These instances of "now," moreover, not being present to anybody, have no
> temporal character and could not occur in sequence. The definition of time
> which is implicit in the comparisons undertaken by common sense, and which
> might be formulated as "a succession of instances of *now*" has not even the
> disadvantage of treating past and future as presents: it is inconsistent, since
> it destroys the very notion of "now," and that of succession.[44]

In other words, time, which is both a moment and an experience of movement
forward into the future, is a paradox. When time moves, it annihilates itself as
a moment. If a "now" exists, then past and present cannot. In Dromio's terms,
time is his own creditor and, failing to pay himself, he turns backward.[45]
Indeed, time fails to move forward for much of this play, as the arrival of the
Syracusan Antipholus begins a circular movement wherein each twin prevents
the other from accomplishing anything he intends. The slapstick is comic repetition, Bergson's "mechanical encrusted upon the living";[46] no wonder that, for
much of the twentieth century, the play was regarded as mechanical, simple,
and as pure farce.

When Aemilia enters for the second time, bringing Antipholus and Dromio
of Syracuse with her, most of the other characters believe at first that they are
seeing another manipulation of space. Adriana perceives their presence as dupli-
cation: "I see two husbands, or mine eyes deceive me" (5.1.332). The Duke,
more canny, suggests, "One of these men is genius to the other: / And so of
these, which is the natural man, / And which the spirit? Who deciphers them?"
(5.1.333–35). Each Dromio is convinced by this hypothesis and asks to have his
spirit conjured away. What the characters themselves see—two Antipholi
onstage simultaneously—is not sufficient to clarify the circumstances that
resulted in this tableau. The characters must treat the tableau as a semiotic field
in order to make sense of the situation.

Aemilia questions not the twins but Egeon, asking him to confirm the story that he has already told about his experiences. The tableau begins to become readable: the Duke recognizes the significance of their exchange. He then reframes the presence of the Antipholi, acknowledging them as the missing twins. In a babble of voices, all the characters piece together the events of the day just past, reinterpreting events with their knowledge of two Antipholi. Their recountal turns the clock back to the day's beginning in an attempt to reorganize "the series of false starts, backtrackings, and collisions by means of which the main action is presented."[47] This brief experience of *déjà vu*, which clarifies rather than confuses the situation, nonetheless cannot mend the torn fabric of Egeon's family life. That task is left to Aemilia.

As I have said, throughout *The Comedy of Errors* the Antipholi seek spatial images to characterize their problems and spatial solutions to resolve those problems. But when Aemilia opens the door of the priory and steps out, the solution is revealed as another medium altogether: the medium of time. The door of the priory, which suggested, though it did not truly offer, the deep perspective of Renaissance interior paintings and famous sixteenth-century Italian theaters, gave the audience the sense of looking back and looking in. As Henri Lefebvre says, "Representational space is alive: it speaks. It has an affective kernel or centre: Ego, bed, bedroom, dwelling, house; or: square, church, graveyard. It embraces the loci of passion, of action and of lived situations, and thus immediately implies time."[48] Shakespeare's borrowings from Roman stage convention reinforce the thematic significance of the third doorway (the priory) as the dwelling of the *dea ex machina* figure, rendering this doorway the passage back to a unified family, bringing together brothers, father, mother, servants, and new wives. But to recognize how the original spectators would have understood what they were seeing, we have to consider what exactly they were looking at. Stage directions presumed original to Shakespeare do designate three houses, generally presumed to be the house of Antipholus, the house of the courtesan, and the priory.[49] How the houses were arranged relative to one another is a matter for debate. If the players wanted to reproduce Plautus's antithesis of courtesan's dwelling versus wife's dwelling, placing the priory in the center would have recreated the balance of the Plautine setting. And if, as Dorsch argues, the priory is the most important building, then it should be in the center; as the priory does provide the play's denouement, this argument is plausible. But if only the central *domus* was indicated by entries in the tiring-house wall, and the other two were more elaborate structures elsewhere on the frame, then other considerations arise. As Proudfoot points out, "It is possible that an upper storey or gallery in the house of Antipholus was also used ... but it is not essential to the play's action."[50] If the upper story was used by Adriana and Antipholus of Syracuse while dining, then having the Phoenix, Antipholus's home, in the center would have made the most sense. All these hypotheses are plausible, but it would be foolish to try to go beyond speculation in the matter.

Another way to examine the staging of *The Comedy of Errors* is to see the number of doorways as less important than their very presence onstage. Whereas

Plautus turned the actors' gaze outward to the audience and beyond, Shakespeare's emphasis on mercantile activity on one hand and domestic intimacy on the other suggests that the onstage doors offered an opportunity to contrast exterior, or social, and interior, or domestic, life. For Plautus's Menaechmi, there is very literally a world elsewhere (to borrow Coriolanus's phrase); that world, the city of Syracuse, is represented by the audience that the alien twin treats as an ally. That world is characterized as a better place, where wives know their place and men have no need to fear the loss of their authority; as Kathleen McCarthy comments, "We are left with a vague sense that life back in Syracuse will be founded only on these 'real' ties and will require no messy economic entanglements."[51] By contrast, in Shakespeare's play the world is complete; society is represented in all its complexity onstage. It seems as if, despite the uniqueness of Ephesus, its society is no different from that of any other community. What Ephesians need is not a way out, but a way of understanding themselves. This need is answered by the Abbess of the priory, whose role resembles that of Father Time in *The Winter's Tale*. Both literally and symbolically, Aemilia provides the synthesis that brings thesis and antithesis (or Antipholus) together.

The play's very emphasis on time and recovery suggests that the original production might have offered some sort of physical representation of these elements. Such a possibility would have been consonant with the similarity between the architectural details of the doorways and those of Renaissance memory theaters, especially those of Robert Fludd. Fludd, who calls his memory buildings "theatres," proposes several different rooms, including a primary theater with ten places, five doorways and five columns, and a secondary one with three doorways.[52] The similarity makes it reasonable, I think, to link Shakespeare's doorways with the tradition of memory theater. Memory theaters were imaginary structures that enabled people to remember lists or series by visualizing each item in a specific place in an elaborate interior. While I am skeptical of Arthur Kinney's suggestion that the doorways represented Hell, Earth, and Heaven, it is reasonable to perceive the places represented as connotative of certain choices. For one or both of the Antipholi, the door of the courtesan represents a way of losing the self; that of the Phoenix suggests the values and practices of domestic life; and that of the priory represents the long way back to one's origins through memory and its recountal. Barbara Freedman suggests that time and redemption are thematically linked in this play, commenting,

> to *redeem* literally means 'to buy back,' to recover only 'by payment of the amount due, or by fulfilling some obligation' (*OED*). The curious financial arrangement implies that Egeon can recover his marital identity only on the condition that he pay neglected marital debts.[53]

He does so, I argue, by paying back the lost time, not in the framework of *The Comedy of Errors*, this drama of Aristotelian unities, but in the time of the abbey, receding into the past where the audience cannot go. Time can only

Figure 1.3 "Ars memoriae," a woodcut representing a memory theater, from Robert Fludd's *Utriusque Cosmi, Maioris scilicet et Minoris, metaphysica, physica, atque technica Historia* (1617–24).
(Oppenheim: de Bry [1619] 2a2: 55)

progress by moving backward first in order to restore Egeon's family as the original family unit. In Aemilia's characterization of the reunion, it is a new birth, from which point they can move forward to the present through the medium of the "gossip's feast" (the traditional celebration of a child's baptism).

My argument that the offstage area behind the priory door may serve as the physical representation of the past is also supported by recourse to the conventions of Dutch genre paintings during the period. In the meaning he creates for the priory doorway, Shakespeare may have drawn on recent developments in perspective painting in order to offer the audience a visual representation of receding but recoverable time. I assert that the three doorways drew on conventions that had already presented time in spatial terms, thereby evoking a schema that urged the audience to "read" the scene allegorically. Karel van Mander's *Het schilder-boeck* (1604) uses the term *perspect* to characterize a vista in the context of an architectural setting, as when "a receding passageway or colonnade is viewed through an archway."[54] Through deep-space interior composition, *perspects* offered the painter an opportunity for dramatic revelation, narrative expansion, and commentary.[55] The art historian Martha Hollander comments, "While an opening in the picture space allows the eyes to 'plunge' into the picture, the 'small background figures and a distant landscape' inside it can be used to enhance the drama."[56] Hollander explains that these vistas can depict additional events in a story, "provid[ing] a narrative context," and she discusses in detail one painting where the *perspect* accomplishes that by illustrating an earlier moment in the story.[57] The relation of secondary to primary subject in the painting is also discussed by the seventeenth-century art theorist Gerard de Lairesse, who says in his *Groot schilderboek* (1707), "The outcome or ending of a story must always be set in the principal place in the composition, and the beginning of it in the background."[58] Hollander compares the deeper understanding a *perspect* provides to the viewer with the purpose of Erasmian *copia*: "variety as a tool of argument. Pictures use the same rhetorical strategies of comparison and opposition."[59] These compositional techniques seem more and more closely related to the uses of the memory theater, and when we recall some of Erasmus's best-known adages, *Veritatem dies aperit* (Time brings the truth to light) and *Tempus omnia revelat* (Time reveals all things), the evidence suggests that a curtained doorway containing the past may itself be a visual emblem of truth or coherence.[60]

In metaphorical terms as well as in the presumed staging, Aemilia's emergence and her words gave the audience a sense of looking in and, by looking in, a sense of looking back in time: after emerging from the doorway, she asks characters to come inside to offer them the opportunity to examine the past in order to fill in the gaps of the present. As both Egeon's wife and a representative of the early Christian church, as both Aemilia and Ladie Abbesse (as she is named in the Folio), this figure serves as the missing piece whose presence finishes the puzzle. Unlike her offspring, she is not twinned, yet she manifests both a present and a past identity—a twinship not of presence but of disparate times.

The significance of the priory doorway is reinforced by action earlier in the play that involves the other doorways. While Antipholus resorts to the courtesan's house in act 3 as an alternative to his own, it is not until the final act that anyone either enters or emerges from the priory. This circumstance could have given the audience the impression that this area was dead space, particularly since the courtesan's house does not play a major part in the action either. But if it was used effectively, the door to the priory could have attained an importance that only built as its use was delayed. Whether her doorway originally stood center stage, as some scholars suggest, or off to one side, Aemilia's emergence from the priory—and, indeed, the priory itself—alters the shape of the stage-space.[61] As Abbess, Aemilia is a holy woman of Ephesus, seemingly energized with powers of Christian redemption specifically affiliated with St. Paul's epistle on Christian marriage. But she is also charged with the pagan powers of Time, turning the clock back to resolve events that have remained unresolved. The door-frame out of which Aemilia, emissary from the past, emerges, provided a visual parallel to the frame story provided by Egeon's presence at the play's opening and conclusion. This connection might have been further reinforced by staging that visually emphasized Egeon's plight, suggesting that the outcome of the comedy must integrate Egeon's story and offer a conclusion more profound than the slapstick that dominates much of the action.

The redemptive qualities of the *coup de théâtre* at the close of *The Comedy of Errors* derive in part from its relation to what has been called an "ideology of time." The perception of time as a concept (rather than a lived medium) was heavily inflected during the Renaissance by religious dogma; in discussing Augustine and his period, the historian Hans Blumenberg asserts "a new concept of human freedom [that places] responsibility for the condition of the world as a challenge relating to the future, not as an original offense in the past."[62] By recapitulating the past, implicitly contained within the abbey, with her expanded family circle, Aemilia hopes to redeem the future, taking her family out of the confusion of human (and therefore faulty) temporal experience into a larger Christian cycle of time (represented by the thirty-three years she refers to). To recover the future, however, it is necessary to go backward in order to achieve the process of recovery that her words presage:

> Reverend Duke, vouchsafe to take the pains
> To go with us into the abbey here,
> And hear at large discoursed all our fortunes ...
> And we shall make full satisfaction.
> Thirty-three years have I but gone in travail
> Of you, my sons, and till this present hour
> My heavy burthen ne'er delivered.

(5.1.394–403)

Aemilia urges that all present go back through the door into the priory, there to hear not the recountal of that day alone but that of the last thirty-three years. Only by the family's shared recountal of the past can they recreate the family circle that existed before their odyssey began. Aemilia's doorway, I propose, represents a kind of "dark backward and abysm of time." Her promise to restore the past, which she characterizes as a birth process, suggests that the doorway represents on some level a passage, the woman's birth passage itself. But it is also a passage back to origins through the medium of memory.

The play's ability to convey the significance of time would depend on the audience's recognition of the need to read the scene allegorically, which is why the staging cues this recognition through the use of space. This new means of staging time would have given the spectators a foundation for how to judge the action and the significance of the conclusion. Moreover, it would direct the spectators to assess the action as the spectators of the medieval morality did, rather than encouraging them to identify with the characters, as in mimetic performance; despite a radically different type of staging, the audiences of moralities were similarly nudged toward recognition of the responsibility to interpret the drama laid before them.[63]

Time progresses here by moving backward in order to restore Egeon's dispersed relatives to their original positions in the family unit. Egeon redeems the time he has lost by recounting the missing years to the family members from whom he had been parted. In Aemilia's characterization, after recounting the past they can reach the present of a new family configuration: two married sons starting new families, presided over by matriarch and patriarch. Past time, or memory, shared among the characters of the play, brings resolution even beyond that shown to the audience. And for the audience, living in their own chronology, the collective memory that the characters piece together represents a closure all the more tantalizing because it is never revealed to them. The emphasis in *The Menaechmi* on the demands of community—and the play's inclusion of the audience as a community—seems to grow organically from the stage design. But the comical problems with time in *The Comedy of Errors* seem to be resolved by elements of the staging evident only when Aemilia emerges from the priory and offers an invitation that clearly *excludes* the theater audience, who must remain outside the priory door even as the characters onstage enter in.

The role of the audience is not merely shaped by the stage design; each play's themes generate a dramatic imperative for the audience as those themes become apparent to the watchers in the course of the performance. *The Menaechmi* is typical of Plautine drama in the interaction between actor and audience; yet the text suggests that the audience of the play developed a highly unusual relationship with Menaechmus of Syracuse. The audiences of *The Comedy of Errors* were not a passive entity but began to fulfill their function only at the moment when watchers were clearly excluded from the action. The subject of community, which is so important to both plays, results in different expectations of the audience. In both plays the audience receives a strong hint at the conclusion that the reunited families of this drama have come to substitute for the communities that were previously constituted onstage. The exclusion of the audience at the end becomes the very mark of closure, whether because observers have become redundant or because their exclusion makes the family a smaller, tighter unit. While community may be the focal concern of Plautus's play and the nuclear family that of Shakespeare's, both plots emphasize the completeness of the family circle at the conclusion.

Notes

1 For David Bevington, one is farce and the other city comedy, whereas for Leo Salingar, Shakespeare's play is more clearly defined by medieval romance. David Bevington, "*The Comedy of Errors* in the Context of the Late 1580s and Early 1590s," in *The Comedy of Errors: Critical Essays*, ed. Robert S. Miola (New York: Garland, 1997), 341–43; L. G. Salingar, "Time and Art in Shakespeare's Romances," *Renaissance Drama* 9 (1966): 12–19.

2 As Marvin Carlson has pointed out, social and cultural messages may be conveyed "through the articulation of space and through the choice of visual, decorative elements" (*Places of Performance* [Ithaca, NY: Cornell University Press, 1989], 9).

3 Stanton B. Garner, Jr., *Bodied Spaces: Phenomenology and Performance in Contemporary Drama* (Ithaca, NY: Cornell University Press, 1994), 4.

4 For a treatment of this concept, see Keir Elam, *The Semiotics of Theatre and Drama* (New York: Routledge, 2002), 78–79.

5 Mary Thomas Crane, *Shakespeare's Brain: Reading with Cognitive Theory* (Princeton: Princeton University Press, 2001), 36–66, and Amanda Piesse, "Space for the Self: Place, Persona and Self-Projection in *The Comedy of Errors* and *Pericles*," in *Renaissance Configurations: Voices, Bodies, Spaces, 1580–1690*, ed. Gordon McMullan (New York: Palgrave, 1998 and 2001): 151–70.

6 Kathleen McCarthy, *Slaves, Masters, and the Art of Authority in Plautine Comedy* (Princeton: Princeton University Press, 2000), 37–38.

7 Cf. George E. Duckworth, *The Nature of Roman Comedy: A Study in Popular Entertainment* (Princeton: Princeton University Press, 1952), 82–85.

8 Ibid., 82. See also Richard C. Beacham, *The Roman Theatre and Its Audience* (Cambridge, MA: Harvard University Press, 1992), 60.

9 Duckworth, *Comedy*, 82–83.

10 Beacham, *Roman Theatre*, 60.

11 Ibid., 61.

12 Ibid., 63.

13 "[G]raecissat, tamen non atticissat"; Plautus, *The Menaechmi*. Latin from *Plautus*, ed. and trans. Paul Nixon (Cambridge, MA: Harvard University Press; The Loeb Classical Library, 1925; reprinted 1988), 366. English from Plautus, *The Menaechmus Twins and Two Other Plays*, ed. and trans. Lionel Casson (New York: Norton, 1971), 2.

14 Niall W. Slater, *Plautus in Performance: The Theater of the Mind* (Princeton: Princeton University Press, 1985), 16.

15 See Slater, *Plautus*, 12, for detailed definitions of these terms.

16 Duckworth, *Comedy*, 82–83.

17 "Quicum haec mulier loquitur?"; Plautus, *The Menaechmi*. Latin, Nixon, *Plautus*, 400. English trans., Casson, *Menaechmus Twins*, 21.

18 "Quis hic est, qui adversus it mihi?"; Plautus, *The Menaechmi*. Latin, Nixon, *Plautus*, 412. All further translations of *The Menaechmi* are from Nixon's version unless otherwise specified.

19 All quotations from the works of William Shakespeare are from *The Riverside Shakespeare*, ed. G. Blakemore Evans (Boston: Houghton Mifflin, 1974) unless otherwise specified.

20 "[S]atine, ut quemque conspicor, / ita me ludificant?"; Nixon, *Plautus*, 414.

21 "Haec me curaturum dicito—/ ut quantum possint quique liceant veneant. / iamne abiit intro? abiit, operuit fores"; ibid., Latin 418; English 419.

22   MATRONA: Non ego istaec tua flagitia possum perpeti.
                 nam med aetatem viduam esse mavelim,
                 quam istaec flagitia tua pati quae tu facis.
        MEN. S: Quid id ad me, tu te nuptam possis perpeti
                 an sis abitura a tuo viro? an mos hic ita est,
                 peregrino ut advenienti narrent fabulas?
        MATRONA: Quas fabulas? non, inquam, patiar praeterhac,
                 quin vidua vivam quam tuos mores perferam.
        MEN S: Mea quidem hercle causa vidua vivito,
                 vel usque dum regnum optinebit Iuppiter.

                                        Ibid., Latin 438; English 439

23 "Quid mihi meliust, quam quando illi me insanire praedicant, / ego med adsimulem insanire, ut illos a me absterream?"; ibid., Latin 448; English 449.

24 "[A]udio, sed non abire possum ab his regionibus, / ita illa me ab laeva rabiosa femina adservat canis, / poste autem illinc hircus calvus"; ibid., Latin 448; English 449.

25 "[N]i occupo aliquid mihi consilium, hi domum me ad se auferent"; ibid., Latin 450; English 451.

26   Multa mi imperas, Apollo; nunc equos iunctos iubes
        capere me indomitos, ferocis, atque in currum inscendere,
        ut ego hunc proteram leonem vetulum, olentem, edentulum.
        iam adstiti in currum, iam lora teneo, iam stimulus in manust.
        agite equi, facitote sonitus ungularum appareat,
        cursu celeri facite inflexa sit pedum pernicitas.

                                        Ibid., Latin 452; English 453

27   Iamne isti abierunt, quaeso, ex conspectu meo,
        qui me vi cogunt, ut validus insaniam?

quid cesso abire ad navem, dum salvo licet?
vosque omnis quaeso, si senex revenerit,
ne me indicetis qua platea hinc aufugerim.

Ibid., Latin 452–54; English 453–55

28 Martin Gardner offers the following comment on the philosophical dilemma posed by the King's dream: "The Tweedle brothers defend Bishop Berkeley's view that all material objects, including ourselves, are only 'sorts of things' in the mind of God. Alice takes the common-sense position of Samuel Johnson, who supposed that he refuted Berkeley by kicking a large stone. ... The Berkeleyan theme troubled Carroll as it troubles all Platonists" (Lewis Carroll, *The Annotated Alice*, ed. Martin Gardner [New York: New American Library, 1974], 238).

29 "Auctio fiet Menaechmi mane sane septimi"; Nixon, *Plautus*, Latin 486; English 487.

30 "[N]unc interim / eamus intro, frater"; ibid., Latin 484; English 485.

31 Andrew Gurr and Mariko Ichikawa, *Staging in Shakespeare's Theatres* (Oxford: Oxford University Press, 2000), 8.

32 Ibid., 27.

33 Ibid., 4.

34 This debate is not new, of course; Sidney Thomas weighed in on the subject in 1956 ("The Date of *The Comedy of Errors*," *Shakespeare Quarterly* 7, no. 4 [1956]: 377–84). More recently, Charles Whitworth, editor of the Oxford edition of the play, said in 2002 that "[a] number of factors, not all of which are hard facts, converge to suggest further that the play, unique in the Shakespeare canon in several important respects, was composed expressly for that occasion, or at least for that Christmas season. ... *The Comedy of Errors* looks like a new composition, purpose-written for the Christmas season, 1594" (William Shakespeare, Introduction, *The Comedy of Errors* [Oxford, Oxford University Press, 2002], 2–4). Yet T. S. Dorsch, editor of The New Cambridge Shakespeare edition of the play, said in 1988 that "it is now generally accepted that the date must be moved back to the first years of the 1590s" (William Shakespeare, Introduction, *The Comedy of Errors*, ed. T. S. Dorsch [Cambridge: Cambridge University Press, 1988], 1). Clearly, the date is still under debate.

35 While stage directions in F1 for *The Comedy of Errors* generally give only the names of the characters entering (e.g. "*Enter Adriana and Luciana*" [4.1.113 s.d.]), some stage directions do indicate a place from which characters are coming (e.g. "*Enter Dromio Sira. from the Bay*" [4.1.84 s.d.]). These and such directions as "*Exeunt to the Priorie*" (5.1.37 s.d.) and "*Enter Antipholus Ephes. Dromio from the Courtizans*" (4.1.13 s.d.) provide strong evidence that Shakespeare is following Roman staging conventions. Two or three doors were common in Roman theater, and the painted boards used at the back could easily have been changed to suit the demands of the production. However, *The Menaechmi* calls for only two doors: one for Menaechmus's house and one for that of his mistress.

The Folio references that specify "*the Courtizans*" and "*the Priorie*" lead Chambers to comment that "at the back of the stage three houses or doors represented to the right and left the Priory with some religious emblem over it, and the Courtesan's house with the sign of the Porpentine, and in the centre the house of Antipholus with the sign of the Phoenix" (E. K. Chambers, *William Shakespeare: A Study of Facts and Problems* [Oxford: Clarendon, 1930], 1: 307), qtd. by R. A. Foakes, ed., Introduction, *The Comedy of Errors* [London: Methuen / The Arden Shakespeare (2nd series), 1968, xxxv]. Foakes also cites "for accounts of the use of 'houses' on medieval and later stages" Allardyce Nicoll, *The Development of the Theatre* (New York: Harcourt Brace, 1952), 65–73, 82–85, 119 (Foakes, Introduction, xxxv).

36 George R. Kernodle considers in *From Art to Theatre* (Chicago: University of Chicago Press, 1944) how the demands of early modern plays with similar needs in staging might have been met (133, 160–63), ctd. in Foakes, Introduction, xxxv.

37 See Erwin Panofsky's *Studies in Iconology: Humanistic Themes in the Art of the Renaissance* (New York: Harper, 1962), 69–91; see also Frederick Kiefer's *Shakespeare's Visual Theatre: Staging the Personified Characters* (Cambridge: Cambridge University Press, 2003), 159–68 for allegorical representations of time in such works as *The Winter's Tale*, *The Thracian Wonder*, *Corona Minervae*, *The Whore of Babylon*, and *The Trial of Treasure*.

38 Benjamin Whorf, "Relation of Thought and Behavior in Language," in *Collected Papers on Metalinguistics* (Washington, DC: Foreign Service Institute, 1952), 153.

39 Yi-fu Tuan, "Space and Place: Humanistic Perspective," in *Philosophy in Geography*, eds. Stephen Gale and Gunnar Olsson (Dordrecht: D. Reidel, 1979), 393.

40 For a fascinating Lacanian reading of this play, see Barbara Freedman's chapter "Reading Errantly: Misrecognition and the Uncanny in *The Comedy of Errors*," in her book *Staging the Gaze: Postmodernism, Psychoanalysis, and Shakespearean Comedy* (Ithaca: Cornell University Press, 1991). This chapter itself is a substantial revision of Freedman's earlier reading of the play, "Egeon's Debt: Self-Division and Self-Redemption in *The Comedy of Errors*," *English Literary Renaissance* 10, no. 3 (1980): 360–83.

41 Cf. Gamini Salgado, "'Time's Deformed Hand': Sequence, Consequence, and Inconsequence in *The Comedy of Errors*," *Shakespeare Survey* 25 (1972), 84, for a similar observation.

42 As Salgado comments, Antipholus of Syracuse makes "a conscious decision to enter the other time of dreams" (87).

43 Ibid., 85.

44 Maurice Merleau-Ponty, *Phenomenology of Perception*, trans. Colin Smith (London: Routledge, 1962), 412.

45 Salgado reads the line quite differently:

> S. Dromio's cryptic line … has often been taken to mean "There is never enough time to do all that occasion offers" but it could equally easily, and with perhaps greater relevance, be understood as saying that time has so exhausted itself that it's more trouble than it's worth to set it straight ("season" neatly combining the two usual senses of "bring to maturity" and "make palatable or agreeable"). Alternatively, if we are not too snobbish to credit the lower orders with quasi-metaphysical intuitions, S. Dromio may be saying that time in itself is empty and owes all its powers and more to "season," the harmonious cyclical regularity of the natural world. In either case the involved and often—admittedly—tedious fooling does have an important bearing on the play's theme and structure.
>
> (89)

46 Henri Bergson, "Laughter," in *Comedy*, ed. Wylie Sypher (Baltimore: Johns Hopkins University Press, 1980), 84.

47 Salgado, "Time", 83.

48 Henri Lefebvre, *The Production of Space*, trans. Donald Nicholson-Smith (Oxford: Blackwell, 1991), 42.

49 Most critics have naturally associated this staging with its Roman antecedents. An exception, Arthur F. Kinney, asserts that "the forms and features of the mystery cycles are pervasive in *The Comedy of Errors*" and sees in the three buildings "the traditional stations of Hell, Earth, and Heaven of mystery and morality traditions" (168, 169). See Arthur F. Kinney, "Shakespeare's *Comedy of Errors* and the Nature

of Kinds," in *The Comedy of Errors: Critical Essays*, ed. Robert S. Miola (New York: Garland, 1997).

While Kinney's Christian reading of the play seems plausible, it relies largely on a few key details such as Aemilia's statement, "Thirty-three years have I but gone in travail / Of you, my sons" (5.1.401–2).

50 Richard Proudfoot, Introduction to *The Comedy of Errors*, in *The Arden Shakespeare Complete Works*, eds. Richard Proudfoot, Ann Thompson, and David Scott Kastan (Walker-on-Thames: Arden, 1998), xxxiv–xxxv.

51 McCarthy, *Slaves, Masters*, 61.

52 In *The Art of Memory* (London: Pimlico, 1992), Frances Yates even suggests that "Fludd meant to use a real 'public theatre' in his memory system; he says so, repeatedly emphasizing that he is using 'real' and not 'fictitious' places. And what he shows us about the stage of the Globe we either know was there, or has been conjectured to be there" (349).

53 Freedman, *Staging the Gaze*, 98–99. Freedman's view of time and redemption is supported by Shankar Raman's comments: "Time divides Egeon, producing a revenant who threatens to undo him and usurp his place. Hence even the first of the successive anagnorises that will ultimately restore Egeon to himself is tinged by doubt: 'Egeon, art thou not? Or else his ghost' (5.1.337), Antipholus of Syracuse uncertainly asks" (Shankar Raman, "Marking Time: Memory and Market in *The Comedy of Errors*," *Shakespeare Quarterly* 56, no. 2 [2005]: 181).

54 Martha Hollander, *An Entrance for the Eyes: Space and Meaning in Seventeenth-Century Dutch Art* (Berkeley: University of California Press, 2002), 9.

55 Ibid., 9.

56 Ibid., 13.

57 Ibid., 14, 16. Hollander connects *perspects* and *doorsiens* to theatrical devices:

> Architectural structures in Renaissance paintings frequently imitate the three-part format of the stage. ... The archway used in stage design was highly adaptable not only for different plays but also for different media. From the 1490s on this classical structure was used for assorted architectural fantasies. Serlio recommended it for windows, doors, gates, tombs, and altars. The three-part archway was also featured in pageants and triumphal entries. ... It even became a popular format for book frontispieces, which expressed the author's intentions in diagrammatic form. The central archway revealed an important motif—a portrait of the author, or a scene, landscape, or symbolic image—flanked by allegorical personifications that were depicted as sculptures and separated from the central arch by columns. Thus stage design and emblems, frontispieces, book illustrations, and paintings incorporated the same organizing principle: partitioning an image into a main scene with one or more ancillary images.
>
> (33–34)

58 Qtd. in Hollander, *Entrance*, 46.

59 Ibid., 18.

60 My reference to a curtained doorway assumes that the doorways were indicated with a minimum of actual structure, created with a minimum of effort. If, as I speculate, they were somewhat more elaborate, with either painted or actual architectural elements, then this effect would be enhanced much further.

61 As Mary Crane so concisely puts it, "There does seem to be some disagreement about the arrangement of the 'houses,' with some editors accepting Chambers' belief that Antipholus's house was in the center, and others ... giving the central place to the Priory" (Crane, *Shakespeare's Brain*, 228). Dorsch confidently states, "In the centre the priory, the most important building, is marked with a cross or

some other religious emblem" (Introduction, 22–23). G. Blakemore Evans places the Phoenix in the center (Shakespeare, *The Riverside Shakespeare*, 83), as does Richard Proudfoot (Introduction, xxxv).

62 Hans Blumenberg, *The Legitimacy of the Modern Age*, trans. Robert M. Wallace (Cambridge, MA: Massachusetts Institute of Technology Press, 1983), 137.
63 Catherine Belsey, *The Subject of Tragedy: Identity and Difference in Renaissance Drama* (New York: Methuen, 1985), 22–23.

2 "Bodied forth"

Spectator, stage, and actor in early modern English theaters

"And as imagination bodies forth / The forms of things unknown, the poet's pen / Turns them to shapes, and gives to aery nothing / A local habitation and a name" (5.1.14–17).[1] So says Shakespeare's Duke Theseus in *A Midsummer Night's Dream*, ascribing to the playwright the power to corporealize the visions of his imagination. In *Henry V*, Shakespeare alludes to another part of the theatrical transaction when the Prologue urges the audience, "'[T]is your thoughts that now must deck our kings" (Pro. 28). In this passage the imagination is that of the audience, who must "piece out [the] imperfections" of the actors with imaginative powers inspired by the playwright's words (Pro. 23). Both passages characterize dramatic text as if it were purely literary—as if there were no theatrical event mediating between text and audience. In fact, the presence of actors in the theater also shapes the experience of the playgoers significantly. Actors' bodies incarnate the playwright's vision, but they add their own qualities to the written part.

Actors affect the playgoer's experience on an additional level. While an actor who comes onstage is said to "take the stage," one could say with more justice that the stage takes him. Actors are performers, but their bodies are stage properties. Just as objects define a spatial area, so do bodies, and in the theater the qualities of a body may be used for effect. Merleau-Ponty notes that the body is always oriented to its surroundings; Edward T. Hall examines the physiological mechanisms that make that orientation possible.[2] These effects operate in theatrical performance: actors' bodies shape the space for other actors, and for nonperformers too. In the words of Stanton B. Garner, Jr.,

> As soon as an actor steps onto the stage and into this imagined theater scenario, a fundamental shift takes place with phenomenological consequences different from those for artistic genres in which the body fails to make an actual appearance. ... On stage, what was oriented in relation to the gaze is now also oriented in relation to the body that inhabits its boundaries.[3]

The perceptions of both actors and playgoers are affected by "the way that the bodies of the actors and other scenic elements move about within the defined stage space, the spatial patterning that is called 'blocking' in modern English and American theatre."[4] The effects depend largely on proxemic experience, the sense of orientation derived from the proximity of other objects. The breadth and depth of a theater's auditorium guarantees that each playgoer's perception of the action onstage will be a little different. From a phenomenological viewpoint, however, the actor's body

> constitutes a subject point from which the other elements receive competing orientation. ... With the actor's entrance, the stage as a whole becomes a differently oriented field in the broader field of spectatorship, refocused in terms of a subjectivity that is never reducible to spectatorial object. The very nature of this internal (dis)orientation adds new (and often divergent) layers of perceptual givenness to the components of mise-en-scène.[5]

The actor's body becomes a focus that draws the attention of the watchers, while multiple actors shape the stage according to verbal and physical involvement in the action. A scene may have a tight focus or a loose one; actors may be strung out along the lip of a stage or massed in one part of the stage like a bloc. Conventions guide the spatial patterning of a production to some extent, but the more significant element is usually the stage design.

Especially when there is little else filling the stage, bodies shape the scene. I examine the public and private stages of early modern England in this chapter because their minimal sets and sparse use of props lend extra weight to the massing of bodies. I focus on the experience these bodies provide and the theme that grows out of their semiotic function: both the subjective experience of embodiment and the subjectivity that was such a frequent motif in early modern drama.

***

To begin, let us picture the original staging of these two death scenes.

In George Chapman's *Bussy D'Ambois* (1603–4), the title character fights off a host of assassins, then turns to combat the man who has hired them. Upon conquering his enemy, Bussy grants mercy to him just as a pistol shot from an assassin standing offstage wounds him mortally. Amazed that his body is "but penetrable flesh," Bussy swears to die standing, like Emperor Vespasian, and then apostrophizes his sword: "Prop me, true sword, as thou hast ever done! / The equal thought I bear of life and death / Shall make me faint on no side; I am up / Here like a Roman statue! I will stand / Till death hath made me marble. O, my fame, / Live in despite of murder" (5.4.78, 93–98).[6] In contrast, the heroine of Shakespeare's *Romeo and Juliet* rises from her catafalque only to learn, as the Friar gestures toward Romeo's body, that "A greater power than we can contradict / Hath thwarted our intents" (5.3.153–54). The Friar almost immediately leaves Juliet. Seeking a means of suicide, she finds Romeo's dagger: "Yea, noise? Then I'll be brief. O happy dagger, / This is thy sheath [*stabs herself*]; there rust, and let me die" (5.3.169–70).

Bussy's death is a public one—Monsieur and Guise look on from above— and his final speeches demonstrate his concern with his position in the social hierarchy rather than with his private life. The action foregrounds his wounded but upright body which, because of the crowd of murderers, must necessarily be located at the forefront of the stage; similarly, because of the combat with Montsurry, he must be close to or at center stage. Although Bussy is surrounded by others, his opponent and the assassins would be sure to stand well out of reach of his sword. Turned to watch him, Montsurry's face would reflect the audience's own interest in the extent of Bussy's injury. Tamyra and the shade of the Friar might clutter up the visual tableau by approaching Bussy—or strengthen it by allowing Bussy to stand unimpeded until his death. Audience involvement would have been affected by two extra-dramatic factors: intensified, perhaps, by their proximity to the indoor stage of St. Paul's and distanced—perhaps—by the fact that the actors were children: the Children of Paul's.

Produced by the Lord Chamberlain's Men around 1597, *Romeo and Juliet* was performed on the public stage.[7] The tomb to which the stage directions refer several times would, logically, have been represented by the tiring-house, receding from the façade at the back of the large platform stage.[8] Audiences might even have had to squint or lean forward to see Juliet's exact gesture in that shadowy recess. Aside from the prone bodies of Romeo inside and Paris just on the threshold, Juliet would have been quite alone as she stabbed herself. The visual focus would have emphasized the narrowing perspective created by distance and detail: a significant but not broad gesture, staged in a visually uncluttered space, far back from the audience. Such staging would have pulled the audience in, forcing their involvement by making them strain to see the action.

Both stagings enclose the death scene. Bussy's is enclosed by the watching actors who mirror for the audience their spectacular involvement. The death scene is also enclosed mimetically (though not visually) by the scene's setting: Tamyra's closet, the small room where she has already received Bussy and the Friar as they rise through a trapdoor. The necessary staging suggests Chapman's enjoyment of visual paradox. Everything about Bussy's death emphasizes its public nature: his concern with fame, the watchers above, the presence of the tangentially involved assassins, the hero's steadfast insistence on dying on his feet (to impress whom if not those watching?); yet it occurs in a private place, the one in which Tamyra has engaged her lover in intimate acts and her husband in intimate conversations.[9] By his theatrical mode of dying, Bussy transforms Tamyra's private room into his showplace, the site of his final enactment of epic fortitude. By reconfiguring its function, Bussy pushes the limits of the imagined space outward. Ringed by the other characters, he is enclosed by the space, but by his words he broadens it, dissolving Tamyra's bedroom into the larger frame of the playhouse of St. Paul's. (Smaller than that of Blackfriars, the stage of St. Paul's was perhaps twenty feet wide and fairly shallow, since the entire auditorium was less than sixty-six feet long.)[10]

In the death scene, Chapman has his theatrical cake and eats it too: he concludes the play in the kind of intimate setting that functioned so effectively on the stage of the private playhouse,[11] yet he permits Bussy the rhetorical gestures that transform Tamyra's closet into an orator's platform. While the setting and the staging of the scene isolate the hero, his performance simultaneously reminds the watchers of their collectivity and their role—as watchers—in apotheosizing him beyond a mere malcontent or bedroom cavalier. His expectation that death will "make [him] marble" alludes to the permanence of statuary and evokes both the vertical space of the statue and the horizontal space of the tomb's carved effigy.[12] Thus, the setting becomes a metatheatrical forum for Bussy's aspirations to epic heroism: the rhetorical equivalent of a modern stage blackout with a spotlight on the face of a soliloquizing actor.

Juliet's death scene is also enclosed—by the setting of the tomb and its stage equivalent, the tiring-house. Shakespeare uses Romeo to emphasize the claustrophobic nature of the place in several ways: by having the youth pry open the door with a mattock and a crowbar (5.3.22 and 48 s.d.); by having him allude to Death as a monstrous Cupid who reenacts the myth's bedroom scene with Juliet (or Romeo himself) as a new Psyche; by vividly evoking the tomb through Romeo's references to "worms that are thy chambermaids" (5.3.109). For a straight Freudian interpreter, this Liebestod is clearly a return to the womb.[13] Romeo returns to his home in Verona and buries himself, his last gesture an orgasmic kiss. Juliet ecstatically stabs herself; like Romeo, her last word is "die," with its obvious double-entendre, and her final gesture transforms her entire body into a sheath (punning on the Latin *vagina*) for Romeo's phallic dagger. The site of her budding fertility becomes a place of death.

Both death scenes complicate the nature of the place in which they occur, going well beyond the usual complication of a stage set. Bussy's speech dissolves the fictional place in which the hero dies; Juliet's tomb metonymizes her body. Theorist Anne Ubersfeld asserts that

> by virtue of the multiplicity of its concrete networks, stage space can simultaneously convey the image of a metaphorical network, a semantic field, and an actantial [activating or energizing] model. ... Likewise, once stage space can be simultaneously the figure of a given text, of a sociocultural or sociopolitical network, or of a topography of the mind, we can be sure that there are substitutive crossovers between these different shaping structures.[14]

As the penetration of Juliet's body has been thematized by imagery and re-presented in her manner of death, it is more generally figured in Romeo's violent entrance into her tomb. Just as he has forced his way into the Capulet home and the Capulet family, he now violates another stronghold of the dynasty: their burial vault. Each of these family structures—including Juliet's body—is figured in Romeo's final, frantic violation of the inner room. Juliet symbolically repeats the process of violation when she stabs her own body. The same symbolic structure appears to operate, though more subtly, throughout *Bussy D'Ambois*, only concluding with Bussy's death. The hero has always entered Tamyra's room (the site of several trysts) by rising up out of a trapdoor from a secret passageway suggesting (to a classic Freudian theorist, at least) the vagina. While Tamyra has blocked her husband throughout the play in every way possible, refusing to grant him the information he asks for even when he stabs her and racks her, she is open to Bussy, even arranging his first visit to her through a transparent stratagem:

> And he I love will loathe me when he sees
> I fly my sex, my virtue, my renown
> To run so madly on a man unknown.
> See, see, a vault is opening that was never
> Known to my lord and husband, nor to any
> But him that brings the man I love, and me.

(2.2.124–29)

The "vault" she refers to is literally the machinery raising Bussy and the Friar from the cellarage below. This is where Freud fails us: though it is tempting to see the passage as a symbol of female genitalia, there is no evidence to suggest that Tamyra denies her husband access to her body. The vault, then, represents something more sophisticated: an aspect of Tamyra hidden from the world, one revealed only to her father confessor. Despite the focus on access to Tamyra's body, the true emphasis is on her subjectivity.[15] As in *Romeo and Juliet*, the playwright uses the fictional space as a figure for the heroine; the hero's penetration of that space, however, is a multivalent act.

The symbolic framework of such stagings, in which the stage-space represents the self of a character in either physical or psychological terms, was by no means an innovation. Such a framework is well known to dramatic scholars today and was quite familiar to the early modern theatergoer as well. Its precedent exists in the morality play, which allegorizes the Christian's struggle against worldliness as a series of external events. In the morality play, while each psychological aspect of the protagonist is personified as a separate character in a classic psychomachia (a representation of the conflict of the soul), the stage serves as a map of the protagonist's self, often drawing on symbolic meanings of the compass points to justify a character's entrance from a specific direction. In such a play, the Christian figure is staged twice: once as an actor in the play's events and once as the performance site upon which the struggle between good and evil is enacted. In Catherine Belsey's words, the Christian figure is "the momentary location" of a cosmic struggle.[16] Though the diagram of the Macro manuscript figures the stage of *The Castle of Perseverance* as a circle, that circle, a microcosm of the world, is also a macrocosm of the Christian himself. Throughout the play, the stage is the site for the wanderings of Mankind, who is enticed by various temptations that stand upon scaffolds set at the stage's perimeter. But these temptations, like the figure of God, can also approach Mankind on the stage, thus penetrating the space representing his self—what is alternately presented as his soul and his consciousness.

At certain moments, early modern plays also use the stage (or part of the stage) to embody the main character. Belsey has pointed out that, at moments of particular tension, early modern playwrights tended to draw on the morality tradition, engendering what she calls a "tension between realism and abstraction," a moment when psychological drama reverts to almost archetypal patterns.[17] Such a pattern often develops in plays that thematize penetration, or repeatedly stage penetrative acts.

I use the term "penetration" advisedly. The word "penetrate" is etymologically related to the phallic "penile" (suggesting a sexual, if not an erotic, component to the act) but also to the geographical "peninsula," deriving from the Latin "pene-trare," which could be used to mean "to place within," "to enter within," or "to pierce." These related terms emphasize the spatial, almost geographical aspect of penetration. "To penetrate" means "to make or find its (or one's) way into the interior of, or right through (something): usually implying force or effort."[18] And even by Shakespeare's time, the word had developed its figurative meaning: "to pierce the ear, heart, or feelings of; to affect deeply; to 'touch'." The Latinate word was a latecomer to English; decried as an inkhorn term, it was defended by George Puttenham, who argues in his handbook on rhetoric, "Also ye finde these words, *penetrate, penetrable, indignitie*, which I cannot see how we may spare them ... for our speach wanteth wordes to such sence so well to be vsed."[19] I would like to bring the multiple valences of the word to bear on various dramatic and thematic instances of penetration in order to suggest the subjectivity inherent in the human being's consciousness of embodiment.

In these dramatic instances, the penetration of space serves as a complex representation of the act of gaining access to a character's interior self. The physical space that is penetrated may be the personal space of a character, the space created by a grouping of actors, the space of the stage as a whole, or even the personal space of the audience. The putative self represented by these spaces may signify, variously, a purely corporeal body; a body part (such as a vagina or a penis); a mind (or subjectivity); or a heart (either the physical organ or the conventional symbol of the desiring self). The varied meanings of the "self" suggested in these spatial intrusions indicate the complexity of the early modern experience of selfhood. We can see the partial nature of each possibility as we move toward developing a view more thoroughly grounded in embodiment.[20]

In Belsey's view, the model of self presented in the morality play precludes the possibility of a speaking subject, since even the main character lacks agency. Belsey not only dismisses the morality play as a possible locus of subjectivity but also presents the links between Renaissance drama and the morality in a way that undermines longstanding critical arguments that literary subjectivity was born on the English Renaissance stage. Belsey draws her definition of sub-jectivity from a liberal humanist model. Based on language and the ability to speak itself, the subject that she envisions, a "discursive hero ... independent of providence and of language," is wholly identified by intellectual apparatuses; the subject's corporeal status is entirely ignored.[21] The Cartesian structures that define such a model also limit it, eliding the phenomenological *habitus*, the experience of being in the body. Despite numerous studies of the body, the interiority of physical experience—Gail Kern Paster's "subjective experience of being-in-the-body"—has been neglected in favor of an "objective" examination of the appearance of experience.[22] This lacuna has only recently been addressed by theorists, and their work is only beginning to be applied to the drama.

In fact, the physical experience of corporeality also generates a type of subjectivity, one that is responsive to constant interaction with the physical world—with the environment, as well as with both animate and inanimate objects. This aspect of subjectivity is key to my argument, both because it renders the "penetration" I see visible and because it broadens the significance of that penetration, enabling us to recognize simultaneous, multiple meanings of "the self." In *The Production of Space*, Henri Lefebvre initiates the reintroduction of the physical self into our understanding of subjectivity. He argues that Descartes' theories marked a crucial dissociation between self and body and led the understanding of the self in the wrong direction, instantiating the germs of an eventual crisis: "With the advent of Cartesian logic … space had entered the realm of the absolute."[23] As Lefebvre explains, the idea of space became entirely abstract, as if the subjective could be eliminated from our perceptions:

> The scientific attitude, understood as the application of "epistemological" thinking to acquired knowledge, is assumed to be "structurally" linked to the spatial sphere. … Blithely indifferent to the charge of circular thinking, that discourse sets up an opposition between the status of space and the status of the "subject," between the thinking "I" and the object thought about. … Epistemological thought … has eliminated the "collective subject," the people as creator of a particular language, as carrier of specific etymological sequences. … It has promoted the impersonal "one" as creator of language in general, as creator of the system. It has failed, however, to eliminate the need for a subject of some kind. Hence the reemergence of the abstract subject, the *cogito* of the philosophers.[24]

In other words, scientific thought, in its dependence upon Descartes, has permitted a longstanding rift between our (i.e. Western culture's) *quantification* of space and our (i.e. each individual's) *experience* of space. Philosophical thought, too, by following Descartes in its examination of selfhood, has lost a fundamental component of the self, accepting the "impersonal 'one'" as a substitute for the social subject and the concrete subject, the individual. Theorists of space as varied as Maurice Merleau-Ponty, Gaston Bachelard, Yi-fu Tuan, and Edward T. Hall have reminded us that space *as we know it* is shaped by the perception of our senses: sight, sound, and touch all play a part. Moreover, as each individual shapes his concept of space, his sense of where he is affects his sense of self. Although space is commonly used in such metaphors as "the social hierarchy" and "the great chain of being," space is a literal experience—an experience of tactility. It is dry or wet, crowded or empty, expansive or compressed, and so forth. Even this brief list of experiential alternatives indicates the extent of the awareness based on physical feeling, an awareness quite separate from one's command of language or will. Like the literary scholar Cynthia Marshall, who sees in early modern culture "any number of signs indicat[ing] an experiential slippage from [the conscious, self-determining individual]," I posit a sense of self that is not at all dependent on reason or will.[25] This experience of subjectivity is located in the unmediated experience of physicality, specifically of proprioception, the interpretation of stimuli concerning one's sense of position and one's experience of the movements of one's limbs and other body parts. As Paster asserts, "bodiliness is the most rudimentary form of self-presence."[26] Everyone's sense of existence comes first from the physical sense of one's own body.

One's experience of one's own physical presence is partly determined by biological factors. The twentieth-century social scientist Edward T. Hall builds on several studies of mammals by such animal psychologists as H. Hediger, C. R. Carpenter, and A. D. Bain in order to develop his analysis of human beings' territoriality. He extensively examines how the nerves in different parts of the body help us to develop a sense of space through auditory, olfactory, and thermal information. As Hollis Huston explains, Hall's theory "describes not a particular code of manners, but an invariant scale of stimulant thresholds, to which individuals and peoples may respond in various ways."[27] The scale refers to physiological experiences consistent across cultures and even across mammalian species; however, different creatures or cultures may respond differently to their stimuli. Hegemonic institutions may attempt to restructure the way that certain groups respond to specific spatial experiences, distinguishing women from men or aristocrats from the underclass or the middling sort, thus dividing a culture along lines of gender or social rank; in such a situation, those involved are engaged in structuring the *doxa* that underlie a physiological response to physiological stimuli. Thus, beliefs may intersect with action, and even sensation, though what is true for *doxa*—that, as Bourdieu points out, "[t]he principles em-bodied in this way are placed beyond the grasp of consciousness, and hence cannot be touched by voluntary, deliberate transformation, cannot even be made explicit"— is even more true of the experience of bodiliness.[28] Such an attempt at imposing rules upon a specific social group is evident in the many early modern conduct books for women: the body of the gentlewoman was no sooner distinguished as her own than it became the subject of many social strictures intended to impose a *habitus* that would become internalized. Women were taught to keep their eyes downcast; timidity was encouraged and the blush considered a sign of reverence and maidenly virtue.[29] Women were also taught not to perceive the physical proximity of others as an intrusion. Adult women, even those of high status, were expected to endure the approach of others, and even to endure disciplinary violence enacted upon their bodies.[30] They were discouraged from physical resistance to aggressive seduction or even sexual coercion.[31]

This thoroughly Foucauldian discipline almost certainly achieved the goal of imposing a sense of self-abnegation upon the women who manifested the demeanor considered appropriate for their sex and status. One aspect of physical experience is the sense of owning or possessing the space around ourselves, what we colloquially call "personal space." Hall developed the term *proxemics* to refer to the study of the individual's structuring of and perception of space. Hall's research indicates that our sense of the extent of the space we possess is structured by such elements as the perception of heat as well as by more purely tactile and visual information. He theorizes that "[u]ntil recently man's space requirements were thought of in terms of the actual amount of air displaced by his body. The fact that man has around him as extensions of his personality the zones described ... has generally been overlooked."[32]

In *'Tis Pity She's a Whore* (published 1633), John Ford's representation of the female *habitus*, or experience of being in the body, manifests significant confusion about the nature of female selfhood.[33] The play's male characters so often allude to Annabella in stock terms that they almost render the heroine a mere plot device: a receptacle, an object of erotic desire that male characters wish to enter. Staging of the erotic object in early modern drama often makes use of mimetic forms such as entrance onto the stage, in fact: physical and/or aggressive intrusion may be enacted in such a way as to suggest erotic bodily penetration. But entering may also, depending on the setting, represent penetrating a character's subjectivity—entering into direct communication with a character's mind, heart, or soul. Though Annabella's body is the focus of several characters in Ford's play, the author himself manifests a concern with the relation between Annabella's body and her "inwardness"; this concern is literally staged throughout the play, as textual images force our attention toward connections between metaphor, staging, and plot.

Throughout *'Tis Pity*, there are a plethora of metaphors about various containers, and many of these figure Annabella as the container.[34] But other images of containment metaphorize the body more generally to express subjectivity in ways that were common during the early modern period. After the siblings have had sexual intercourse, Annabella tells Giovanni, "Go where thou wilt, in mind I'll keep thee here" (2.1.39).[35] The idea that the beloved is contained as an image within the mind or the mind's eye of the lover frequently recurs (and is read today as a sign of subjectivity) in Shakespeare's and Sidney's sonnet sequences. Later, Ford strikingly echoes Antony's opening lines in *Antony and Cleopatra* (as well as the lyrics of John Donne, his contemporary) when Giovanni says, "Let poring book-men dream of other worlds, / My world, and all of happiness, is here" (5.3.13–14). It would be false and reductive to suggest that this reference to Annabella is purely sexual.

Related imagery appears when other characters anxiously examine Annabella's motives. After advising Annabella, the Friar comments, "But soft, methinks I see repentance work / New motions in your heart" (3.6.31–32). Her heart represents her interior state; his vision, his ability to see beyond her physical appearance. This reference to Annabella's interiority is repeated when Soranzo discovers his new wife's pregnancy. Eventually, dissembling his rage, Soranzo distinguishes between himself and her supposed lover: "Well might he lust, but never lov'd like me. / He doted on the pictures that hung out / Upon thy cheeks ... Not on the part I lov'd, which was thy heart, / And, as I thought, thy virtues" (4.3.125–29). These characters evince a desire for a different, nonsexual penetration: discovery of the truth of Annabella's heart. Her consciousness, her subjectivity become as much of a focus of the play as her body.

This concern is dramatized by staging and by verbal references to stage action. In a play that begins with a speech about bodily space and continues with a complaint about violent intrusions upon one's space of private property, we might expect to see intrusion staged repeatedly. Indeed, one of the characters, Annabella's maidservant, actually states this expectation: "How like you this, child? Here's threat'ning, challenging, quarreling, and fighting, on every side, and all is for your sake; you had need look to yourself, charge, you'll be stol'n away sleeping else shortly" (1.2.63–66).

Yet there are few, if any, scenes in which Annabella's suitors aggressively enter upon her solitude.[36] When Giovanni and Annabella discover their mutual affection, they do so in their father's hall. This space, which is neutral ground to each, enables them to meet without intrusion on the part of either. (Indeed, one could read Annabella's willingness to make her brother her erotic choice as an extreme example of endogamy that makes it unnecessary for her ever to leave the family circle.) When the two have pledged their love, they exit, presumably to consummate their vow. But the next scene stages not their act of love but the low comedy of Bergetto's indifference to Annabella. Directly following that scene, Giovanni and Annabella enter "as from their chamber"; they renew their vows and agree to remain faithful to one another. Thus, the audience is denied the revelation of Annabella's body. Instead, it enjoys a parodic inversion of Giovanni's courtship. The staging reflects back on the audience its prurient desire for the unveiled sex scene that the play initially seemed to promise. As Patricia Fumerton argues, the subject at this time

> lived in public view but always withheld for itself a "secret" room, cabinet, case, or other recess locked away (in full view) in one corner of the house. ... the aristocratic self arose in a sort of reflex of retreat, an instinct to withdraw into privacy so pervasive even in the most trivial matters that there never could be any final moment of privacy.[37]

It seems that this private room will never be revealed. Even to Putana, Annabella pointedly refuses to offer any confidence about the details of what has passed.

Despite their urgent desire to win the prize, Annabella's other suitors gain little access to her. Almost the only contact that Grimaldi achieves occurs when Annabella and Putana enter "above" after his fight with Vasques. The stage direction strongly implies that the two women peer down at the fight from an upper window or a balcony overlooking the street. Annabella remains "above" the violence, and apart from it—never seriously threatened. Her meeting with Bergetto is only recounted, not staged; true, Annabella is later summoned by her father to read the youth's letter, but after doing so, she is permitted to dismiss the suitor without further ado. When Soranzo courts Annabella, they walk in her father's hall; her sense of security is evident in her raillery. Even when her husband discovers her previous sexual activity, Annabella remains calm. Stage directions indicate their entrance: "*Enter Soranzo unbrac'd, and Annabella dragg'd in*" (4.3.1 s.d.). We can deduce that they enter from a shared bedchamber after their mutual disrobing reveals Annabella's condition. The fact that Ford does not stage the scene in the bedchamber itself emphasizes that Soranzo fails to penetrate Annabella's defenses. She steadfastly refuses to name her lover and sings a song that indicates her indifference to death. Despite their wedding, Soranzo never gains access to Annabella's interior self.

Annabella's bedchamber is not represented onstage until the scene of her repentance. The stage direction says, "*Enter the Friar sitting in a chair, Annabella kneeling and whispering to him: a table before them and wax-lights: she weeps and wrings her hands*" (3.6.1 s.d.).[38] The scene plunges *in medias res* as the Friar comments, "You have unripp'd a soul so foul and guilty ... I marvel how / The earth hath borne you up" (3.6.2–4). He dominates the scene with speeches punctuated only occasionally by exclamations from Annabella, graphically describing hell and its torments until Annabella asks, "Is there no way left to redeem my miseries?" (3.6.33).[39] His answer persuades her that marrying Soranzo is the right choice: when the Friar asks if she is content, she replies, "I am" (3.6.42).[40]

Though the stage direction indicates that Annabella and the Friar appear onstage together, the pose described and the speeches that follow indicate that Annabella's concealed subjectivity has finally been revealed. The scene depicts what we have long desired to see: Annabella's bedchamber. This feminized space is indeed penetrated by an aggressive male—the Friar, whose coercive speeches constitute an assault upon Annabella's privacy. But what is exposed inside this *sancta sanctorum* is not Annabella's body but her soul. The long-awaited revelation of Annabella's self presents not an overly willing woman but a thoughtful one. The Friar's concern gains him access to a purely spiritual interior.

Yet this understanding of Annabella is undermined by the play's conclusion. Ford parts the bed-curtains in 5.5, revealing Giovanni and Annabella in bed once again.[41] There is no need for Giovanni to make an aggressive entrance; he has already taken possession of Annabella's body. Now, on this bed, Annabella's inner space is reconstituted, this time in an erotic guise, and, as the lovers use the time they have, they reenact the primal act, staging Annabella as a body entered and conquered by a male. Stabbing her, Giovanni penetrates the body violently as well as sexually, killing the fetus, the interloper whose presence brought Soranzo into Annabella's sphere ("The hapless fruit / That in her womb receiv'd its life from me / Hath had from me a cradle and a grave" [5.5.94–96]). Annabella's interiority is turned inside out, as the staging places her body on display and the script suggests that what matters for Giovanni is not his sister's soul, but her body. The space of the stage represents Annabella's interior once again, but that interior seems more appropriately figured by her genitalia than by her heart.

The heart itself reappears at the end. Shrunk down to the actual organ, however, interiority retains unknowability. What is internal is, as Katharine Maus says, "beyond scrutiny, concealed where other people cannot perceive it. And it *surpasses* the visible—its validity is unimpeachable."[42] When Giovanni enters the stage "*with a heart upon his dagger*" (5.5.7 s.d.), the tableau inevitably recalls the scene in which Giovanni urged Annabella to discover the truth of his feelings by cutting open his body to see his heart. The trope of the heart as the seat of love, so common in the verses of Sidney, Shakespeare, and Donne, is here literalized. Thus, Giovanni presents to all his triumph:

> The glory of my deed
> Darken'd the midday sun, made noon as night. ...
> I came to feast too, but I digg'd for food
> In a much richer mine than gold or stone
> Of any value balanc'd; 'tis a heart,
> A heart, my lords, in which is mine entomb'd:
> Look well upon't; d'ee know't?
>
> (5.6.22–29)

The speech leads us to expect a bawdy pun—surely the "richer mine" must refer to Annabella's queynt. But Ford surprises us by altering the meaning of the container once again: Giovanni is proud that he has conquered Annabella's *affections*. The "case" is not the vulva but the heart, which Giovanni believes will offer the pure, unequivocal sign of authentic feeling that he desires. But of course it does not. Even Giovanni's father fails to recognize Annabella's heart (as Giovanni says, "Why d'ee startle? / I vow 'tis hers" [5.6.31–32]). When presented onstage, the heart is just a bloody hunk of flesh: it lacks any identifying trait, let alone the symbolic value that it has for Giovanni himself.[43]

On a theatrical level, one that comprises both plot and staging, the revelation of Annabella's interiority, though deferred for a while, is finally reached—and is reached, in fact, more than once. Annabella's interiority is not only visible, but actually staged when her room and her bed are revealed onstage. As Georgiana Ziegler has said in her discussion of "The Rape of Lucrece," "the chamber metaphorically represents her 'self,' her body with its threatened chastity."[44] But in this play, the "self" is represented as several different constructs. It may be the soul, the conscience, the genitals, the womb. Is fancy bred in the heart, in the head, inside the vagina? Ford cannot decide: his stagings shift the seat of the self from one thing to another. Annabella's interiority remains a moving target; her characterization is nowhere more ambiguous than at the play's end.

'Tis Pity draws on the stage conventions of the morality play to represent the female aristocratic body and to examine the nature of the subjectivity represented by that body. It also resembles the morality play in the psychological distance that it maintains between the characters and the audience. Despite, or perhaps because of, the play's sensationalism, *'Tis Pity* remains largely an intellectual exercise for the audience member, a quest for the nature of Annabella's subjectivity. Unlike *Macbeth*, for example, *'Tis Pity* offers no entrance into the focal character's experience but remains a cautionary lesson, not unlike morality plays themselves.

If *'Tis Pity* does offer the audience a role, it is that of the onlooker, the Peeping Tom whose desires have been legitimized because commodified. What aspect of Annabella do *we* desire to see? Giovanni's desire may awaken our prurience, but the incestuous nature of his desire makes us experience any touch of kinship with Giovanni as distasteful. Even more than its gore and its subject matter, the position in which it places its audience members may be the element that links *'Tis Pity* with an Artaudian Theatre of Cruelty. Do we watch *with* Giovanni or over his shoulder? And in which of these capacities are we more (or less) akin to him? This challenge to the spectator's role—when we are both enticed and sickened by our willingness to be enticed—leads to larger questions about theatrical transactions between actors and spectators. What draws us into the action? And how are our relations with the characters altered when we are? Do we empathize with each character seriatim or with only one, enjoying a dual viewpoint as we relate to the other characters through the lens that "our" character provides? No matter what the action, it is evident that as soon as one actor establishes a relation to another, he alters their spatial relations and realigns the audience with each of them. As Hollis Huston explains,

> To transfer Hall's comprehensive analysis of behavior directly to the stage [would be] a catastrophic mistake. A stage differs from real life in a way that is essentially proxemic. ... [T]he fundamental relationship of the theater is not between two actors, but between the two of them and those who watch: when the contract of mutual responsibility is broken, the stage dies and the theater is void.[45]

Any consideration of staging is incomplete without a discussion of its effect upon the spectators. By extension, discussion of the body and its use in the theater should also include the spectator as a third element, forming a triad of related concerns.

Many early modern antitheatrical pamphleteers who feared that dramas could have a bad effect upon audience members inveighed against what they perceived as a loss of control that resulted from watching plays. Stephen Gosson, for example, writes repeatedly of the danger of "gazing." In *Playes Confuted in Five Actions* (1582), he alludes four times to the effect of the spectacle—or, more exactly, to the effects of gazing upon a spectacle:

> yf we be carefull that no pollution of idoles enter by the mouth into our bodies, how diligent, how circumspect, how wary ought we to be, that no corruption of idols, enter by the passage of our eyes & eares into the soule? ... that which entreth into us by the eyes and eares, muste bee digested by the spirite.[46]

Phillip Stubbes perceives the theatrical experience similarly: "For such is our grosse and dull nature, that what thing we see opposite before our eyes, to pearce further, and printe deeper in our harts and minds, than that thing, which is hard [sic] onely with the eares."[47] Both these writers characterize sight as a way of opening up the body, as if the eye were a mouth that ingests visual stimuli. Sight becomes an invitation for stimuli to enter into the body: a "piercing," or penetration. To make sense of the assault upon the self that these writers see in the very experience of play-watching, I revert to the relation between what Hall calls "distance receptors—those concerned with examination of distant objects— the eyes, the ears, and the nose" and "immediate receptors—those used to examine the world close up—the world of touch, the sensations we receive from the skin, membranes, and muscles" for early modern theatergoers.[48]

How would early modern audience members have experienced the drama at the physiological and visceral levels? At the sensorial level? Based on the contract for constructing the Fortune Theatre, Bruce Smith asserts that "no one in the Fortune or the 1599 Globe was more than fifty feet from an actor standing downstage, at the focal center of the space."[49] Though this distance may have been small in terms of auditory experience, it is experienced proxemically as somewhat remote, falling under the category that Hall calls "public distance," the distance at which people lose a sense of connectedness with one another.[50] According to Hall's research, actors attempting to make their performance touch the spectator work with the limitations established by that distance:

> Most actors know that at thirty or more feet the subtle shades of meaning conveyed by the normal voice are lost as are the details of facial expression and movement. Not only the voice but everything else must be exaggerated or amplified. Much of the nonverbal part of the communication shifts to gestures and body stance. In addition, the tempo of the voice drops [and] words are enunciated more clearly.[51]

But for groundlings already in intimate contact with the stage, the actor's approach onto the *platea* (downstage area) of the stage would intensify the experience of closeness resulting from the actor's approach within social dis- tance. Hall characterizes the physical experience of such intimacy as somewhat uncomfortable—certainly, it takes active observation to form an impression of what is nearby. At a close social distance,

> the area of sharp focus extends to the nose and parts of both eyes; or the whole mouth, one eye, and the nose are sharply seen. Many Americans shift their gaze back and forth from eye to eye or from eyes to mouth. ... At a 60-degree visual angle, the head, shoulders, and upper trunk are seen at a distance of four feet.[52]

Perhaps most significantly, Hall notes that "to stand and look down at a person at this distance has a domineering effect."[53] One can easily extrapolate from this (and from one's personal experience) that craning one's neck upward to watch a performance would render one submissive to impressions.

In the public theaters, the thrust stage aggressively appropriated the standing- room of the audience. A raised platform jutting twenty-seven feet out into a bare area, the stage must have served as a physical intrusion upon the personal space of those spectators pressed close to it.[54] Despite the excitement of proximity, those who stood around its actual perimeter would have been uncomfortable at being pressed against the hard wooden platform—more so than those more distant spectators who were pressed back against the walls of the amphitheater. Surrounded by groundlings on three sides, an actor could not possibly achieve the same visual effect as one performing toward only one side. Yet in this case, the audience would be much more affected by actors' entrances, particularly when they passed from *locus* (upstage area) to *platea* (downstage area) for greater intimacy. These paired concepts are particularly suggestive in this context. Robert Weimann argues that the *platea* "becomes part of the symbolic meaning of the play world, and the *locus* is made to support the dialectic of self-expression and representation." In moving from one to another, actors employed "transitions between illusion and convention, representation and self-expression, high seriousness, and low comedy—each drawing physically, socially, and dramatically on the interplay." Further, Weimann suggests, an early modern actor "uses certain conventions of speech and movement that roughly correspond to *locus* and *platea*, conventions by which the audience's world is made part of the play and the play is brought into the world of the audience."[55]

How might specific scenarios or stagings further compel the audience to open themselves up in the way that Gosson and Stubbes describe? Can the audience themselves be *penetrated* by their experience of the theater? Not, one might suspect, sitting at a nineteenth-century proscenium arch theater, watching actors in a cluttered box set, but perhaps in the crowd surrounding the early modern amphitheater's thrust stage, when a bare stage awaits the actor's entrance, which will shape the area into meaningful space.

Not all theatrical entrances convey a sense of aggressive penetration, of course (least of all when characters enter in the midst of conversation), but a solitary actor might achieve this effect, particularly when the scene was set for aggressive entry by previous imagery, dialogue, setting, or the mode of earlier entrances.[56] Further, in moving from *locus* to *platea*, an actor not only penetrates an empty stage but also steps into and above space that the audience would experience as their own. Gurr seems to support this view when he argues, "The chief feature of the staging and its interaction with the audience was the intimate connection between them. The spectators were as visible as the players, and even more potently they completely surrounded the players on their platform."[57]

More than once throughout his dramatic career, Shakespeare created a representative body onstage that stands in for the audience, thereby enabling him to use the material conditions of his theater to manipulate the spectator's proxemic experience. How might the linkage of stage entrances to thematic concerns with penetration and invasion of the body have brought the audience to share the proxemic experience of the onstage (intra-dramatic) spectator?

Shakespeare's *Coriolanus* not only makes use of a mob as an intra-dramatic spectator, it constantly thematizes the relationship between crowds and individuals, parts and wholes, closed bodies and open bodies. Piercing and penetration remain an underlying theme of the play, as Shakespeare constantly draws our attention to openness, vulnerability, autonomy, and the necessity for solidarity. In *Coriolanus*, the hero wins his name by penetrating and opening up the town of Corioles, but he refuses to render himself vulnerable to figurative penetration. He resists the traditional theatrical vulnerability of the soliloquizer, in itself a metaphorical openness to penetration;[58] he refuses to show his wounds to the populace, blocking their gaze (a visual and symbolic form of penetration); and he ignores the needs of both the metaphorical stomach (the desires of the Roman populace) and those of the literal stomach (food as fuel for the body), thereby refusing to acknowledge that the body can be affected by external, or even internal, stimuli.[59] Martius's refusal to acknowledge his vulnerability is most notable in the showstopping scene in which he successfully penetrates the town of Corioles entirely alone.

Entrances and exits almost immediately become symbolic of thematic concerns throughout the play. *Coriolanus* begins with action, possibly reinforced by confused sound: "Enter a company of mutinous Citizens, with staves, clubs, and other weapons."[60] This is, as Arden editor Philip Brockbank notes, the only play of the period to open with public violence.[61] And, as the critic Jarrett Walker points out, the audience experiences this beginning as "a frontal assault of bodies."[62] From an empty stage, we change to a confused milling about of hostile, angry characters—as many extras as the King's Men had on hand. This would have been experienced as violence, as attack; the audience would have felt the shock of reverberating boards, of crowdedness very different from that of the spectators crammed together.[63]

Indeed, Zvi Jagendorf suggests that Shakespeare purposely contrasts the "isolated and discrete body of the man who stands alone" with the common body of the people:[64]

> Both are prominent features of the play's spectacle. The crowd—the citizens in the street and marketplace, the common soldiers on the battlefield—is a constant feature of the action. We hear their shouts on and offstage. We are encouraged to imagine them jostling for space in the victory parades, and we both see and hear them in the mob scenes.[65]

Shakespeare, I am suggesting, brings together crowds and the figure of the body by creating scenes in which crowds and (ultimately) the whole stage come to "stand in" for a body, as Ford does through different techniques in *'Tis Pity She's a Whore*. Throughout the play, the thrust stage and the actors create situations in which penetration of groups of bodies occurs. The opening is a case in point: after the unruly multitude have assembled, they are called to order by the First Citizen, who addresses the crowd. Whether they stand in small clusters or assemble in a circle or semicircle, it is natural for the next character who appears, Menenius, to enter from the back and push through to the center of the crowd that then surrounds him. His penetration of the crowd is his first move toward controlling and dispersing it. In entering and taking center stage, in fact, he seems to provide a visual emblem of the belly in his fable. He becomes the visual center, around which there would be a circle of empty space because the plebeians would have to stand far enough off so that they could turn their eyes upon him.[66] When Caius Martius enters, he too would necessarily thrust his way through the crowd of plebeians, but his presence would confuse the effect of the tableau. The conversation would cease to be a dialogue between individual and crowd; it would become more diffuse, less of a clear exchange, as Martius quarrels both with Menenius and with members of the crowd.

Entering and exiting become the subject of discussion a scant two scenes later, when Virgilia insists, "I'll not over the threshold till my lord return from the wars" (1.3.74–75). Although Valeria argues, "Fie, you confine yourself most unreasonably," Virgilia stands firm (1.3.76). Refusing to visit "the good lady that lies in" (1.3.77), Virgilia insists on her own enclosure, her own containment. Walker actually comments that Virgilia's silence itself is visual and emblematic when framed by her talkative friend and her mother-in-law:

> She is never fully separable from the women who surround her. Accordingly, when I refer to Virgilia as a presence onstage, it is with the understanding that Volumnia and Valeria are essential to draw our attention to that presence and are thus, in phenomenal terms, inseparable from it.[67]

Even in this scene, a closed circle is more than once broken in upon: Volumnia and Virgilia enter together, their paired-ness making us focus on their interaction rather than on their penetration of the empty stage. But the stage directions (which textual critics as venerable as Greg and as recent as Werstine believe to have been written by Shakespeare himself) indicate that the pair seat themselves on stools and begin to sew silently, creating a sense of intimacy and community broken by Volumnia's first line: "I pray you, daughter, sing, or express yourself" (1.3.1–2). The circle is again disrupted when a servant enters to announce Valeria's arrival and Virgilia is with difficulty prevented from exiting the stage. When Valeria appears with an Usher and a Gentlewoman (presumably Valeria's servant), the previous intimacy is dissolved by the presence of too many bodies on stage.

In the next scene, the sense of the stage-space that I have described is reversed. Scene 1.4 stages the Roman attack upon Corioles. As well as the main actors, the stage directions specify *"Drum and Colours* [extras], *with Captains and Soldiers ... to them a Messenger."* The army of the Volsces, which soon pours out of the tiring-house door, further confuses the visual picture. They beat the Romans "to their trenches," and then Martius appears, "cursing"; he pursues the Volsces, who flee back to the gates of Corioles (the doors of the tiring-house), and he follows them in. As the gates are shut and the Roman general Titus Lartius immediately focuses on the possible loss of Martius, the characters and the audience can only speculate on what is going on behind the door in "Corioles." Martius's own powers of penetration are best perceived by the audience not when he is fighting onstage but now, when he is absent and all eyes are fixed upon the door through which he has passed. Ironically, the audience's attention is not directed toward the penetration of swords piercing bodies behind the door; instead, the watchers see the city of Corioles itself as the thing that Martius has penetrated by entering it. Thus, the city becomes a larger emblem of the cutting, wounding, and opening up of individual bodies that Martius traditionally enacts in battle. As I have shown elsewhere, the penetration indicated by the wound's blood is a matter for shame, as it reveals masculine vulnerability—a vulnerability associated, according to Paster, with a woman's menstrual flow.[68]

When Martius emerges, *"bleeding, assaulted by the enemy"* (1.4.61 s.d.), the general Titus Lartius exclaims, "O, 'tis Martius! / Let's fetch him off, or make remain alike," and the company of Roman soldiers rush toward Martius, who turns and leads them all back into the city (1.4.61–62). This action inverts the more usual sense of the stage as an area that can be penetrated; instead, it focuses on the watchers' attention on a single point of exit or entry. The possibility of forced penetration is outward—through the tiring-house doors—but yet away from the audience. Thus, as Titus Lartius enters, the extras pause, facing toward the door through which Martius has passed. When he reenters and turns about, they all follow him, and the flow of actors abruptly pushes toward the single, central door, leaving the stage as empty as if it had been evacuated. I hypothesize an effect as of tumescence and detumescence—not in literal terms, but in the audience's experience of the stage.[69] As the circulation of bodies onstage focuses on action occurring directly behind the doors, the audience would not only focus on what the doors concealed, but would experience the cessation of action as an abrupt slowdown—one that they might even understand as resembling a sudden chill to flowing blood. They would feel the stage's detumescence as a sudden emptying out, an absence of tension in the immediate vicinity and a sense of closure to the scene that is suggested by the outflow, which, on a primitive level, would carry a sense of the Romans' attack as almost inevitably successful.

In architectonic terms, the staging implied by the action of *Coriolanus* manifests two different ways of dwelling in space. Edward S. Casey characterizes two extremes of architectural experience as "hestial" and "hermetic":

> Any built place that aims at encouraging hestial dwelling will ... tend to be at once centered and self-enclosed. The implicit directionality will be from the center toward the periphery and will thus obey the architectural counsel to "extend inner order outward."[70]

In contrast, "the hermetic moves out resolutely"; it "represents the far-out view, a view from a moving position."[71] Shakespeare offers both these experiences to his audiences through the proxemics inherent in the staging examined here. As David Wiles comments, "While the modern spectator may be content to go to *see* a play, the premodern spectator went rather to inhabit a theatrical place."[72] Both hestial and hermetic forms of experience affect watchers viscerally, and each one develops a sense of self substantially different from that of the region "between or behind the eyes."[73]

The staging of the body affects the audience's experience on many levels. While related to proxemic concerns, the effect of entrances and exits goes beyond that single dimension; it depends not only on proximity but on the design and use of the stage within the theater itself. Thus, the stage-space, whether that of the thrust stage or the proscenium arch, organically affects the experience of the spectator, as each stage design creates a different relation between the audience and the action.

The self implicated by early modern metaphors of the body is not easily defined, any more than is the self that comes into being through proxemic experience. Yet the validity of applying proprioceptive analysis to staging should be evident. Freud's paradigms have so thoroughly infused our culture that one is likely to describe the audience's proprioception as an unconscious response to the staging of the action. Such a term denies the nature of the experience, which is unrelated to psychic structures or intellectual activity. The "bodiliness" (if you will) of the individual is an important constitutive element of subjectivity—a subjectivity that must be recognized as a broader experience than has been understood hitherto.

Scholars who have written about the early modern spectator's experience have often intuitively done so in the context of considering bodily, even proprioceptive, elements onstage. Not only does Belsey discuss the uses of psychomachiae in *The Subject of Tragedy*, she treats similar issues in her analysis of *The Duchess of Malfi*, a play whose focus could be defined as the question, "Who controls the body of the Duchess?" When Huston Diehl addresses audience experience, she does so in the context of her discussion of stage violence.[74] We must continue to examine how spatial elements construct the subject, using the drama both as a mimetic form and as an intra-performative transaction between actors and audience members. The staged nature of dramatic theater offers a unique opportunity to examine this dimension of human experience.

Notes

1 Quotations from *A Midsummer Night's Dream* and other Shakespeare plays refer to William Shakespeare, *The Riverside Shakespeare*, ed. G. Blakemore Evans (Boston: Houghton Mifflin, 1974) unless otherwise noted.

2 Maurice Merleau-Ponty, *Phenomenology of Perception*, trans. Colin Smith (London: Routledge, 1962), 206; Edward T. Hall, *The Hidden Dimension* (Garden City, NY: Doubleday, 1966), 10–37.

3 Stanton B. Garner, Jr., *Bodied Spaces: Phenomenology and Performance in Contemporary Drama* (Ithaca: Cornell University Press, 1994), 46.

4 Marvin Carlson, "Space and Theatre History," in Charlotte M. Canning and Thomas Postlewait, eds. *Representing the Past: Essays in Performance Historiography* (Iowa City: University of Iowa Press, 2010), 199.

5 Garner, *Bodied Spaces*, 47.

6 Quotations from *Bussy D'Ambois* refer to George Chapman, *Bussy D'Ambois*, ed. Robert J. Lordi (Lincoln, NE: Nebraska University Press, 1964). This edition is based on Q2, published in 1641.

7 The first quarto of *Romeo and Juliet*, published in 1597, is generally judged to be a "bad quarto," probably a pirated version sourced from one of the actors. Editors consider the second quarto, published in 1599, more reliable and authoritative; it is possibly set from the author's own draft or "foul papers."

8 At 5.3.48 s.d., Q1 states, "*Romeo begins to open the tomb.*" At 5.3.87, Theobald includes the stage direction, "*Laying Paris in the tomb.*" Q1 also specifies at 5.3.139 the stage direction "*Friar stoops and looks on the blood and weapons*" directly before the Friar's line, "Alack, alack, what blood is this, which stains / The stony entrance of this sepulchre?" (140–41). Two lines later, the Douai MS offers the stage direction, "*Enters the tomb.*" The many references to the tomb indicate that it was represented by a physical structure, for which the obvious choice would have been the tiring-house. Based on similar circumstantial evidence, Gurr confidently asserts that the tiring-house front "served as the Capulet house when Romeo climbed to its balcony" (Andrew Gurr, *The Shakespearean Stage, 1574–1642* [Cambridge: Cambridge University Press, 1992], 182).

9 The idea of the bedchamber as a private place may be somewhat negated by the argument about bedchambers espoused by Michael Danahy in "Social, Sexual, and Human Spaces in *La Princesse de Cleves*" (*French Forum* 6, no. 9 [1981]: 212–24). Yet Danahy's point is also mine: when female courtiers lack any private space, and even lack the ability to decide who may enter their bedroom and who may not, they may fail adequately to develop an *interior* space, a sense of self that is distinct from the directions and wishes of others.

10 See Gurr, *The Shakespearean Stage*, 160. As Gurr points out, "after the adults took [the Blackfriars playhouse] over in 1608 swordplay was confined to the occasional fencing bout and ... battles and what Shirley called 'target fighting' were never tried there" (157). The size of the stage provides one explanation for why Bussy's epic duel in act 2 is described, not staged.

11 Consider the "boudoir atmosphere" (to coin a useful anachronism) of such settings as Clerimont's dressing room in Jonson's *Epicoene*, the Duchess's closet in Webster's *Duchess of Malfi*, and Tamyra's closet in this play.

12 Indeed, the line may even have been intended as a reference to the golden statues that apotheosize the lovers at the close of *Romeo and Juliet*.

13 Sigmund Freud, *Introductory Lectures on Psychoanalysis*, trans. and ed. James Strachey (New York: Norton, 1966), 156.

14 Anne Ubersfeld, *Reading Theatre*, trans. Frank Collins, eds. Paul Perron and Patrick Debbèche (Toronto: Toronto University Press, 1999), 110.

15 These symbolic structures persist beyond Bussy's death. After her lover's decease, Tamyra begs to depart from her husband's house. Having failed to keep her affair hidden, her bedroom matters private, she urges her husband to let her depart until her stab-wounds—"that never balm shall close / Till death hath enter'd at them, so I love them, / Being opened by your hands"—heal (5.4.194–96). Having been grotesquely penetrated by her husband's phallic knife, Tamyra promises to bear lovingly these signs of his ownership, his right to enter her body exclusively, and in any way he wishes. She pledges, "I never more will grieve you with my sight, / Never endure that any roof shall part / Mine eyes and heaven; but to the open deserts, / Like to a hunted tigress, I will fly" (5.4.197–200). Leaving behind the empty shell of a place that failed to offer her protection, she seeks the promise of nakedness that the wilderness seems to offer. After Bussy's death, she no longer needs any private place. Violated by her husband's knife and by his base murder of her lover, Tamyra becomes a walking emblem of someone who has nothing to hide, a woman whose interiority contains nothing but a bleakness that she is willing to share with the world.

16 Catherine Belsey, *The Subject of Tragedy: Identity and Difference in Renaissance Drama* (London: Methuen, 1985), 13. Michael Hattaway looks to the future, borrowing the term "gest" from Brecht to characterize "moments when the visual elements of

the scene combine with the dialogue in a significant form that reveals the condition of life in the play" (*Elizabethan Popular Theatre: Plays in Performance* [London: Routledge, 1982], 57).

17 Catherine Belsey, "Emblem and Antithesis in *The Duchess of Malfi*," *Renaissance Drama* 11 (1980): 117.

18 As an example, the *OED* cites Hall's *Chronicles*, from Richard III, 56: "With out resistence, [we] have penetrate the ample region ... of Wales." The French cognate was also commonly used at this time to mean "to enter into a space."

19 George Puttenham, *The Arte of English Poesie* (1589; rpt. Kent, OH: Kent State University Press, 1970), 159.

20 Many critics, following Gail Kern Paster's groundbreaking book, *The Body Embarrassed: Drama and the Disciplines of Shame in Early Modern England* (Ithaca: Cornell University Press, 1993), have investigated the relation between selfhood and early modern humoral theory. My approach emphasizes phenomenology's concern with actual physical perception rather than the physiological discourse of the time.

21 Belsey, *The Subject of Tragedy*, 14.

22 Paster, *The Body Embarrassed*, 3.

23 Henri Lefebvre, *The Production of Space*, trans. Donald Nicholson-Smith (Oxford: Blackwell, 1991), 1.

24 Ibid., 4.

25 Cynthia Marshall, *The Shattering of the Self: Violence, Subjectivity, and Early Modern Texts* (Baltimore: Johns Hopkins University Press, 2002), 14.

26 Paster, *The Body Embarrassed*, 5.

27 Hollis Huston, *The Actor's Instrument: Body, Theory, Stage* (Ann Arbor: University of Michigan Press, 1992), 112. For more specifics, see Edward T. Hall, *The Hidden Dimension*. Hall discusses different cultures in Europe (123–38), Japan (139–44), and the Middle East (144–53).

28 Pierre Bourdieu, *Outline of a Theory of Practice*, trans. Richard Nice (Cambridge: Cambridge University Press, 1977), 94.

29 Ruth Kelso, *Doctrine for the Lady of the Renaissance* (Urbana, IL: University of Illinois Press, 1956), 43–44.

30 In *The Family, Sex, and Marriage in England, 1500–1800* (New York: Harper, 1977), Lawrence Stone quotes Lady Jane Grey as complaining of her parents' rigorous and even apparently spiteful discipline:

> When I am in presence either of father or mother, whether I speak, keep silence, sit, stand or go, eat, drink, be merry or sad, be sewing, playing, dancing, or doing anything else, I must do it, as it were, in such weight, measure, and number, even so perfectly as God made the world, else I am so sharply taunted, so cruelly threatened, yea presently sometimes with pinches, nips and bobs, and some ways I will not name for the honour I bear them, so without measure misordered that I think myself in Hell.
>
> (Quotation at 167)

31 Jennifer A. Low, *Manhood and the Duel: Masculinity in Early Modern Drama and Culture* (New York: Palgrave, 2003), 73–74.

32 Hall, *The Hidden Dimension*, 121.

33 As N. W. Bawcutt points out, the statement on the title page of *'Tis Pity She's a Whore* that the play was "Acted by the Queenes Maiesties Seruants, at The Phoenix in Drury-Lane" indicates that it was first performed anywhere between 1626 and its publication date, 1633. John Ford, *'Tis Pity She's a Whore*, ed. N. W. Bawcutt (Lincoln, NE: Nebraska University Press, 1966), xi.

34 In 1.1, Giovanni asks the Friar whether "A customary form ... [should] be a bar / 'Twixt my perpetual happiness and me?" (1.1.25–27). Since his happiness is in the

enjoyment of Annabella's body, his reference to a bar implies that he conceives of his sister's body as a room with the entrance barred by the traditional prohibition against incest. Later, when Giovanni learns of Annabella's pregnancy, he asks Putana, horrified, "But in what case is she?" (3.3.17). In this instance, the double meaning is the author's, not the character's. The term clearly refers to Annabella's body as container—not, this time, an empty container with space for the phallus but a full container, bearing the child that is the result of his "filling" her.

35 All quotations from *'Tis Pity She's a Whore* refer to the Bawcutt edition.

36 In contrast, consider the scene in *The Duchess of Malfi* when Ferdinand enters the Duchess's chamber just as she, speaking to Antonio, says, "You have cause to love me, I ent'red you into my heart" (John Webster, *The Duchess of Malfi*, ed. Elizabeth Brennan [New York: Norton, 1993], 3.2.61). As Judith Haber comments, "When Ferdinand enters that space, uninvited and 'unseen,' he forcibly reappropriates her body/room/stage and defines it as his container—the empty, passive receptacle that is the ground of his existence. ... At this point, understandably, the Duchess's speech undergoes a radical change" ("'My Body Bestow upon My Women': The Space of the Feminine in *The Duchess of Malfi*," *Renaissance Drama* n.s. 28 [1997]: 144). Georgianna Ziegler also pursues this line of reasoning in her discussion of *Cymbeline*: "For Iachimo, a woman's body is part and parcel of her room and can be similarly violated. Though he does not physically rape Imogen, we nevertheless feel that a rape has been committed in his voyeuristic intrusion on her privacy" ("My Lady's Chamber: Female Space, Female Chastity in Shakespeare," *Textual Practice* 4, no. 1 [1990]: 82).

37 Patricia Fumerton, *Cultural Aesthetics: Renaissance Literature and the Practice of Social Ornament* (Chicago: University of Chicago Press, 1991), 69.

38 N. W. Bawcutt comments, "Q's *in his study* clearly seems an error, as the scene takes place in Annabella's bedroom (see III.iv.33)" (Ford, *'Tis Pity*, 57). At the cited line, Florio says to the Friar, "Come, father, I'll conduct you to her chamber."

39 According to editor Mark Stavig, the Friar's speech draws substantially on Ford's poem *Christ's Bloody Sweat*. See Stavig, Introduction, *'Tis Pity She's a Whore* (Arlington Heights, IL: AHM, 1966), vii–xix.

40 Claudine Defaye sees the scene as a representation of psychological enclosure for which the Friar provides an egress: "It is as if, by conforming to the role of sinner assigned by religion, terrible and constraining though it be, Annabella succeeded in escaping from her own intimate and immediate torment, from a kind of existential anguish, where all issues seem blocked" ("Annabella's Unborn Baby: The Heart in the Womb in *'Tis Pity She's a Whore*," *Cahiers Élisabéthains* 15 [1979]: 37).

41 The scene is almost surely set in the main bedchamber in Soranzo's house.

42 Katharine Eisaman Maus, *Inwardness and Theater in the English Renaissance* (Chicago: University of Chicago Press, 1995), 4.

43 Many critics have attempted to clarify the personal symbolism of Giovanni's sensationalistic gesture. Among them are Ronald Huebert, who argues that the gesture literalizes a flawed analogy between discovering a secret and ripping up a bosom (*John Ford, Baroque English Dramatist* [Montreal: McGill-Queen's University Press, 1977], 145); Michael Neill, who makes some of the same points that I do in his effort to sort out the "welter of competing definitions and explanations [that the gesture] invites" ("'What Strange Riddle's This?': Deciphering *'Tis Pity She's a Whore*," in *John Ford: Critical Re-Visions*, ed. Michael Neill [Cambridge: Cambridge University Press, 1988], 165); and Susan J. Wiseman, who asserts that Annabella's heart, for Giovanni, is "endowed ... with all the private and confused meanings of incest" ("*'Tis Pity She's a Whore*: Representing the Incestuous Body," in *Revenge Tragedy*, ed. Stevie Simkin [New York: Palgrave, 2001], 222). Wiseman's article, excellent in many ways, nonetheless unthinkingly uses spatial concepts as metaphor in a way that runs directly contrary to my goal of noting how space shapes

consciousness and vice versa. Most notably, Wiseman seems to collude with Ford's own rhetoric when she asserts that, in *'Tis Pity*, "the female body is represented as an ethical, financial, spiritual, amatory and psychological territory" and that Annabella's body "is located and relocated within these competing ways of looking at the body" (215). Like me, however, Wiseman asserts that "the significance of Annabella's body is repeatedly transformed during the play by the powerful discourses which ... define it" (216).

44 Ziegler, "My Lady's Chamber," 80.
45 Huston, *The Actor's Instrument*, 113.
46 Stephen Gosson, *Playes Confuted in Five Actions*, (1582, rpt. New York: Garland, 1972), B8$_v$.
47 Phillip Stubbes, *The Anatomie of Abuses* (1583; rpt. New York: Garland, 1973), "A Preface to the Reader"; qtd. in Marshall, *Shattering of the Self*, 17.
48 Hall, *The Hidden Dimension*, 40.
49 Bruce R. Smith, *The Acoustic World of Early Modern England: Attending to the O-Factor* (Chicago: University of Chicago Press, 1999), 206.
50 Hall, *The Hidden Dimension*, 120.
51 Ibid., 117.
52 Ibid., 114.
53 Ibid., 114.
54 Twenty-seven feet is the measurement Gurr derives from the builder's contract for the Fortune (*The Shakespearean Stage*, 138). Not every stage, of course, would share these dimensions.
55 Robert Weimann, *Shakespeare and the Popular Tradition in the Theater: Studies in the Social Dimension of the Dramatic Form and Function* (Baltimore: Johns Hopkins University Press, 1978), 83.
56 As Gay McAuley says,

> The moment of entering the presentational space is extremely important for the actor as is evident from the fact that conventions have been developed in many different performance genres to heighten or mark the moment of entrance. These may involve the material reality of the performance (the drum roll, musical flourish, and spotlight of circus or music hall) or be activated from within the fiction ... but the function is similar: to draw the spectators' attention to the physical point of entrance into the space and to mark the moment in some way.
>
> *Space in Performance*, 96

57 Gurr, *The Shakespearean Stage*, 179.
58 Cynthia Marshall alludes to this issue in "Wound-man: *Coriolanus*, Gender, and the Theatrical Construction of Interiority," in *Feminist Readings of Early Modern Culture*, eds. Valerie Traub, M. Lindsay Kaplan, and Dympna Callaghan (Cambridge: Cambridge University Press, 1996), 95.
59 "Penetration" is not the right word here, of course. Jarrett Walker's comment is useful: "Ultimately, [Coriolanus] does not distinguish between being nourished and being wounded. Both are kinds of incorporation, and in both cases he responds by 'spitting back' at the world in an automatic reciprocal action, a compulsive denial of receptiveness" ("Voiceless Bodies and Bodiless Voices: The Drama of Human Perception in *Coriolanus*," *Shakespeare Quarterly* 43, no. 2 [Summer 1992]: 176). These terms enable us, I think, to perceive more accurately what mechanism is at work. "Starving," a related term that invokes the process of digestion, is one of the principal foci of Stanley Cavell's groundbreaking article "'Who does the wolf love?': *Coriolanus* and the Interpretations of Politics," in *Shakespeare and the Question of Theory*, eds. Patricia Parker and Geoffrey Hartman (New York: Routledge, 1985), 245–72.

60 William Shakespeare, *Coriolanus*, ed. Philip Brockbank (New York: Arden, 1976, rpt. Routledge, 1988), 95.

61 Brockbank, *Coriolanus*, 95.

62 Walker, "Voiceless Bodies," 172.

63 In discussing group experiential space, Yi-Fu Tuan asserts that crowds may "not detract, but enhance the significance of the events: vast numbers of people do not necessarily generate the feeling of spatial oppressiveness" if the people's reasons for being present are identical and are not directly opposed to the presence of others ("Space and Place: A Humanist Perspective," in *Philosophy in Geography*, eds. Stephen Gale and Gunnar Olsson [Dordrecht: D. Reidel, 1979], 404).

64 Zvi Jagendorf, "*Coriolanus*: Body Politic and Private Parts," *Shakespeare Quarterly* 41, no. 4 (Winter 1990): 462. Similarly, Arthur Riss argues that the play develops a "nexus between the land and the body," establishing "a correspondence between the impulse to enclose public land and Coriolanus's urge to enclose his body" ("The Belly Politic: *Coriolanus* and the Revolt of Language," *English Literary History* 59, no. 1 [Spring 1992]: 55).

65 Jagendorf, "Body Politic," 462. For a different point of view, see Ralph Berry, who analyzes the opening and concludes "that the Roman crowd ... is not the fearsome manifestation of the popular will that it might at first appear. There is nothing here like the brutal capriciousness of ... the blood lust that Antony arouses during the Forum scene. On the contrary, we see a collective of indeterminate and variable characteristics" ("Casting the Crowd: *Coriolanus* in Performance," *Assaph* C4 [1988]: 114).

66 An alternative interpretation of the scene would present the dialogue between 1. Cit. and 2. Cit. center stage, surrounded by the mob. This staging would create a small bubble of intimacy which would either be broken by Menenius's entrance or dissolve as the two citizens faded into the crowd. Michael Warren considers various possibilities for staging the citizens in his article "The Perception of Error: The Editing and the Performance of the Opening of *Coriolanus*," in *Textual Performances: The Modern Reproduction of Shakespeare's Drama*, eds. Lukas Erne and Margaret Jane Kidnie (Cambridge: Cambridge University Press, 2004), 127–42.

67 Walker, "Voiceless Bodies," 179, n. 16.

68 Paster, *The Body Embarrassed*, 92.

69 Janet Adelman strongly endorses this view, though she is quite uninterested in staging and uses a psychoanalytic framework for her argument. Adelman asserts that

> the scene at Corioli represents a glorious transformation of the nightmare of oral vulnerability ... into a phallic adventure that both assures and demonstrates his independence. Coriolanus' battlecry as he storms the gates sexualizes the scene: "Come on; / If you'll stand fast, we'll beat them to their wives" (I.iv.40–41). But the dramatic action itself presents the conquest of Corioli as an image not of rape but of triumphant rebirth.
>
> "'Anger's My Meat': Feeding, Dependency, and Aggression in *Coriolanus*,"
> in *Representing Shakespeare: New Psychoanalytic Essays*, eds.
> Murray M. Schwartz and Coppélia Kahn (Baltimore:
> Johns Hopkins University Press, 1980), 134.

70 Edward S. Casey, *Getting Back into Place: Toward a Renewed Understanding of the Place-World* (Bloomington: Indiana University Press, 1993), 133.

71 Ibid., 137–38.

72 David Wiles, "Seeing is Believing: The Historian's Use of Images," in *Representing the Past: Essays in Performance Historiography*, eds. Charlotte M. Canning and Thomas Postlewait (Iowa City: University of Iowa Press, 2010), 215.

73 Edward Casey meditates on "hereness": "even *within* my lived body, I can distinguish a corporeally localized here from the here that is coextensive with my body as a whole. At this level, my here is often identified with my head, and even more particularly with a region between or behind the eyes" (*Getting Back into Place*, 52).

74 See Belsey, *The Subject of Tragedy*; Belsey, "Emblem and Antithesis"; and Diehl, "The Iconography of Violence in English Renaissance Tragedy," *Renaissance Drama* 11 (1980): 27–44.

3   Audience performance

The claque in nineteenth-century French theater

In act 2 of Shakespeare's *As You Like It*, Jaques creates a performance space out of audience members. As Amiens sings the first verse of "Under the Greenwood Tree," the Duke's companions gather round and, at Jaques's urging, they join in on the second verse.[1] Finally, Jaques sings a third verse alone, concluding with the lines

> Ducdame, ducdame, ducdame:
> Heere shall he see, grosse fooles as he,
> And if he will come to me.[2]

> (2.5.54–57)

Amiens, curious, inquires, "What's that Ducdame?", to which Jaques replies, "'Tis a Greek invocation, to call fools into a circle" (2.5.58–60). In performance the companions are generally scattered in a loose formation across the stage when the song is begun but gather into a tight circle around Jaques by the song's end. Jaques's comment prompts the staging, but the presence of the other characters prompts his words and his performance. His maneuver creates an inset performance: the song becomes a play-within-a-play as well as an "invocation" when the group forms around the singer, as passers-by do around a street performer. The space of his performance is defined by the bodies of the companions surrounding him.[3]

To some extent, their action simply demonstrates the truth of Eric Bentley's assertion that theater occurs whenever "A impersonates B while C looks on."[4] While most of this book considers the impact of space or performance on audience experience, this chapter considers how the theater space is reshaped by audience behavior—and how that reshaping in turn affects the audience. Carlson urges that "text-performance-audience interaction should not be considered in a vacuum, but rather as an event embedded in a complex matrix of social concerns and actions, all of which 'communicate' or contribute to giving the theatre experience its particular 'meaning'."[5] As he says, the audience itself contributes to the way each member "makes sense" of the event. My argument is that audience behavior—audience performance—can reshape a performance space.

The audience of *The Real Inspector Hound* seems in their own way to shape the experience of the play. The opening stage directions state,

> The first thing is that the audience appear to be confronted by their own reflection in a huge mirror. Impossible. However, back there in the gloom—not at the footlights—a bank of plush seats and pale smudges of faces. The total effect having been established, it can be progressively faded out as the play goes on, until the front row remains to remind us of the rest and then, finally, merely two seats in that row—one of which is now occupied by Moon. Between Moon and the auditorium is an acting area.[6]

Audience members see what looks like a transverse stage—one in which the audience, seated in two opposing banks of seats, face each other across a long, narrow acting area (often on a plinth). It is, instead, a visual gag crucial to the play's commentary on the troubled relationship between actor, audience member, and critic. Moon, apparently an audience member, turns out to be a critic who is a character in Stoppard's play. He is a false reflection of the audience.

The audience more truly interacts with the performance in the second act of the 1975 musical *A Chorus Line*, when Cassie dances as mirrored panels descend from the flies at the rear of the stage, transforming the theater into a dance studio. The mirrors reflect both Cassie and the footlights; while the audience cannot be seen, the doubled image is a constant reminder of their ghostly presence as observers who judge and assess Cassie's performance, just like the invisible director, Zach, who is heard but not frequently seen during a long day of dance auditions for a Broadway show.[7] The audience at *A Chorus Line* is not part of the mimetic illusion, since the show is about the audition process. Yet, because an audition is a continual reference to the show that will be performed, the audience's role must be absurdly self-conscious. Without a role in the context of the play, they are Peeping Toms, watching the audition process. In the realistic framework they inhabit, however, their presence validates a show about auditioning: their presence confirms Brook's statement that an act of theater occurs whenever "a man walks across [an] empty space whilst someone else is watching him."[8] Based on Brook's statement, their presence also validates the concept of this musical, implying that for each show that is conceived, cast, and rehearsed, there is an audience poised to enter, seat themselves, and observe.

That the audience may shape the stage-space is commonly understood by some types of scholars and entirely overlooked by others. When Stephen Greenblatt, the early modern scholar who coined the term "a new historicism," alludes in a throwaway line to "the relative nonparticipation of the audience" while characterizing London's public theater in Shakespeare's time, his comment is not only inaccurate but also indicative of a failure to perceive how and in what contexts audiences affected the dramas of their time.[9] As I have said elsewhere, "Imagined audiences shaped dramas at the inception of the compositional process. ... Expected audiences at different venues caused early modern players to alter the dramas in their repertoire."[10] Once performance is reconceived as a dialectical activity, our awareness of theatrical audiences expands considerably.

In *The Semiotics of Theatre and Drama*, Keir Elam notes that in the sociologist Erving Goffman's terms, the audience's role is itself performative; Patrice Pavis and Pavel Campeanu both discuss the receptive and active roles of the theatrical spectator.[11] More recently, Anne Ubersfeld has pointed out in *Reading Theatre* that spectators are continuously assessing a performance, reading its signs as it takes place, and responding in ways that the actors perceive as feedback. However, she notes, there is a multiplicity of spectators; all of these react to one another as well as to the actors themselves.[12]

Part of what creates a unified audience is the theatergoers' role as applauders. As the theater scholar and theater professional Jimi Vialaret points out,

> No one makes us applaud, yet we all do it. ... "At the moment when the curtain rises, the crowd has already undergone a series of preparatory moments at the level of physiology". ... To applaud is a social energy; the crowd produces a collective. We observe that humans do not merely applaud; like any energy, it can be diffused, recovered, controlled, and dispensed for purposes not always fully admitted.[13]

Vialaret describes applause as joy—a party, a transgression—and asserts that spontaneous applause is "always on the edge of ecstasy and the impalpable."[14] This account of an almost solipsistic pleasure in applause runs contrary to the social interaction Bernard Beckerman sees in his conception of

> a three-way communication: between the play, the individual and collective audience. The play projects doubly, to each member of the audience as an individual ... and to the audience as a whole, in that distinctive configuration that it has assumed for a particular occasion.[15]

While Beckerman's basic conception is valid, it needs further refinement. Although the audience may be a totality, it is made up of individual playgoers. If they perceive their role as performers (as they do to varying degrees in the plays I have already described in this chapter), if they recognize their role as *performative*, then they may cease to be primarily spectators and become actors in their own right. Moreover, these responses, though they may be enacted in concert, are often initiated by small groups or isolated watchers in concert with others who share a similar disposition. The determination to act breaks up the unity of the audience. If the individual playgoer arrives determined to perform, he separates himself from the group, preventing any possibility of unity among the audience.

Such a situation becomes formalized by the presence of the claque, semi-professional clappers brought in to enhance audience response through their own exaggerated performance of enthusiasm. They are described more broadly by Arthur Saxon as "any organized body of persons who, either for hire or other motives, band together to applaud or deride a performance which generally is of a public nature, and who attempt to influence the audience."[16] This chapter focuses on the role of the claque. Because the members of the claque function as both audience members and performers, the phenomenon blurs what is nominally a fairly clear division. The claque redefines the position of the spectator and, in doing so, redefines the theatrical space, extending it beyond the edge of the proscenium stage commonly in use during the time when the claque was most common.

The claque attained its apogee in the theaters of nineteenth-century Paris, though the nickname for claqueurs at that time, "the Romans," calls attention to the origin of the practice during the time of Nero.[17] But it is generally agreed that the phenomenon of the professional claque emerged in the French theater in the late eighteenth or early nineteenth century. The design of theaters at that time renders the claque and other forms of audience interaction particularly significant. The Théâtre-Français, the primary theater I shall focus on in this chapter, is typical in featuring the proscenium stage. With a vast, horseshoe-shaped auditorium, this theater seated nearly two thousand spectators in the space provided by the orchestra, loge, boxes, and three levels of galleries. The stage was divided from the audience by a vast arch, from which an enormous curtain descended. Though not completed until 1874, the Paris Opera theater was similar in scale; it featured an arch 55 feet wide, with a slightly raked stage 175 feet wide by 85 feet deep. Stage design in the nineteenth century emphasized spectacle with a series of flats; illusionism and historical accuracy were the most important artistic values. For interior scenes, box sets came into fashion early in the century, but these imitated the scale of the theater as a whole and should not be imagined as representing the cramped Victorian interiors of Ibsen.

Such front-facing theater design (in contrast to the thrust stage) creates a clear division between performer and theatergoer. It has been assumed that such a design alienated spectators from the action and forced a passive role on them. Thus, consideration of the existence of a responsive group within the audience upends standard expectations of how the relation between audience and actor functioned at that time. It challenges our previous sense of a clear spatial division structured by use and behavior.

Before considering specific instances of the claque within the history of French drama, however, it is necessary to see it in the political and social context of that history. The claque arose during a time of profound social upheaval: the century came to birth in the midst of the French Revolution and the rise of Napoleon; after the fall of Napoleon, the monarchy was restored, though king followed king in what was hardly an orderly line of succession. Despite Louis-Philippe's attempts at broad-based reform, he, like his predecessors, was ousted in the revolution of 1848, which brought in the Second Republic. The rise of Napoleon III, first as President, then as self-declared Emperor, brought the country some stability (as well as Haussmann's massive rebuilding of Paris). The rule of Napoleon III concluded ignominiously, however, with the loss of the war against Prussia. What followed was the Third Republic, which, however

Figure 3.1 Eighteenth-century watercolor of the Théâtre-Français by A. Meunier. Wikipedia: https://en.wikipedia.org/wiki/Comédie-Française#mediaviewer/File: Paris_Comedie-Francaise.jpg.

problematic, lasted longer than any government in France since the start of the Revolution. The fashion of the claque in nineteenth-century French theater emerged after Napoleon's defeat and seems to be in part a response to changing social conditions and their effect on the economics of the theater industry.

Scholars differ on when and why claques became common in French theaters. Amateur claques (sometimes described as cabals) often formed as partisan groups that wished to support or condemn particular playwrights, performers, or styles of performance. Occasionally, theater devotees attempted to serve as arbiters of the public taste, but more often amateur claques were inspired by loyalty to show their support for the object of their admiration. Saxon suggests that the claques "attained to some degree of permanence" in 1802 with the formation of two claques during the artistic contest between Mlle. Georges and Mlle. Duchesnois, two actresses of the Comédie-Française. Even after Mlle. Georges left Paris for Russia, the claques "had acquired considerable discipline and organization, and instead of disbanding, as such groups had always done before, they remained together, *chefs* were chosen to lead them, and the first permanent claques were born."[18] This view suggests that claques grew out of the system of theatrical troupes that provided regular work for their members, some of whom eventually generated a substantial fan base. On the other hand, F. W. J. Hemmings asserts that claques in France grew out of the practice of playwrights purchasing extra "authors' tickets" to distribute among friends and acquaintances willing to come and clap for the play on opening night.[19] This view suggests that claques originated in the playwright's involvement (and investment) in theatrical production.

Hemmings has documented that by 1809, petty criminals were making money by blackmailing playwrights to pay a fee to hired supporters. Those who refused were hissed by the thirty or forty recruits in regular attendance at the theaters. Later, actors were similarly blackmailed. By the mid-1820s, most theaters had a permanent claque paid by the management, and the system became more orderly: "it was finally decided to incorporate the claque officially, so that the *chef de claque* became, in Paul Ginisty's words, 'an employee at the disposal of the administration and drawing a monthly salary.'"[20]

The fact that the claque of the Comédie-Française were on salary from the theater does not mean that older practices of payment had ceased. The first-tier actors, or *sociétaires*, of the company generally paid the *chef de claque* a regular sum whenever they were in a current production; in addition, the *chef de claque* received complimentary tickets ("comps") that he was free to sell at a discount to theatergoers or to use to recruit additional members of the claque. Louis-Désiré Véron, director of the Opera, recounts in his memoir that Levasseur, the *chef de claque*, regularly received tips from masculine admirers of specific female performers; male theatergoers hoped to ingratiate themselves with the singer or dancer they admired by tipping the applause leader.[21]

While the members of the claque are simultaneously both performers and audience members, they do not function as intermediaries between the two; rather, they complicate each of those categories. Audience members who chatter, preen, and pose have often been characterized in terms of the actors' failure, but they are more properly recognized as people offering alternative performances. Theater was a more genuinely social event in the nineteenth century than it is today, and, as gaslight suffused the rooms, the lights around the auditorium could not be dimmed. Particularly because audience members felt they were on show, they often hesitated to demonstrate enthusiasm for a performance even when it was an honest response.

Though there were frequent outcries against the claque, theater administrators in Paris generally agreed that audience members were fearful of appearing provincial by mistakenly applauding what was mediocre or second-rate. Periodically attempts were made to outlaw the claque, but audience responses without this encouragement were so dismal that the claque was soon reinstated. In *The Theatres of Paris*, published in 1847, Charles Hervey urges,

It is time that this intolerable nuisance should be banished from the theatres, and yet no manager dares to set the example. The public, say they, have been so long accustomed to applaud by proxy, that they have become cold and indifferent, and seldom manifest any feeling of approbation, lest they themselves should be considered in league with *la claque*. The listless apathy of the frequenters of the Italian Opera … is cited as a proof of the absolute necessity of a *claque*. … "Let others begin, and I will follow," is the only answer given to the repeated remonstrances of the press and the public.[22]

Such a change was unlikely to occur, however, so long as neither the theater industry nor the audience themselves trusted a paying public to react with appropriate discrimination to what was occurring onstage. Though a few theaters (the Italian Opera among them) chose not to permit the practice, the theater in France's capital was deeply enmeshed in a complex system that extended the area of performance from the stage to the auditorium. One could even argue that the journalists, who often documented audience responses and even the behavior of the claque in their reviews of openings nights, were engaged in their own responsive performances in the pages of the newspapers for which they wrote.

While the claque's performance was always responsive, based on what was going on onstage, its techniques could be nuanced or rigid, depending on the type of theater it served:

> In state theatres [the claque] became more discreet, obtruding itself hardly at all, concentrating on encouraging the indecisive spectators to overcome their hesitation and give a well-merited ripple of applause; elsewhere it still remained, even at the end of the century, "noisy, intervening frequently, insupportable and of a nature to antagonize the spectators and turn them against the play, the actors, and even the theatre." In such circumstances the claque became themselves, as Jouslin de la Salle observed, "actors destined to play their part opposite those playing on the stage; it was a play within a play. Is it not comical to watch a few pairs of hands rhythmically clapping and creating a furore in the midst of an audience whom the dramatic work and its interpreters often leave in the dead calm of complete indifference?"[23]

By the very nature of their responsibilities, claqueurs engage in performance, whether or not it is forceful enough to be noted by the audience. My interest in the claque is based on the triangulated relationship it creates, where there are actors onstage, an audience in the auditorium, and a segment of the audience who are also performers in their role as claqueurs.

The claque's performance in the state-run theaters was intended to blend in with the response of the audience as much as possible. Initially the claque was massed together near the *chef de claque* under the gas-lit chandelier that overhung the auditoriums (thereby earning the nickname *chevaliers du lustre*). Later, in order to avoid notice, they broke up into groups of two or three scattered throughout the pit and upper galleries. In some cases they rehearsed along with the onstage performers; in many theaters, the *chef de claque* sat in on rehearsals, where he took notes on how he wanted the claque to perform.[24] Documentation from the 1830s indicates that at the Paris Opera the *chef de claque* Auguste Levasseur conferred with the *régisseur* after the opening performance to discuss possible modifications of the claque's performance.[25] A claque might easily be expanded by adding unpaid members who joined in order to avoid long ticket lines; however, the core of the claque could be relatively small. Records from the 1870s indicate that the claque of the Comédie-Française consisted of only about eighteen regulars.[26]

The claque's role included a great deal beyond actual applause. Claques did not merely express approval or disdain for a performance; as their job was to enhance the audience's enthusiasm (and perhaps to perform enthusiasm for drama critics attending the performance), they performed to encourage a warm response on the part of other audience members, consciously enacting the behavior that leads to enthusiasm. Hervey alludes to the *chatouilleur* (or tickler), a functionary of the claque in smaller theaters whose job is

> to laugh at all the jokes, especially the bad ones, in the different pieces, and to utter sundry exclamations of delight at short intervals, with the view of exciting a similar manifestation of satisfaction on the part of the audience.[27]

A dictionary of the period documents *claqueurs* who performed a similar role, the *rigolards*—jokers or laughers: "This specialty requires tact, good humor, and something Rabelaisian in mimicry and communication. ... When the laughs were frequent, the critic wrote in his columns of the 'Success of good, frank gaiety.'"[28] Saxon also mentions *commissaires*, who "call their neighbors' attention to the more noteworthy scenes."[29]

Within the claque, a specific role was assigned to women, who were employed as *pleureuses*, criers. They were placed in the most visible seats in the second and third galleries:

> One has noted that at rehearsals, at one heartrending scene ... the weepers who had pulled out their handkerchiefs, bit at them convulsively and, wiping their eyes, blew their noses with emotion, and the female part of the paying public were soon sobbing freely as well, a skill that comes naturally to them. "*Success of tears!*" said the well-informed critics the following Monday.[30]

In a contemporary memoir, *La Vie d'un théâtre*, Paul Ginisty recounts that once a *pleureuse* received a request from two performers "who promised her one hundred francs if she would sob in the second act, weep in the fourth, and faint at the denouement, all in the most emotional manner" so that journalists would relate the fact in their pages the next day.[31]

The sociologist Erving Goffman would undoubtedly categorize members of the claque as shills, a shill being "someone who acts as though he were an ordinary member of the audience but is in fact in league with the performers."[32] As I do, Goffman defines this role as providing "a visible model for the audience of the kind of response the performers are seeking or ... the kind of audience response that is necessary at the moment for the development of the performance."[33] His description is astute but fails to note that the role of the claque blurs social and professional performance. The claque are not merely improvising, they are improvising within a framework of rehearsals and advance planning that structures both when they perform and how enthusiastically they do so. This performance, then, combines improvisation and set behaviors in an unusual way. As watchers who respond to what they see, they continue to be spectators even when they perform, but at the same time they perform much as actors do: in response to specific cues and in previously agreed-upon ways.

The claque's performance at the Théâtre-Français could be extraordinarily nuanced; this extract from the memoir of "Robert" (Robert Castel or Robert Saisburg) demonstrates the care taken to be responsive to the needs or desires of each sociétaire:

> Mlle. Demerson commands the bravo by a way of acting that is frank, and a joy that is contagious. Mlle. Dupont calls forth the claque by her determined walk, and the spicy agitation of a dark eye and an excessively powerful glance. There was a time where Mlle. Bourgoin only had to show herself to get the public started; today, a little bit of help is necessary, because while losing the youthful blush in her complexion, she has kept most of the faults that had been justly reproached at the beginning of her career. These faults are, for example, to deliver almost all her lines in the same tone; to round her arms at each period; and to precede each concluding feminine syllable with a pause, particularly in verse plays. Thus, this is how she delivers the following:
>
> Vous n'avez devant vous qu'une jeune princes-se.
>
> Or:
>
> Trouverai-je l'amant glacé comme le pè-re.
>
> It is therefore essential that the claque starts before the end of the word.[34]

The performance on the part of the claque described here may be subordinate to that of the actors onstage; however, it redefines the nature of the audience's experience, greatly expanding the conception of spectacle beyond the contributions of set designers or musicians. The claque creates one kind of experience for the actors themselves, and another, a kind of immersive experience, for the playgoers, who are enveloped in a larger sense of illusion. Oddly enough, this performance was generally successful. Maximin Roll, author of *Souvenirs d'un claqueur et d'un figurant* (1904), recounts that

> The head of the claqueurs of this epoch, Father Chapeau, told me one day that his supreme joy was to hear it once said by a paying visitor … "What pleases me about the Comédie-Française is that there is no claque there." Then Father Chapeau, with an accent of the most unshakeable conviction, said, "If there were a claque at the Comédie-Française, I would not set foot there!"[35]

The point of the claque was to provide the perfect theatrical experience. If we accept the idea that the audience pays money not merely to see a specific play enacted but also to enjoy "theatrical experience" as such, this broader concept almost justifies the company's decision to put a house claque on salary.

Robert's commentary on his experience as a member of the claque at the Théâtre-Français also demonstrates the degree to which the *chef de claque* had to attend to the response of the audience he was there to encourage:

> It is necessary to feel and guess what the spectator feels, in order to slow down or accelerate according to the circumstance. In this case, we talk with our neighbors and we leave only when we see them ready to follow our lead. This article concerns only the brigadiers [leaders]; because soldiers must keep following the orders they are given. Nonetheless, either one or the other are, as we have already said, only machines, marionettes, automatons whose strings the general holds between his hands.[36]

Note the distinction Robert makes between the *chefs de claque* and the rank-and-file members. The leader must be sensitive to nuance, but the latter must automatically follow his direction as if they were machines rather than flesh and blood. The reference is to wind-up toys, though Robert will soon shift to a different series of images. Here he refers to brigadiers and soldiers; as we shall see, war imagery dominates his description of the work of the claqueurs.

Later, Robert recounts his first experience as a claqueur on the occasion of the premiere of the Vicomte of Arlincourt's tragedy *Le Siège de Paris* at the Théâtre-Français, which occurred on April 8, 1826. He notes with surprise that Mouchival makes his "plan of campaign with the calm and dignity of a general of an army" and goes on to express his pleasure at making his "first test of arms at such a beautiful siege."[37] Once the performance begins, all goes well until an ill-made verse makes the audience laugh:

> Mouchival paled, but without despairing of victory: so he gave us the signal to give a salvo of applause to repair this small failure. We had gotten the advantage back, when another verse, "*L'infortune auprès d'elle eût glissé sur sa vie*," made the author fall down again. Our chief, furious, gave the signal for a line of fire, which, repeated by the galleries, imposed silence on the mean-spirited jokers; but these sly "*coquins de cabaleurs*" don't stop at laughing, they are whistling, and I had the grief of hearing a few whistles from two people dominate the thunder of our applause. In the excess of our rage, we would have liked to fight these cowardly enemies of the glory of M. le Vicompte, but we were alone on the floor while they, retrenched in their boxes, were mocking us as much as the play. ... we had just maneuvered so as to stay the masters of the field of battle, when a verse came suddenly and forced us to retreat with losses. ... From the second act until the denouement, we smoked incessantly at the breach. ... As for Mouchival, he was an unshakeable rock; he contented himself with crying out to us, like M. Lafon in *Le Cid*, "If we vanquish without peril, we triumph without glory!"[38]

Why does Robert use this warlike imagery so extensively to characterize the claque's behavior toward those whom they were expected to cajole? Part, at least, may have been Robert's attempt to pick up and expand on the siege imagery of the play itself. Interestingly, Robert recounts that afterward he regretted their failure to Mouchival, who responded that in fact the premiere was a success.[39] But the imagery used also seems to echo the conventions of courtly love, and the connection suggests the complex relationship between the claque and the audience, whose relationship with the claque is like that of a beloved whom the claque must conquer.

The rough wooing of the audience is intended to win them over, to convince them to show their solidarity with the claque by following its applause and mimicking its patterns of response. Though both are performing or responding to a third entity, the actors onstage, the claque is not merely trying to drown out dissenting auditors, it is attempting to sway them psychologically. Though there were times in the century's theatrical history that the claque simply tried to overwhelm an unappreciative audience, for the most part their applause was meant both to lead by example and to encourage audience members to rethink their views of the performance. For a claque to be successful, audience members had to doubt their own perceptions of a play and yield up their own judgment to the promptings of the claque. Just as the beloved is supposed to be over-whelmed by the passionate expressions that Petrarchan lovers drew upon, the audience was manipulated by their ignorance to take the claque's views for their own. The success, then, was psychological as well as auditory, though the one was not perceptible unless it was followed by the other. Audience members must yield, then, much as the beloved does (from weariness, if nothing else, as some students of Petrarch may remark).[40]

The idea of overwhelming the perceptions of the audience was as offensive in the time of the claque as the idea of overwhelming a woman's resistance with attentions is today. While some people at that time felt that audiences needed to be led, others believed that the compulsion to respond as a group was coercive. Hemmings, in fact, notes Malliot's comment on audiences outside the capital:

> The most pacific provincial is very touchy on this point, he won't permit anyone to do his thinking for him and he would be capable of dealing with the claque in no uncertain way if they tried to organize themselves at his theatre as they do in the capital.[41]

Though Robert's expressions may amuse us now, his language helps us to recognize the obverse side of the theater industry's desire to create a full theatrical experience that pushes audience members into accepting the theater's own repre-sentation of the value of its productions. The encouragement to go along with the claque could override a tepid response to second-rate material; even the Théâtre-Français could not be relied upon to produce a masterpiece every night.

The system was highly artificial, of course, and resulted in many disasters. When the renowned male sociétaire Joanny refused to pay the claque prior to his performance of the title role in Corneille's *Cinna*, he found he received no applause at all. He wrote that he wished to do without "the hired services of this riff-raff. This is what I do; so, no claque for me! On the other hand—and there is some consolation in this, shameful though it is—I hear some truly shocking acting wildly applauded."[42] In this case, the claque's lack of performance *was* a performance, though it was directed more toward the stage than to the other members of the audience.

Despite, or perhaps because of, the social turmoil of the nineteenth century, theater professionals sometimes engaged in revolutions of their own.[43] The onset of theatrical Romanticism, initially viewed by the French as a German import, created a number of stormy scenes. Those audience members who were committed neither to Neoclassicism nor to Romanticism did not know how to react. Their reservations created what theater professionals regarded as a need for professional appreciators of their art, people who stood as examples, if not actual pedagogues, for how to behave at the theater. While the claque probably played to the audience more often than not, they frequently engaged in antagonistic responses to other factions as well. Rather than trying to win over an audience to enjoyment of a play, they might simply try to overwhelm another group to make a point.

The tumultuous night of the premiere of Victor Hugo's *Hernani* is a case in point. This event, characterized by Marvin Carlson as "the best known date in French theatre history between the seventeenth and the twentieth centuries," took place on February 25, 1830.[44] The repertoire of the Théâtre-Français had been dominated for years by second-rate playwrights whose work imitated Corneille and Racine in all particulars. The production of Hugo's play, for which there had been more than fifty rehearsals, was a bold stroke on the part of Baron Taylor, director of the theater since 1825. This play was widely regarded as a test case for the success of a new form of theater—the Romantic drama, which the French had widely resisted as part of a movement that had originated with their longstanding enemy, Prussia.

Use of the company's claque would seem to have been a natural choice. However, Hugo recognized that resorting to that hidebound institution might be a mistake. According to Marguerite Treille, "The *chef de claque* had applauded colorless pieces of a pseudo-classical style for such a long time that he had become classical by habit and he only applauded the first romantic attempts with the tips of the fingers."[45] Moreover, Hugo feared that the *chef de claque* might sell out to his enemies for the right price—he had already seen his previous play *Amy Robsart* fail at the Odéon Theater in 1828.[46]

Consequently, Hugo allowed his friends to muster their own forces. Baron Taylor agreed to give out the usual authors' tickets to Hugo's friends rather than to the claque, and a group of between three hundred and four hundred persons "ready to intervene at any time to crush the old classics" came, many wearing wigs as a moderate form of concealment.[47] This group, which included Théophile Gautier, Gérard de Nerval, and Petrus Borel, constituted a loosely formed cabal, a proud army eager to prove their allegiance to the new literary style. In his

Histoire du romantisme, Gautier ecstatically opens the section about *Hernani* by exclaiming, "February 25, 1830! That date stands out in my past in letters of fire."[48] He goes on to say how difficult it is to describe the effect on the audience of

> the striking, virile, vigorous verse, that had so strange a ring ... for nowadays the very innovations that then were considered barbarisms are accounted classical. It must also be carefully borne in mind that in France, at that time, abhorrence of plain speaking and of the use of crude words was carried to a fairly unimaginable extent.[49]

Writing in 1872, Gautier found it difficult to convey the experience of a moment when French literature was on the cusp of a great change. He concludes his account by saying,

> It needed only to cast a glance at the public to learn that this was no ordinary performance; that two systems, two parties, two armies, even two civilizations—it is no exaggeration to put it so—were facing each other, filled with cordial reciprocal hatred of the intense literary kind, ready to come to blows and longing for a fight.[50]

Gautier's account makes it clear that there *was* a war on, a war between passionate factions determined to decide the character of the national literature. Looking back with forty years' distance, he claims he is astonished at how the passages that provoked obloquy are the ones that, by 1872, were applauded; yet he vividly recalls them as

> passages that were then fields of battle well trampled over, redoubts that were stormed and retaken, ambushes where one lay in wait round the corner of an epithet, relays of hounds ready to spring at the throat of a hunted metaphor.[51]

The opening provokes his comment, "With the very first words the orgy is already in full swing!"[52] For the French classicist, the play's opening, in which the hemistich line is broken into two parts and spoken by two speakers, as well as the enjambment into the second line, was "like a professional swashbuckler, a Saltabadil, a Scoronconcolo smacking the face of Classicism and challenging it to a duel."[53] Marvin Carlson more recently offered his own list of what was at stake: a battle

> between those who felt French art should draw primarily on its own classic tradition and those who would seek inspiration elsewhere, between a theatre based on language and one sharing that emphasis with spectacle, and perhaps most fundamentally between a theatre of tradition and one of innovation.[54]

Essentially, as Carlson explains, the play challenges classical French tradition on several fronts: it violates the sacrosanct poetic conventions of the verse drama of its day; it shows a monarch "asking what time it is in the language of a commoner, and answered as though he were a clodhopper";[55] it violated the three unities; and it challenged the structure of classical usage by violating "the traditional arrangement of scenes [and] the alternation of set speeches and dialogue."[56] In addition, Hugo acted in the capacity of the modern theater director, providing innovative blocking that violated the standard practice of having a row of actors stand downstage and simply declaim their lines to the audience.[57]

The result of these challenges to the conventions of classical theater was that almost every line provoked an audible response. André Le Breton describes the scene in this way:

> The clashes began among the spectators. Almost every line was simultaneously cheered and hissed, hissed by the loges, cheered by the second gallery occupants and those of the parterre. And as happens in any passionate discussion, the audience cheered and hissed with great confidence, even without having heard the actor ... The battle lasted the entire evening.[58]

Theater historians generally agree that, though the outcries continued for the run of the play, the very controversy was a victory for the Romantics. *Hernani* ran for thirty-nine performances that year, and its success prompted managers to put on other Romantic dramas by the new men. Though Hugo complained in his memoirs of what he felt were universally negative reactions, he also noted that the receipts for each performance came to five thousand francs. By the time that Gautier wrote about a revival in 1867, the many challenges to accepted practice in *Hernani* had become common, and the play itself had become as celebrated as Corneille's *Le Cid*, the great French classical drama.

In a case like the premiere of *Hernani*, social performance becomes the primary goal of applause. Applause is an aggressive act, not an attempt to alter the perceptions of those who might be sitting on the fence. On occasion, riots could ensue, as aural competition becomes literal violence. Hemmings tells the story of a performance at the Odéon in which disagreement between the claque and a group of students grew so heated that it concluded in a punch-up. A review of the play in *La Quotidienne* recounts, "Clenched fists rose and fell with such velocity that the eye could barely follow them. ... Meanwhile, the spectators who had remained neutral ... clambered through the orchestra and took refuge on the stage."[59] The violence might have been expected to give a sense that the claque had failed; on the contrary, however, further events at that theater suggest that the claque was trying to make an impression with its own power, and that the success of the play was not so much a concern as the claque's goal of forcing the audience to accept their efforts as part of the experience of attending a theatrical performance. Thus the efforts of the claque could shade into acts of physical aggression. While the claque may not have had an ideological commitment to any element of a specific performance, they were committed to enforcing their knowledge and skill. Their actions could manifest a self-aggrandizing function, though a well-trained claque would certainly be expected to act more circumspectly.

If the presence of the claque restructures the use of the theater building so that stage and auditorium face one another in mutual performance, what changes when the production onstage is a self-reflective artwork like *A Chorus Line*, in which the mimetic space doubles the actual space? With *Adrienne Lecouvreur*, first performed at the Théâtre-Français in 1849, the playwrights Eugène Scribe and Ernest Legouvé created a melodrama about an actress who had performed at the same theater 120 years earlier. One act is set in the Théâtre-Français's green room (the waiting room and lounge area where performers rest when they are not onstage); another occurs at a noblewoman's drawing-room where Adrienne has been invited to recite after dinner. The experience of seeing the play would have broadly offered the pleasure of being "in the know," not merely because theatrical secrets were being revealed but also because many audience members would have seen their previous knowledge of Lecouvreur dramatized on the stage. Spatially, the production turned the theater inside out, temporarily transforming the performance area into a replica of the concealed work area. The presence of the claque in the auditorium, coupled with this drama's theatrical self-consciousness, created an extended performance space that lessened the significance of the spatial divide between performers and watchers. In one scene, set in the green-room of the Théâtre-Français, actors playing actors listened onstage for aural indications that their peers, who were performing (on a stage that supposedly existed next to the green-room), were reaping applause for their performances. The claque was doubled by actors applauding offstage to represent the offstage audience, and the claque's self-effacing performance of unplanned enthusiasm contrasted with the play's presentation of self-conscious theatricality in social performance.

Scribe and Legouvé's *Adrienne Lecouvreur* is a celebration of the diva of the title; it was written as a vehicle for Rachel, one of the most illustrious French actresses of the century, who was later compared with Bernhardt. Brander Matthews's anecdote about the inspiration for the play indicates the extent to which the drama is embedded in a theatrical context: Scribe was initially doubtful that Rachel would "either be easy herself, or be accepted by the public" in comedy, but his collaborator urged, "'It will be enough to put into a new frame and another period Rachel's ordinary qualities. The public will believe it a transformation, while it will be only a change of costume.'"[60] When Legouvé came upon the story of Lecouvreur reciting a speech from *Phèdre* and directing the line, "I am not one of those hardened ones, / Who, proud e'en of their infamy, do boast a brow / which lieth ever, but ne'er wears a blush," to her rival in love, a noblewoman attending the theater, Legouvé told the story to Scribe, who "fell on his neck in delight, crying, 'A hundred performances at six thousand francs!'"[61] The incident served as the basis of the fourth-act climax.

Initially, Rachel hesitated to take the role; she convinced the management not to produce the play, fearing that her fans would be displeased at seeing her outside of the Neoclassical settings in which, until that time, she had invariably appeared. But the play was revisited six months later and the company agreed to produce it.

The social context of *Adrienne Lecouvreur* enables us to examine the function of the claque from many angles. Jules Lan, a member of the claque, recounts in his 1883 memoir that ever since her debut at the Comédie-Française, Rachel had purchased extra tickets. Aided by an "intimate friend ... a celebrated lawyer who had become Minister of Justice," Rachel passed these tickets to friends and supporters who entered the theater by a special door. Lan comments gleefully that the eulogies upon the man's death should really have included mention of his accomplishments as a *chef de claque*.[62] Critics of Rachel argued that the actress's reputation was solely a matter of publicity and the claque (whether salaried or brought in for her performances alone). A review from the *Courrier du théâtre* in January 1840 that mocked her with hyperbole, alluding to "Le Puff Rachel" and, more ironically, to the "Genius, Goddess of Love, liberator of Racine, Toast of the salons, the Théâtre-Français personified, the teacher of its actors, cosmopolitan tragedienne, idol of the Jews, spoiled child of the aristocracy, eighth wonder of the world," seems to be typical in its suggestion that the claque and the press made her the phenomenon she was at the time.[63] Contemporary documents, however, suggest that the claque deserves little credit for her success. Hervey goes so far as to say that her performances confounded the claque, who were unable to play their part in response to her:

> She does not come on the stage to recite a lesson, but to speak as the spirit prompts her; she does not *act*, she *feels*. ... She has a power ... of riveting the attention of her audience. ... She imitates no one, not even herself. ... The very *claqueurs* themselves are puzzled; they know not when to applaud or when to be silent. While reserving their hired enthusiasm until some cabalistic word, the preconcerted signal for its explosion shall have been pronounced, they are confounded by the legitimate bravos of the audience, who are impelled, by some magical and wholly unexpected effect of her acting, to applaud for *themselves*.[64]

Some audience members complained of her coldness: Brownstein cites the contempt of the painter Courbet for what he called the party of "Ingres, Mlle. Rachel, and M. Scribe," a list that suggests he viewed all three as mannered, formulaic, and bloodless.[65] Hervey, however, gives us a way of understanding Courbet's reaction (the credibility of which, in any case, is undermined by Gautier's enthusiastic response to her acting):

> Mlle. Rachel must not be judged by her first performance of a character; on such occasions she is often uncertain and consequently unequal, whereas it is perhaps only on the third or fourth representation, when she has acquired greater confidence in herself or in her own conception of the part, that she is in full possession of her powers.[66]

In writing about Rachel, Hervey characterizes her quirks of performance while defending her from her critics:

> Among other defects with which this admirable actress has been charged is that of "crumbling and chewing" her words, for the sake of making an effect by abruptly pausing at the close of a sentence. This is unjust: her utterance, even when she lowers her voice to a whisper, is peculiarly distinct, and her delivery, though bearing no earthly resemblance to the monotonous sing-song of modern French tragedians, with whom the *rhyme* is everything and the *sense* nothing, is neither wanting in poetry nor in precision.[67]

The contemporary actress Aleksandra Shubert commented that Rachel's voice was naturally a contralto that could shift to a harsh, metallic, grating tone in the expression of jealousy or concentrated fury.[68]

Rachel's success derived from her Romantic style of performing Neoclassical roles; Hervey comments that "Nature has endowed her with a face and form modelled after the statues of ancient Greece" and says that "the fire mounts from her soul to her eye, her heart throbs violently, and sends forth the breath of passion and energy. She appears like an animated Grecian statue, so classic is her form."[69] Gautier makes a similar comparison when he remarks on her features and her manner, which "arranged themselves naturally in a sculptural manner, and broke down into a series of bas-reliefs."[70] Accordingly, Scribe and Legouvé designed *Adrienne Lecouvreur* to emphasize Rachel's ability to bridge old and new theatrical styles. Neil Arvin describes the play as "a series of compromises between the contradictory ideas of the Classicists and those of the Romanticists" and posits that Scribe "must have been incited by the passion of the moment to take into account the renaissance of the classical spirit caused by Rachel's art, and at the same time to cater to the taste developed ... by the romantic drama."[71] The play violates the unities somewhat but stands firm on unity of action, presenting a series of events that take place in only thirty-four hours. It blends comedy and tragedy, thus following the Romantic disregard for purity of genre; yet it quotes fourteen different Neoclassical dramas (all tragedies). In *Adrienne Lecouvreur*, Adrienne is first depicted performing Roxane in *Bajazet*, a role that helped make Rachel herself famous. Later, however, Adrienne's star turn is her monologue from *Phèdre*, in a role that established the fame of Lecouvreur as well as that of the later actress.

One theme of the play is expressed in Lecouvreur's *bon mot*, which is quoted by the Princess de Bouillon in act 1: "The advantages possessed by *theatrical* princesses over *real* ones consisted in the fact that *we* perform of evenings only, while *they* assume characters all day long."[72] The entire play emphasizes the constant social performance that results from a rigid social hierarchy that enmeshes everyone in systems of patronage and privilege. The Princess, who later becomes Adrienne's rival for the love of the Count of Saxony, tacitly endorses her husband's affair with an actress who is Adrienne's dramatic rival because it gains her greater freedom and license to pursue her own interests.

Consequently, she initially supports that actress, Duclos, for personal reasons and asserts that Lecouvreur's success proceeds "from mere frenzy and blind obstinacy on the part of the public" (9). A dispute soon begins between the Princess and her friend the Duchess d'Aumont, who admires Lecouvreur:

DUCHESS: [Lecouvreur] is indeed a wondrous woman! She has brought about a wondrous revolution in tragedy. She is natural and unaffected. ... I must inform you that Madame de Bouillon by no means shares my enthusiasm. She is a staunch admirer of La Duclos, whose emphatic style of declamation amounts to mere singing.
PRINCESS: 'Tis the very essence of tragedy.
ABBE: By all means! Do not all poets commence by—"I sing"?
PRINCE: "Arma virumque cano."
PRINCESS: What's that, I pray?
ABBE: 'Tis either *Horace* or *Virgil*. ...
PRINCESS: Hence, you see, the more tragedy is *sung*, the better.

(13)

The quarrel sets the terms not only of the theatrical debates of 1730 but squarely in the quarrels of the mid-nineteenth century. The playwrights write as much about Rachel herself as about her celebrated predecessor.

Early in the second act, Lecouvreur's closest friend, the *régisseur* (stage-manager) Michonet, urges the actress to maintain her self-control as she performs. He exhorts her to calm herself: "O heavens! In your present state of agitation you will not be able duly to calculate your effects, or make your points" (23). The line seems an implicit acknowledgment of the compact between the actor and the claque. As Robert said in 1830, "There is no problem with giving a thirteenth round of applause to ladies and young women, because we can if needed attribute it to the gallantry of the public. The same maneuver ought to be effective in sorties with the nuances commanded by the rank of each artist."[73] Michonet wants to be sure that Lecouvreur will pause at certain places just as she has in rehearsal so that the claque can recognize the right moments to applaud. He fears that her abandon will make her overrun the claque's cues, making it impossible for them to support her performance properly. That this is a matter of rival factions is also evident: Michonet warns Lecouvreur, "You need coolness and self-possession, even during inspiration. La Duclos will take the lead—will profit by her advantages—whilst you will think of naught but [your lover]" (23). Since Duclos's acting emphasized regularity and the suppression of emotion, her style would make it particularly easy for the claque to work with her rhythm.

When the Count of Saxony comes to the green room, telling Lecouvreur that he came extra early, she laughingly suggests that he must have been mistaken for a poverty-stricken claqueur: "Mercy, oh me! They must have taken you for a lawyer's clerk!" The Count, implicitly denying that Lecouvreur's success is the result of the claque, responds, "Let them: lawyers' clerks understand these matters as well as most people. At the very name of Adrienne, all shout Bravo!" (24). Because this scene occurs in the Théâtre-Français, known for the subtlety of its claque, the line indicates the difficulty of discovering what response derives from professionals or personal supporters, and what response results from over- whelming enthusiasm from an audience. The difficulty hinted at here is one of the play's frequent reversions to the theme of self-conscious artifice, which occurs once more when Adrienne insists that her lover has a future as a military hero:

> I have already seen you sword in hand, and when I listen to your half playful descriptions of your warlike deeds—now do not laugh at my predictions—I cannot help foreseeing in you a great warrior—a future hero! … Oh—I'm a judge of heroes, I can tell you! I live among heroes of every age and every country! Now do you know there's something in the tone of your voice, the glance of your eye, which reminds me of Rodrigues, of Nicodemes, and, mark my words, success awaits you!
>
> (25)

If the Count of Saxony may be expected to enjoy a brilliant military career based on his resemblance to actors' depictions of classical military heroes, then Lecouvreur's success may be assured whether it depends on actual applause or merely on skillful imitation of it. To go one level further, the drama also suggests that Rachel's success must be real, whether her resemblance to Lecouvreur is profound or superficial.

Michonet's soliloquy at the end of the act reveals the play's blurring of the line between performers and audience members. Almost with bated breath, he listens to the performance, marking both Lecouvreur's delivery and the response of the audience:

> Ah, now she begins the soliloquy! What profound silence! How breathlessly they hang on her every word! Well, very well! Ah, not so fast, not so fast! Ah, that's it, bravo! What emphasis, what truth! Why don't you applaud, you fools! (*applause heard*) At last! She's immense this evening, unapproachable! … (*listening*) Ah, how she gave that line! I'm going out of my senses—I laugh—I cry—I'm sinking from grief and joy! Oh, Adrienne, while I listen to thee I forget everything.
>
> (29)

He is both critic and audience, responding to the performances of both the actress and the theatergoers. He is particularly attentive to the interaction of performer and audience and shows he is aware of his own role as responder to Lecouvreur as well. Significantly, it is in his role as responder that he loses sight of both his environment and his responsibility to keep track of the props. As Vialaret says, applause blends audience members into a single entity; applause is ecstatic, joyous, transgressive. A moment later, Michonet observes Lecouvreur's response as she picks up a prop letter that, unknown to him, bears a real message from her lover; his commentary reiterates the play's theme of the difficulty of distinguishing what is real from what is performance:

> Ah! Fatima enters. Deuce take it, she hasn't her letter! Yes she has, though—she hands it to Roxane [Lecouvreur]. Heavens! What an effect! She trembles—she can scarcely stand—her emotion is so great that while reading the letter her rouge has positively disappeared. 'Tis really marvelous! (*Tremendous applause heard.*)
>
> (30–31)

The concept of the claque as an element alien to the audience is challenged by the premise of this play, which reinforces the idea that it is impossible to distinguish between performance and true feeling. Adrienne's performance cannot be divided from the feelings she experiences, which carry her along; the claque cannot truly be separated out from the audience, as it merely leads the rest of the audience to express enthusiasm it already feels.

The claque is portrayed quite differently in a play in which it is actually the subject: William Busnach's frothy one-act musical *La Claque! La Claque!*, performed in 1862 at the Théâtre de la Société artistique, a small theater characterized as "a new institution deserving the favor and approbation of all the friends of music and theater."[74] The play reflects the up-to-the-minute changes in French society in its time. Its subject is a middle-aged entrepreneur who has established a photography studio. The plot concerns his desire for fame and influence in the art world, which is gratified by his daughter and her lover, the young photographer who runs the studio. The play begins with the time-honored New Comedy plot of a young girl and her lover whose union is blocked by a disapproving parent. But the rest of the play is very modern, emphasizing both commercial photography and the theatrical claque as new forms of promotion that bring fame to both promoter and promoted.

The plot begins when Julie's father, Collodion, enters theatrically, like a figure in a melodrama, complaining of a peculiar torment: "To feel in oneself the stuff of a man of genius, and not to be able to catch a break!"[75] He hands his daughter a newspaper and points out an ad for a photographer's album containing "more than 12,000 portraits of contemporary celebrities," none of whom, unfortunately, he knows. He dreams of creating a similar album that would make him famous:

> What would be put in this album? Something new, something original is necessary; that is what I have been looking for, in vain, for eight days. ... What I am looking for is a newsworthy item to bring to the public's attention. ... it is ... I don't know what![76]

Later, Collodion soliloquizes:

> To be illustrious! The price isn't important. To be a great man! Ah, that is what I have desired all my life. So, having left the field of commerce, I have

sought a branch where I could become illustrious. I had thought to make my name as an ambassador, but the official robes are so expensive! So I have thrown myself headlong into photography.[77]

Playing on his employer's desire for fame, Julie's lover, Bain-de-Fer, mysteriously promises to aid Collodion in creating a photograph album of well-known people, thereby winning Collodion the fame he desires in exchange for Julie's hand. Once Collodion agrees, he is approached by Romulus, a *chef de claque* whose presence is heralded by the noise of whistles, hisses, and shouts of "Bravo!". As the result of an agreement between the two, Collodion finds his establishment visited by a variety of oddities including the quick-tempered actor Chabannais, the Tendril, the King of Auraucania, a Comet, and the Thread of the Plot. The play reaches its climax when Collodion expresses a wish to see a theatrical revue and the Thread of the Plot offers him a chance to see one, introduced by their own Théâtre Bellefond (the name of the actual theater where the play occurred). The finale celebrates the theater and its claque and, before the final song, Bain-de-Fer presents Collodion with the completed album and receives Julie's hand in return.

Though the title of the musical is *The Claque! The Claque!* and the primary focus is Bain-de-Fer's bargain with Collodion, the true subject of the play is notoriety and how to gain it. The play links photography and the claque as forms of public relations that frequently influence reviewers and diverse forms of audience. The general audience for theater, photography, and newspapers was the growing bourgeoisie, whose tastes were shaped by these purveyors of popular culture and simultaneously catered to. In Busnach's play, the "audience" of theatergoers is purportedly idealized, but the plot reckons them as a body of consumers to be manipulated. Rather than characterizing the claque and the audience as indistinguishable, the play envisions the claque as performing both the immediate, rather minor job of encouraging the actors and the broader, much larger job of helping to create a "buzz" about a play.

Collodion's choice of photography as a career path that will win him fame is an intriguing one. The process of fixing and retaining images produced by a camera obscura was developed more or less simultaneously in France, Brazil, and England in the 1820s and 1830s through the manipulation of chemical processes. Daguerre is one candidate for producer of the first photograph; France awarded him 6,000 francs in 1839 in order to persuade him to allow their government to offer the process to the world as a gift.[78] The potential of the photographic process was immediately recognized by scientists and national security forces; equally, its possibilities were explored by artists and a variety of commercial entrepreneurs. Since then, its potential has been exploited in such divergent forms of business as fashion, advertising, architecture, conservation, forensics, medicine, cartography, astronomy, and journalism. Busnach's Collodion leaves a business career in rubber for the photography business, which he hopes will make him famous. The choice indicates the degree to which photography was in vogue at the time; early

French photographers such as Daguerre and Nadar were world-famous in their time and are still known today.

Busnach's character names render the characters mere types. The *chef de claque* Romulus is named after one of the legendary founders of ancient Rome in a reference to the slang term for claqueurs, the "Romans." The name "Collodion" is the word for both a chemical and a method of combining it with silver iodide solution to sensitize glass plates in the photography process. Collodion is "a viscous solution of nitrocellulose in alcohol and ether."[79] The use of it in photography is called the wet collodion process; after this method was developed in 1851, it replaced egg white as the substance spread on glass photographic plates because its use reduced the exposure time needed to fix an image. A different form of collodion was used in theatrical makeup.[80]

Throughout the musical, Busnach astutely comments on the similarities between photography and the claque. Upon meeting Collodion, Romulus sings a song about "the profession of the latest fashion." As he says,

> Long live photography!
> Such is the general cry.
> Each wants his image
> Sitting, standing, on horseback.
> Old masks with fresh faces. ...
> Men of spirit, fools, madmen, and sages,
> The lens reproduces all of it.[81]

The French term for lens, "l'objectif," is identical with the word's adjectival form, which shares the meaning of the English term "objective": unbiased, impartial, neutral in observance. But the impression of objectivity resulting from the linkage of the noun with its identical brother is undermined by the series of verbal images that follow: "The portrait of Talleyrand, / A scrupulous virtue," a warrior who "holds in his right hand / The baton of a Marshall."[82] From twentieth-century hindsight, the list seems to prefigure Jean Genet's portraits of social institutions that substitute appearance for the actual functioning of power in order to maximize their broader functioning through reputation. The song concludes by expressing the desire of each tradesman to represent his essence through photography: "The butcher wants his brawn, / And each author, the Institute. / ... Soon, more photographers; / The true -tographer will come."[83] Repeatedly the song emphasizes the link between photography and objectivity, naively equating appearance and truth despite the references to commercial photography's idealized images. But clearly, what creates the mania for a posed photograph is the recognition that the image must be staged (if not actually manipulated) through props and preparation— rehearsal, if you will. The song's opening phrase, "Vive la photographie!", anticipates the final lines of "Vive la claque!", suggesting that both practices manipulate the impressions of the spectators. In Busnach's view, the claque is aligned not with the audience but with the actors, as the claque, like photography, is a theatrical practice—a rehearsed representation that taints the clarity of the audience's perceptions.

Despite this acknowledgment of deceptive practices, Busnach's characters are essentially good-natured in their deceptions. Almost everyone in the play is a bit of a deceiver, while the self-important Collodion is a dupe of his daughter and her lover, who are scheming to please the old man in order to avoid her being disinherited. Bain-de-Fer sets the stage for the introduction of Romulus with the aside, "If Romulus, our ancient model, has understood me, it will work—and put down Father Collodion!"[84] Collodion, who believes he is protecting his daughter's purity by forbidding her to read the daily papers, finds himself manipulated by her, and he is surprised in the end to find that she is the star performer in the climactic show, in which she plays the part of the theater itself.

When Romulus introduces himself to Collodion, he describes himself as "one of those who are charged with showing to authors and artists the satisfaction of the public" (13). This term is more comprehensible to Collodion than the slangier terms he uses ("a descendant of an illustrious Roman," "a blackbird"). Though Romulus says that he has trained under Melingue and Vavasseur, he offers none of the nonsense about wanting to conceal his existence; at Bain-de-Fer's recommendation, he has come because of his professed wish "to leave my traits for posterity": "It is for that that I have come to your house. I wish to have my portrait with this characteristic costume, and this line near my feet: 'The greatest of the Romans, here's what's left of him!'"[85]

Busnach's portrayal of this *chef de claque* suggests that the *chef de claque* memoirists' usual modest expressions and stated wishes to remain unobtrusive and unrecognized may be merely a pose. Certainly this *chef de claque* shows no desire for anonymity—on the contrary, he wants to be remembered, and he regards himself as a personage worthy of remembrance. When he explains that he regards his plan as the rendering of a service to Collodion rather than the reverse, Collodion immediately takes the bait: "Heavens! What do I hear? What? So my dream can be realized? My album ... here ... Album Collodion! Revue of 1861. Ah, my dear Nero!"[86] Collodion accepts Romulus's rather extraordinary assertion that a photo of Romulus will lead others to remark upon his photography salon and lead "all the celebrities of the past year ... to come here to pose" for him.[87] The *chef de claque*, according to Romulus at least, is not a semi-respectable figure but a well-known man whose behavior will prompt others to follow the fashion he sets. Collodion is overjoyed at the prospect of netting this first and most crucial celebrity, the "blackbird" of the boards. A round of demonstrative applause from Romulus prompts the arrival of the second "celebrity," the quarrelsome actor Chabannais, whose fame, despite his bad temper, seems to demonstrate the success of the claque as a form of advertisement.

Romulus concludes the scene with a song in celebration of the claque, which is described as pursuing actors like paparazzi:

The claque, the claque, the claque!
You do not hear anything other than that!

> Everywhere, each stalking you
> With this same refrain.
> Once in the underworld
> We spoke nothing but Javanese.
> Now, at this moment,
> We speak "Chabannais."[88]

Romulus jocularly urges his own merits, convincing Collodion that, just as he has made Chabannais notorious, he can do the same for Collodion.

The play ends under the benevolent control of the play's good spirit, the Thread of the Plot. When Collodion asks to finish his story with a musical revue, the Thread obliges with "a new theater piece, very little, very modest." The Theater sings a song largely in its own praise ("No grand scenery on our boards, / No carpets on our parquets, / But the fresh young folk gambol / At their rendez-vous under the lamps").[89] The song turns, toward the end, though, to a veiled reference to the role of the claque among the theater staff:

> Mustachio'd lips, pink lips,
> All have cried to us, "Bravo!"
> And our success imposes on us now
> A new obligation.
> [...]
> All of you who dream of the ecstasy
> Of the first applause,
> You who are rounding up phrases!
> Where Bressantes is, without commitments?
> Great names of the future: actors, poets,
> Who we push back, still unknown,
> We will give you, during our parties,
> A little noise, if not a little gold.[90]

The verses imply that no theater can get by without the aid of the claque. For ongoing runs, the claque encourages the actors and fills in less-than-ideal performances. The harmless claque augments the response of the theatergoers and gives "a little noise" to help the performers along.

The point is reemphasized even further in the play's finale, which begins with the cheer, "Long live the claque, long live the claque! / In order that we might attack! / Long live the claque!"[91] "Attack" serves as metonymy for "triumph," for the successful "putting over" of a performance. The claque is part of the theater, playing a supporting role to the onstage actors. In verses sung by the various characters, the claque is compared to various items initially perceived as unnecessary or excessive but which become, through the influence of fashion, a perceived necessity. The Comet compares the claque to a long train on a dress; Brule-Pavé compares it to a showy equipage. Parisians, according to the Frégate-École, "go to see the sea, which rises and falls—an astonishing thing!—as if no one had rent to pay."[92] Romulus's comparison is most clearly expressed:

> The theaters on the water's edge,
> To save many a tumble,
> Ought to replace their lightning rods
> With a good parachute.[93]

He means that every theater needs a back-up system—a parachute. Rather than having a lightning rod to stave off bad reviews, theaters need a system that prevents their shows from failing. The claque is a safety system—it prevents occasional failures from becoming disasters.

At the last verse, the Thread of the Plot reiterates the point that the claque's role is to support the actors:

> At the little Theater Bellefond,
> If we brighten up sad faces,
> We will see what the beauties do
> In order to encourage the artists.
> Long live the claque! Long live the claque!
> That we may attack!
> Long live the claque![94]

The claque here is described in terms of its narrow role—its specific role as supporter, as "encouragers" of the actors. But the claque's larger role is featured throughout the play. Just as Collodion's album is intended to direct the public's attention to stars that he has created through the publicity engendered by the album, the claque engenders the success of the theatrical production by generating an enthusiasm that is noted in journals and newspapers. Both applause and celebrity photography are a form of performance, phenomena that are parasitic in relation to more purely creative art but which enhance the success of those creative efforts exponentially. The two modes stand in relation to one another as representatives of the old and the new: the claque, the old form of public relations, is enhanced by photography, the newer mode of representation. If theater is representation and the claque battens on that art form as an attendant type of representation, the photograph of Romulus goes one remove beyond the claque as a parasite of the theater, enhancing the reputation of Collodion as photographer while it makes Romulus, *chef de claque*, more notorious as well.

Busnach offers a good-natured portrayal of the nature of public relations. What he doesn't necessarily realize is that his depiction of these modes of representation reveals a cynical manipulation of the public. Photography and the claque are economic phenomena, part of a debased system in which the profits of promotion are concealed by the mechanism of fame.

That the claque is a parasitical phenomenon is no news. But the claque is not merely parasitical. The phenomenon of the claque demonstrates that we cannot unproblematically characterize the audience as a single entity. Maurice Descotes wisely observes that mass behavior among theatergoers is a kind of assent to collectivity: "Tears are a mode of expression, a collective convention, and the viewer really experiences what he imagines experiencing: they become a sort of reflex conditioned by the existence of rules of which the individual has no awareness."[95] But the experience of French theatergoers in the nineteenth century reveals many circumstances in which the audience acted as respondents to pressures among themselves, pressures related to but in some ways separate from the relation between the audience and the actors onstage. The division proposed by Gay McAuley based on the terms "audience" and "spectators," in which McAuley perceives linguistic implications "as though hearing were a communal act but seeing an individual one" seems inadequate. McAuley further examines related terms in French and German, however, pointing out that the French term "l'assistance" "is a much richer term than *audience*," referring "primarily to the spectators' physical presence, to the being there, but the secondary meaning of *assister* (to help) is also relevant."[96] In fact, "assister à" means "to be present at," as McAuley notes, but it also means "to participate in." The term acknowledges the theatrical experience as a transaction between actors and audience.

Significantly, the role of the claque also restructures the shape of the stage-space, the "place of performance" (to use Marvin Carlson's term). This place is remade when performers are stationed throughout the auditorium, and it is restructured further when their performance is directed toward the actors, to opposing parties in the auditorium, or to passive or receptive people in the auditorium. The stage-space is expanded to encompass the full theater under these circumstances and, when self-reflexive dramas are portrayed onstage, the offstage area is in some sense included or flipped by its representation onstage. But the circle of onlookers with which I began is also made more complex by the actions of the claque. Rendered symbolic by those actions, the circle dissolves into a more amorphous shape whose influence may be said to terminate at the walls of the architectural structure. A more radical view might even perceive the stage-space as extending to the environment affected by the "buzz" generated by claques, promotional photos, and the news media, whether in paper or even (today) in electronic form.

Notes

1 The stage directions indicate "*Altogether here*," meaning "all together here."
2 All quotations from *As You Like It* are from William Shakespeare, *The Riverside Shakespeare*, ed. G. Blakemore Evans (Boston: Houghton Mifflin, 1974), 369–402. All further citations will appear in text.
3 See Richard Southern's comment on how the kind of performance offered by buskers will shape the way the crowd gathers. Richard Southern, "Unusual Forms of Stage," in *Actor and Architect*, ed. Stephen Joseph (Manchester: Manchester University Press, 1964), 48.
4 Eric Bentley, *The Life of the Drama* (New York: Atheneum, 1964), 150.

5 Marvin Carlson, *Places of Performance: The Semiotics of Theatre Architecture* (Ithaca: Cornell University Press, 1989), 5.

6 Tom Stoppard, *The Real Inspector Hound*, in *The Real Inspector Hound* and *After Magritte* (New York: Grove, 1975), 7.

7 Michael Bennett, James Kirkwood, and Nicholas Dante, *A Chorus Line* (New York: Applause, 1975).

8 Peter Brook, *The Empty Space* (New York: Touchstone, 1968), 9. Like Eric Bentley, Brook implies that the essential element of theater is the presence of a spectator.

9 Stephen Greenblatt, *Shakespearean Negotiations: The Circulation of Social Energy in Renaissance England* (Berkeley: University of California Press, 1988), 13.

10 Jennifer A. Low and Nova Myhill, "Introduction: Audience and Audiences," in *Imagining the Audience in Early Modern Drama, 1558–1642* (New York: Palgrave, 2011), 1.

11 Keir Elam, *The Semiotics of Theatre and Drama* (London: Routledge, 1988). See also Patrice Pavis, "Pour une esthétique de la réception théâtrale: Variations sur quelques relations," in *La Relation théâtrale*, ed. Régis Durand (Lille, France: Presses Universitaires de Lille, 1980), 27–54; and Pavel Campeanu, "Un Role secondaire: le spectateur," in *Sémiologie de la representation*, ed. Andre Helbo (Brussels: Complexe, 1975).

12 Anne Ubersfeld, *Reading Theatre*, trans. Frank Collins, ed. Paul Perron and Patrick Debbèche (Toronto: University of Toronto Press, 1999), 23.

13 "Personne ne nous oblige à applauder, et pourtant nous le faisons tous. ... 'A l'instant où le rideau se lève, la foule a déjà subi une série d'états préparatoires, d'ordres physiologiques'. ... Applaudir est une énergie sociale; en ce sens la foule produit du collectif. Seuls, nous l'observerons, les humains n'applaudissent pas, et comme toute énergie, elle peut être diffuse, récupérée, contrôlée, et dispensée dans des buts pas toujours avouables"; Jimi B. Vialaret, *L'Applaudissement: claques et cabales* (Paris: Harmattan, 2008), 9–10. Vialaret quotes Charles Lalo, *La Beauté et l'instinct sexuel* (Paris: Flammarion, 1922), 297. Here and throughout this chapter, translations from the French are mine unless otherwise indicated.

14 Ibid., 10.

15 Bernard Beckerman, *Dynamics of Drama* (New York: Knopf, 1970), 133.

16 A. H. Saxon, "A Brief History of the Claque," *Theatre Survey* 5, no. 1 (May 1964): 11.

17 Saxon cites the accounts of Tacitus and Suetonius, who record not only Nero's appearance onstage but his hiring of "young men of the equestrian order, and above 5,000 robust young fellows from the common people" and training them to applaud his performances as encouragement to the rest of the audience (Suetonius, *The Lives of the Twelve Caesars*, ed. J. Eugène Reed, trans. Alexander Thomson [Philadelphia: Gebbie, 1889], II: 21; Tacitus, *The Complete Works of Tacitus*, 401, *Annals* 16.5; cited in Saxon, "History of the Claque," 12–13).

18 Saxon, "History of the Claque," 17.

19 F. W. J. Hemmings, *The Theatre Industry in Nineteenth-Century France* (Cambridge: Cambridge University Press, 1993), 102. See also John Lough, *Paris Theatre Audiences in the Seventeenth and Eighteenth Centuries* (Oxford: Oxford University Press, 1957), 190–95 and 203.

20 Hemmings, *Theatre Industry*, 105; Paul Ginisty, *La Vie d'un théâtre* (Paris: Schleicher Freres, 1898), 103.

21 Louis-Désiré Veron, *Mémoires d'un bourgeois de Paris* (Paris: G. de Gonet, 1853–55), 313–14; qtd. in Hemmings, *Theatre Industry*, 104.

22 Charles Hervey, *The Theatres of Paris* (Paris: Galignani & Co., 1847), 27. See also Arsène Houssaye, *Les Confessions: souvenirs d'un demi-siècle, 1830–1880* (Paris: E. Dentu, 1885), III: 148; and P. A. Fiorentino, *Comédies et comédiens* (Paris: Michel Lévy Frères, 1866), II: 178; qtd. in Hemmings, *Theatre Industry*, 114.

23 Hemmings, *Theatre Industry*, 105, quoting Astruc, *Le Droit privé du théâtre ou rapports des directeurs avec les auteurs, les artistes, et le public* (Macon:

Protat frères, 1897), 278; and Armand-François Jouslin de la Salle, *Souvenirs sur le Théâtre-Français* (Paris: E. Paul, 1900), 84.

24 Hemmings, *Theatre Industry*, 109, 116.

25 Ibid., 116; Saxon, "History of the Claque," 20.

26 Hemmings, *Theatre Industry*, 109.

27 Hervey, *The Theatres of Paris*, 27–28.

28 "Cette spécialité exige du tact, de la belle humeur, quelque chose de rabelaisien dans la mimique et de communicatif. ... quand les *rigolades* ont été fréquentes, le feuilleton écrit dans ses colonnes: *succès de bonne et franche gaieté*"; *Grand Dictionnaire Universel du XIXe Siècle* (Paris: Larousse, 1869), 385.

29 Saxon, "History of the Claque," 19.

30 "On a noté, aux répétitions, une scène *déchirante* ... les *pleureuses*, qui ont tiré leur mouchoir, le mordent convulsivement, se tamponnent les yeux, se mouchent avec émotion, et la partie féminine du public payant de sangloter aussitôt, avec cette facilité qui lui est naturelle: *succès de larmes!* disent le lundi suivant les critiques bien informés"; *Dictionnaire*, 385.

31 "Il y a quelque temps que l'une des plus sensibles fut mandée par un révérend père-noble et une ci-devant jeune première, qui lui promirent cent francs si elle voulait sangloter au second acte de la pièce nouvelle, pleurer au quatrième, se trouver mal au dénouement, le tout d'une manière sensible, afin que les journalistes pussent, le lendemain, relater le fait dans leurs feuilles"; Ginisty, *La Vie d'un théâtre*, 66.

32 Erving Goffman, *The Presentation of Self in Everyday Life* (Garden City, NY: Anchor, 1959), 146.

33 Ibid., 146.

34 "Mlle. Demerson commande le bravo par un jeu franc et un gaîté communicative. Mlle. Dupont appelle la claque par sa démarche décidée, et la piquante agacerie d'un oeil noir excessivement fendu. Il fut un temps où Mlle. Bourgoin n'avait qu'à se montrer pour faire partir le public; aujourd'hui un peu d'aide est nécessaire, car, tout en perdant la majorité des roses de son teint, elle a gardé la plupart des défauts qu'on lui a justement reprochés lors de ses débuts: ces defauts sont, par example, de débiter presque tout sur le meme ton, d'arrondir les bras à chaque période, et de faire précéder d'un repos les dernières syllabes féminines, particulièrement dans les pièces en vers. C'est ainsi qu'elle dit: 'Vous n'avez devant vous qu'une jeune princes-se.' Ou bien: 'Trouverai-je l'amant glacé comme le pè-re.' Il est donc indispensable que la claque parte avant la fin du mot"; Robert Saisburg, *Mémoires d'un claqueur* (Paris: Constant-Chantpie, 1829), 37–38.

35 "Le doyen des claqueurs de cette époque, le père Chapeau, m'avoua un jour que sa joie suprême était d'entendre dire parfois à un de ses voisins de stalle, un voisin 'payant' ... 'Ce qui me plait à la Comédie-Française, c'est qu'il n'y a pas de claque.' Lors, le père Chapeau, avec l'accent de la plus inébranlable conviction! 'S'il y avait de la claque à la Comédie-Française je n'y mettrais pas les pieds!'"; Maximin Roll (Jean Raphanel), *Souvenirs d'un claqueur et d'un figurant* (Paris: Aux bureau du magasin pittoresque, 1904), 64.

36 "Il faut sentir, deviner ce qu'éprouve le spectateur, afin de ralentir ou de presser, selon la circonstance. Dans ce cas, on cause avec ses voisins et on ne part que lorsqu'on les voit disposés à marcher d'accord. Cet article ne concerne que les brigadiers, les soldats devant se borner à suivre les impulsions qu'on leur donne. Néanmoins, les uns et les autres ne sont, ainsi qu'on l'a déjà dit, que des machines, des marionettes, des automates, dont le général tient le fil entre ses mains"; Robert, *Mémoires d'un claqueur*, 36.

37 Ibid., 41, 43.

38 "Mouchival pâlit, mais sans désespérer de la victoire: alors il donna le signal d'une salve qui répara ce petit échec. Nous avions ressaisi l'avantage, lorsque cet autre

vers: '*L'infortune auprès d'elle eût glissé sur sa vie,*' fit encore dégringoler l'auteur. Notre chef furieux donna le signal d'un feu de file qui, répété par les galeries, imposa silence aux mauvais plaisants; mais bientôt ces coquins de cabaleurs ne se contentent pas de rire, ils sifflent, et j'ai la douleur d'entendre quelques sifflets de deux liards dominer le tonnerre de nos applaudissement. Dans l'excès de notre rage nous aurions voulu boxer ces lâches ennemis de la gloire de M. le vicomte; mais nous étions seuls au parterre, tandis que, retranchés dans leurs loges, ils se moquaient de nous autant que de la pièce. … avions-nous manœuvré de manière à rester les maîtres du champ de bataille, qu'un vers arrivait tout-à-coup et nous forçait à reculer avec perte. … Depuis le second acte jusqu'au dénouement, nous fûmes sans cesse sur la brèche. … Quant à Mouchival, c'était un roc inébranlable; il se contentait de nous crier comme M. Lafon dans Le Cid: '*A vaincre sans péril on triomphe sans gloire!*'"; Ibid., 45–47.

39 Robert says that the play ran for ten successive nights and would have run for longer if the author had supported it more wholeheartedly.

40 The situation must have been particularly amusing for those who knew the work of Arlincourt. Known for the syntactic inversions in his prose, he was dubbed "the inversive Viscount"; it was this propensity in *The Siege of Paris* that prompted the spectators' laughter and derision of specific lines.

41 A. L. Malliot, *La Musique au théâtre* (Paris: Amyot, 1863), 337; qtd. in Hemmings, *Theatre Industry*, 115.

42 Maurice Descotes, *L'Acteur Joanny et son journal inédit* (Paris: Presses Universitaires de France, 1956), 63; qtd. in Hemmings, *Theatre Industry*, 104.

43 Hemmings asserts, "Behind every serious theatre riot in the nineteenth century there lay some immediate political grievance. … sometimes the audience was united in damning a particular play, either because its political message was considered offensive or because the author was felt to be too closely associated with those who were working to promote an undesirable political development" (82).

44 Marvin Carlson, "*Hernani*'s Revolt from the Tradition of French Stage Composition," *Theatre Survey* 13, no. 1 (May 1972): 1.

45 "Le chef de claque applaudissait depuis si longtemps les pièces incolores des pseudo-classiques qu'il en était devenu classique par habitude et qu'il n'applaudissait que du bout des doigts les premiers essais romantiques"; Marguerite Treille, *Le Conflit dramatique en France de 1823 à 1830 d'après les journaux de l'époque et les revues du temps* (Paris: Picart Editeur, 1929), 41.

46 Marvin Carlson, *The French Stage in the Nineteenth Century* (Metuchen, NJ: Scarecrow, 1972), 64.

47 Vialaret, *L'Applaudissement*, 113.

48 Théophile Gautier, *A History of Romanticism*, vol. 16 of *The Works of Théophile Gautier*, ed. and trans. Frederick C. de Sumichrast (New York: George D. Sproul, 1902), 137.

49 Ibid., 149.

50 Ibid., 153.

51 Ibid., 150.

52 Ibid., 148.

53 Ibid., 147.

54 Carlson, "*Hernani*'s Revolt," 3.

55 Gautier, *A History of Romanticism*, 151.

56 Carlson, "*Hernani*'s Revolt," 4.

57 Ibid., 5–26.

58 "Les altercations commencèrent entre les spectateurs. Presque chaque vers était en même temps acclamé et sifflé, sifflé par les loges, acclamé par les secondes galeries et le parterre. Et, comme il arrive dans toute discussion passionnée, on acclamait et on sifflait de confiance, sans même avoir entendu l'acteur. … La bataille se prolongea

jusqu'à la fin de la soirée"; André Le Breton, *Le Théâtre romantique* (Paris: Boivin et Cie, 1928), 59–60.

59 Qtd. in Hemmings, *Theatre Industry*, 111.
60 Brander Matthews, *French Dramatists of the Nineteenth Century*, 3rd ed. (New York: Benjamin Blom, 1968), 96.
61 Ibid., 96.
62 Jules Lan, *Mémoires d'un chef de claque* (Paris: Librairie Nouvelle, 1883), 55.
63 Qtd. in Rachel Brownstein, *Tragic Muse: Rachel of the Comédie-Française* (New York: Knopf, 1993), 136.
64 Hervey, *The Theatres of Paris*, 99–100.
65 Cf. Brownstein, *Tragic Muse*, 135.
66 Hervey, *The Theatres of Paris*, 100.
67 Ibid., 99.
68 Cited in Hemmings, *Theatre Industry*, 218.
69 Hervey, *The Theatres of Paris*, 100, 97.
70 Gautier; qtd. in Brownstein, *Tragic Muse*, 173.
71 Neil Cole Arvin, *Eugène Scribe and the French Theatre, 1815–1860*, 2nd ed. (New York: Benjamin Blom, 1967), 162.
72 Eugène Scribe and Ernest Legouvé, *Adrienne Lecouvreur,* trans. unknown (New York: Baker and Godwin, 1866), 10. All quotations from *Adrienne Lecouvreur* are from this edition.
73 "Il n'y a pourtant pas d'inconvénient à donner la treizième à ces dames et demoi-selles, parce qu'on peut, au besoin, l'attribuer à la galanterie du public. Mêmes manoeuvres doivent s'effectuer aux *sorties* avec les nuances commandées par le rang de chaque artiste"; Robert, *Mémoires d'un claqueur*, 35.
74 *Les Beaux-Arts, revue nouvelle* 3 (1861): 26.
75 "Sentir en soi l'étoffe d'un homme de génie, et ne pouvoir parvenir à percer!"; 9. All quotations are from William Busnach, *La Claque! La Claque! Un Folie-revue en un acte* (Paris: Librairie Theatrale, 1862).
76 "Mais qu' y mettre dans cet album? … Il faudrait quelque chose de neuf, d'original; c'est ce que je cherche en vain, depuis huit jours. … Ce que je voudrais c'est une actualité quelconque, à mettre au jour … c'est … je ne sais quoi enfin!" (ellipses in text); ibid., 10.
77 "Être illustre! … N'importe à quel prix … Être un grand homme … Ah! ce fut le désir de toute ma vie! Aussi, en quittant le commerce, j'ai cherché dans quelle branche je pourrais m'illustrer … J'avais bien pensé à me faire nommer ambassa-deur, mais les costumes officiels sont si chers! Alors je me suis jeté à corps perdu dans la photographie"; ibid., 12.
78 Alma Davenport, *The History of Photography: An Overview* (Boston and London: Focal Press, 1991), 8.
79 Beaumont Newhall, *The History of Photography from 1839 to the Present* (New York: Museum of Modern Art, 1982), 59.
80 Helmut Gernsheim, *A Concise History of Photography* (London: Thames & Hudson, 1965; rpt. New York: Dover, 1986).
81   Vive la photographie!
       Tel est le cri général;
       Chacun veut son effigie:
       Assis, debout, à cheval.
       Vieux masques aux frais visages. …
       Gens d'ésprit, sots, fous ou sages,
       L'objectif reproduit tout!

                                    Busnach, *La Claque! La Claque!*, 14.

82 "Le portrait de Talleyrand, / Une vertu scrupuleuse … Ce guerrier tient dans sa dextre / Un bâton de maréchal"; ibid., 14.

83 "L'charcutier voudra sa hure, / Et chaque auteur l'Institut. / ... Bientôt plus de *photographes*; / Le vrai tographe viendra"; ibid., 15.

84 "Si Romulus, notre ancien modèle, m'a bien compris, ça va marcher, et enfoncé le père Collodion!"; ibid., 12.

85 "C'est pour cela que vous me voyez chez vous ... Je veux avoir mon portrait avec ce costume caractéristique, et ce vers à mes pieds: Du plus gros des Romains, voilà tout ce qu'il reste!"; ibid., 15.

86 "Ciel! qu'entends-je? ... Quoi! ... mais alors mon rêve se réaliserait ... Mon album ... le voilà ... Album Collodion ... Revue de 1861. Ah! mon cher Néron!"; ibid., 15.

87 Ibid., 15.

88   La claque, la claque, la claque!
       On n'entend plus que ça;
       Partout chacun vous traque
       Avec ce refrain-là.
       Jadis, dans l'demi-monde,
       On n'parlait qu'javanais;
       À présent, à la ronde,
       On parle chabannais.

                                                          Ibid., 17.

89 "Point de grands décors sur nos planches, / Point de tapis sur nos parquets, / Mais les gaîtés jeunes et franches / Ont rendez-vous sous nos quinquets"; ibid., 41.

90   Lèvre à moustache et lèvre rose,
       Tout nous ont crié ... Bravo!
       Et notre succès nous impose
       Maintenant un devoir nouveau!
       [...]
       Vous tous qui rêvez les extases
       Des premiers applaudissements!
       Vous tous arrondisseurs de phrases!
       Ou Bressants ... sans engagements?
       Grands noms futurs ... acteurs, poètes,
       Qu'on rebute, inconnus encor,
       Nous vous donnerons dans nos fêtes,
       Un peu de bruit ... sinon de l'or!

                                                          Ibid., 41–42.

91 "Vive la claque, Vive la claque! / Que l'on attaque! Vive la claque!"; ibid., 43.

92   Le Parisien s'dérange bêt'ment
       Pour aller voir, chose étonnante
       La mer qui monte et qui descend,
       Com' si nous n'avions pas le rente.

                                                          Ibid., 43.

93   Les théâtres du bord de l'eau,
       Pour s'épargner mainte culbute
       D'vraient remplacer leurs parato. ...
       Nuerre par un bon parachute.

                                                          Ibid., 44.

94   Au p'tit théâtre Bellefond,
       Si nous déridons les fronts tristes,
       Nous verrons c' que les belles font
       Pour encourager les artistes!
       Vive la claque, Vive la claque!

Que l'on attaque!
Vive la claque!

Ibid., 44.

95 "Les larmes sont un mode d'expression, une convention collective, et le spectateur
    éprouve vraiment ce qu'il imagine éprouver: elles deviennent une sorte de réflexe
    conditionné par l'existence de règles dont l'individu n'a plus conscience"; Maurice
    Descotes, *Le Public de théâtre et son histoire* (Paris: Presses Universitaires de France,
    1964), 190.
96 Gay McAuley, *Space in Performance: Making Meaning in the Theatre* (Ann Arbor:
    University of Michigan Press, 1999), 251.

4   How Modernism played in Berlin

Moholy-Nagy's *Hoffmann* at the Kroll Opera House

Thus far I have examined original productions in order to see how playwrights respond to the theater design and theater industry of their times. In later periods of dramatic history, however, as theatrical production becomes increasingly complex, more people are involved in creating a performance; theories of mimesis and theatrical experience become more codified, and the production team becomes much more self-conscious in their manipulation of the stage-space. To learn about the interplay of text and staging in the creation of a performative artifact, it can be useful to study the contributions of figures involved less with the text than with the staging itself. In this chapter I examine how a theater project embedded in its culture challenged a national audience to see itself freshly. My object of study is the 1929 Kroll Opera production of Jacques Offenbach's opera *The Tales of Hoffmann* in Berlin, with set designs by László Moholy-Nagy.

Part of what makes this production notable is that, like the premiere of Hugo's *Hernani*, it challenged deeply held assumptions about what national art and the national character should be. Both productions received vitriolic con-demnation in some quarters and extraordinary enthusiasm from others.[1] The controversy over *Hernani*, however, derived from the playwright's choices: Hugo's innovations in verse and subject matter were the elements that made French traditionalists react against the performance. The outrage expressed in response to the Kroll production of *Hoffmann* seems to result from the contrast between Moholy-Nagy's technical innovations and what the opera's subject, the early Romantic author E. T. A. Hoffmann, had paradoxically come to emblema-tize for the German people: a Biedermeier sensibility based on bourgeois values and *Gemütlichkeit*. (This perception misreads Hoffmann; paradoxically, his work manifests a perverse sensibility and an antipathy toward bourgeois pieties.) Moholy-Nagy designed the sets in response to Hoffmann's ideas about the artist and the role of science in the modern world, which had been refracted through more than one dramatization before this new production. His treatment of these themes offered a new vision that came from his own work and training. Moholy-Nagy's designs for *Hoffmann* are also historically significant in that they exemplify what Stanton B. Garner, Jr. has called "an emerging aesthetics of environment," in which the proscenium stage ceases to manifest a pictorial conception of theatrical space and evinces "a new conception of the stage world as material field."[2]

The Kroll's production convened a number of authors—the German writer-critic E. T. A. Hoffmann, whose fantasy tales provide the basis of the opera and whose life provides the opera's frame narrative; Jules Barbier and Michel Carré, the Frenchmen who wrote a drama based on Hoffmann's life and work and, in the case of Barbier, the libretto for Offenbach's opera as well;[3] and Offenbach himself, a figure not unlike Hoffmann in some ways. An expanded definition of the term "author" would allow us to include in that category Hans Curjel, the dramaturge of the new Kroll Opera, and the set designer, László Moholy-Nagy, Modernist artist and member of the Bauhaus faculty.

In designing the sets for the Kroll's production of *Tales of Hoffmann*, Moholy-Nagy gave form to the experimental ideas about space and motion that he and his colleague Oskar Schlemmer had developed. Moholy consciously considered spatial issues as he worked; indeed, he was affiliated with an influential artistic movement that theorized the nature and functions of art, theater, and spectatorship.[4] Until the twentieth century, most theories of the theater were embedded in more general treatises about art or aesthetics.[5] The views of philosophers, orators, scholars, and divines dominate the field. While playwrights sometimes comment on audiences or the purpose of the theater through dramatic prologues, satiric poems, or characters who served as their mouthpieces, theater professionals prior to the twentieth century were seldom the ones constructing a poetics of theater, mimesis, or art. Moholy-Nagy, however, had very decided views on theater; as a Constructivist and a member of the Bauhaus school, he belonged to two aesthetic movements that tried to redefine the nature of art. The media in which Moholy worked were numerous: painting, typography and book design, photography, collage, and sculptural "constructions." Moholy's theater designs were influenced both by Constructivists like Vladimir Tatlin, Alexandra Exter, Naum Pevsner (Gabo), and Liubov Popova, and by Bauhaus colleagues—most notably Oskar Schlemmer, who served as the Master of Form for the Bauhaus theater workshop. Schlemmer and Moholy-Nagy, as well as Walter Gropius, wrote manifestos about the relation of theater to arts such as sculpture and architecture. They were deeply concerned with the reception of art, conceiving the spectator as an active participant in artistic creation. This chapter investigates how Bauhaus theories about space, theatricality, technology, and spectatorship were employed in the design of the Kroll's production of *Hoffmann*.

In the productions treated in earlier chapters, spatial issues were far from the primary concern. Their staging was structured by the current ideas and practices of their day. Most of the choices concerning the theater, the stage design, the sets, and the blocking followed common practice rather than conscious decisions; a standard approach to staging was the norm, with casual improvisation in response to specific material conditions. But by the late nineteenth century, theater professionals had begun to think about the aesthetic potential of space. This production of *Tales of Hoffmann* was part of a bold program of experimentation; Moholy-Nagy's contribution was very consciously solicited, and his designs manifest the Bauhaus interest in spatial expression—what might be called the semiotics of space. Moholy attempted to include the experience of industrial society in the opera through his designs, using movable planes and multiple stage levels. He used geometric forms to structure his spaces and orient the viewer. His stage design included deliberate consideration of the positioning of bodies, as the designer recognized that bodies themselves shaped the space in which they were located.

Though Moholy was not responsible for every part of the production, the Kroll's dramaturge, Hans Curjel, art historian, musicologist, and aspirant conductor, oversaw most of the new productions.[6] According to the biographer Peter Heyworth, with the artistic director Otto Klemperer taking a lesser role in the Kroll Opera House in 1929, Curjel "put into effect his plans to bring about a renewal of scenic design in the opera house which was to go far beyond anything that Klemperer and [the Kroll's in-house stage designer Ewald] Dülberg had envisaged."[7] Modernism, as Gerald Köhler explains, "was a part of the house's programmatic orientation. ... The unconventional stagings were intended to have an exemplary character and help to establish the new style, which was true to the work in a different way."[8] With this program in mind, Curjel selected the Bauhaus faculty member Moholy-Nagy as set designer for *Hoffmann*.

The controversy stirred up by the production of *Hoffmann* was, to some extent, a planned assault on established tastes. The Kroll had been founded in 1919 as a *Grosse Volksoper* (the Great People's Opera House) to provide "good performances at cheap prices in a theater ... that would seat four thousand people."[9] The new State Opera House (i.e. the Kroll) was a joint venture between the *Kultusministerium* (Ministry of Culture) and the Berlin Volksbühne, "an organization close to the German Social Democratic Party (SPD) that had been set up in 1890 to make good theatre available to the masses at a price they could afford."[10] Despite troublesome party politics, by 1927 an administration who shared an interest in promoting cultural renewal was assembled.[11] According to Hans Curjel, Harry Graf Kessler, the art patron who had collaborated with Hoffmannsthal on the libretto for Richard Strauss's *Der Rosenkavalier*, commented,

> Klemperer [the Kroll's artistic director] designed a path of activity for the Kroll Opera that, in my opinion, is of the greatest importance not only for German music, but for the German drama. He frees us from all the muff, with the polluted bourgeois, hollow-sentimentals that for a long time pestered the German opera stages.[12]

Kessler proved to be correct that "[i]n a few years people [would] not understand how it had been possible to take this dusty opposition seriously"; however, the road to success was a bumpy one.[13]

In his review of the Kroll's *Hoffmann*, the critic Paul Zschorlich complained bitterly of the new company as a whole, perceiving the treatment of Offenbach's opera as a Jewish plot: "Three-quarters of the audience were Jews, and they were very impressed with their Klemperer Ensemble. Those snobs lusting for sensationalism are not interested in Art, rather surprises, thrills, and director's gimmicks."[14] Moholy-Nagy's designs might not have evoked such unequivocal condemnation from critics like Zschorlich if they had been made for a different opera, however. By 1929, E. T. A. Hoffmann had gained considerable cultural significance for Germans; in fact, he had become one of the representative artists of his nation. The nineteenth century had been a century of nation-building in Europe; both Italy and Germany became nation-states during this period. In unifying the country, the cultural work of defining a national identity was almost as important as the more obvious political work of unification; the development of the term *soziale Kunstpflege*, meaning the cultivation of the social functions of art, indicates the importance assigned to this work. Hoffmann was recognized as a significant writer in the German Romantic movement, though his grotesquerie and his focus on tortured, spiritualistic fantasies provoked some negative commentary. However, his reputation in his native land rose sharply after it was more widely recognized in the rest of Europe: first in France in the 1830s, then in Russia in the 1840s.[15] His work was praised by the advocates of *l'art pour l'art*, "championed by French writers and critics who wanted to free creativity from fetters of moralism and good taste."[16] Charles Baudelaire wrote about Hoffmann's work in the highest terms. By the twentieth century, Germany was ready to embrace its native son.[17] While opinion about Hoffmann would be understandably sharply divided during the National Socialist regime, his work was highly praised during the Weimar Republic as the country came to valorize its leading role in the Romantic movement.

Barbier and Carré's dramatic version of *The Tales of Hoffmann*, which premiered in 1851, grew out of the *l'art pour l'art* movement in France. Their play glorified the artist's poverty and his alcohol consumption, strongly implying that the poet's literary greatness grows naturally out of purely social shortcomings. Jacques Offenbach (1819–1881), though born in Cologne, adopted France as his homeland; the light operas he composed for Parisians came to define his era. Attracted to the Barbier and Carré drama, he chose at the end of his life to write an operatic version of the play in collaboration with Barbier, who served as his librettist. Barbier and Offenbach produced a work in which the German aesthetic was heavily overlaid by culture of the French *fin-de-siècle*. Photographs and prints representing the opera's premiere at the Opera Comique in 1881 indicate the use of perspective sets, with costumes in the style of contemporary dress of the 1880s. The sets were all interiors, but with the size of the theater (the second Salle Favart), which seated 1,500, the designs understandably made use of massive architectural elements, deep perspective, and the stage's lofty proscenium.

With his designs for *Hoffmann*, as with so much of his work, Moholy-Nagy challenged the public to revise their view of art and the artist's relation to technology. Critics of the Kroll Opera production may have justifiably identified Constructivist influences in Moholy-Nagy's designs (as several did),[18] but the designs were equally inspired by the principles of the Bauhaus academy.[19] The Bauhaus is one of the groups whose work defined high Modernism; while the Bauhaus existed as an actual arts academy in Germany for less than fifteen years, its principal members may be called a "school" in the sense of being adherents of a recognized artistic movement. The philosophy and the goals of the Bauhaus had a pronounced effect upon the development of industrial design, painting, and, more broadly, upon industrialized society itself.[20]

The Bauhaus school was originally founded to bring together what we term commercial art and the fine arts, and it was intended to end the isolation of each branch of the arts from all others.[21] Art and craftsmanship were reconceived in the school as a seamless continuum. Students were to learn their craft according to a system that would free them from Romantic ideas about the unique status of the artist. Art itself was redefined by the school's goals: "to bring together all creative effort into one whole, to reunify all the disciplines of practical art—sculpture, painting, handicrafts, and the crafts—as inseparable components of a new architecture."[22] Aesthetics were highly valued; at the same time, one of the school's principles was that art was more valuable if it could serve some practical use in the household or the public sphere.

According to Henri Lefebvre, the Bauhaus was responsible for the emergence "of an awareness of space and its production" that resulted in a new conception of space.[23] Lefebvre credits the members of the Bauhaus with recognizing the link "between industrialization and urbanization, between workplaces and dwelling places" that constituted the *production* of space.[24] In Lefebvre's words, "The Bauhaus people understood that things could not be created independently of each other in space ... without taking into account their interrelationships and their relationship to the whole."[25] With this knowledge, figures like Gropius were able to see that social practice was changing: one mastered global space "by bringing forms, functions, and structures together in accordance with a unitary conception."[26]

While a number of designers and directors in the early twentieth century were experimenting with new ways of shaping the stage-space, Moholy-Nagy's designs did so in ways that, as Lefebvre says of the Bauhaus group more broadly, opened up space "to perception, to conceptualization, just as it did to practical action."[27] At the surface level, Moholy's designs changed the vaguely nineteenth-century Franco-Prussian settings to a German Modernist locale—indeed, to Bauhaus-style interiors. The effect was achieved by a shaping of space through the deliberate use of light and shadow. Through most of the 1920s, Moholy worked on a machine that became one of his masterpieces: the Light-Space Modulator, described by Jack W. Burnham as "a six-foot high apparatus of moving aluminum and chrome-plated surfaces driven by an electric motor and a series of chain belts."[28] The machine creates "a myriad of dissolving shadows passing over walls and ceiling."[29] This device was not used at the Kroll, but Moholy used metal frames, semi-transparent panels, and up-to-date lights to shape space and suggest a variety of ideas. Even the critic Oscar Bie, who asserted that Moholy's concept was not organically related to the opera, praised the lighting: "The light is the most willing instrument of this Bauhaus stage. It achieves wonderful effects and is above all musical."[30]

Moholy-Nagy's vision was decidedly evocative. Though it did not represent the settings of the opera realistically, it brought out many individual details. But it was, above all, a Modernist vision. The critic Bernhard Diebold, writing for the *Frankfurter Zeitung*, sagely notes the stakes involved:

> One can become the enemy of such powerful modernizing with ease and good reason, for here, two styles run parallel: one from Paris and one from Dessau [referring to the location of the second Bauhaus school]. Offenbach is turning in his grave, not because he doesn't understand the new style, but because he doesn't understand the new times that created this new style. We are given the thought to consider—that the Parisian version of German Romanticism has taken a blow and that the musical style between lyric opera and the sound of German trumpeting has entered into a not altogether harmless relationship. ... Therein it lies. Will this music remain music for the people of 1929? The test is called Dessau.[31]

Diebold challenged the audiences of the Kroll to decide "whether this Dessauer Type 1929 will endure beyond the music." This question became the central one raised by the innovative production, challenging Germans to decide whether or not they were ready for their culture to move into the modern era.

In another idiom, the right-leaning Paul Zschorlich says almost the same thing:

> What happened there had absolutely nothing to do with German artistic endeavor. ... it is a shame for the originally lovely, thematically rich music. If old Offenbach could see this caricature of his seriously-minded work, he would most probably say, "God, save me from my friends."[32]

Zschorlich, of course, believes the production fails. He even regards it as un-German, perhaps because it was convenient to link Moholy's aesthetic to his foreign nationality. Diebold, on the other hand, challenged his countrymen to decide what kind of Germany they envisioned for the future.

A true assessment of whether or not the designs related organically to the opera must be grounded in an understanding of what Moholy-Nagy brought to the production from his prior work and experience. Though Russian Constructivist influences are evident, Moholy-Nagy's set designs hew to principles that were very much his own. Throughout his long career, which extended well beyond that of the Bauhaus school, Moholy explored the limits of space and form. In his essay "The New Vision" (1928), Moholy-Nagy defines space as "a reality of sensory experience" and "the relation between the position of bodies."[33] He asserts that "spatial creation is the creation of relationships of position of bodies (volumes)" and describes in specific terms how spatial experience is provided by our senses:

> Each of the senses with which we record the position of bodies helps us to grasp space. Space is known first of all by the sense of vision.

This experience of the visible relations of bodies may be checked by movement—by the alteration of one's position—and by means of touch.[34]

These principles were manifested in Moholy-Nagy's paintings as well as his sculptures, his typography, and his photography. His paintings also exhibit a strong Constructivist influence: though abstract, they frequently offer perspectival views of what appears to be a world of geometric figures in landscape.

Moholy-Nagy noted that the act of space creation is not generally a conscious act on the part of the individuals except in the field of performance: dance, sports, and acrobatics.[35] However, he was fascinated by the possibilities of circus performance, cinema, and theater, and he saw in these an opportunity to combine two kinds of space creation: that which the body engages in and that which is enacted through architectural design. As Walter Gropius explains, "The aim of [Moholy-Nagy's] creations was to observe 'vision in motion' in order to find a new space conception," and Gropius asserts that Moholy-Nagy's set designs grew "[o]ut of his theoretical laboratory experiments in the Bauhaus."[36] For the Bauhaus members involved in theatrical experimentation, "The art of the stage [was] a spatial art"; as Oskar Schlemmer explained, "The stage, including the auditorium, is above all an architectonic-spatial organism where all things happening to it and within it exist in a spatially conditioned relationship."[37] These theories, expounded in such works as Moholy-Nagy's *Vision in Motion*, and his essays "Theater, Circus, Variety" and "The New Vision," prefigure the thinking of the phenomenologist Maurice Merleau-Ponty and the many theater scholars he influenced.[38] Scenographers such as Josef Svoboda were influenced by Moholy-Nagy as well, though perhaps as much by his designs as his writing.

Like so many figures in twentieth-century theater, Moholy-Nagy agitated for performance and performance spaces that did not divide performers from audience members:

> In today's theater, STAGE AND SPECTATOR are too much separated, too obviously divided into active and passive, to be able to produce creative relationships and reciprocal tensions. It is time to produce a kind of stage activity which will no longer permit the masses to be silent spectators, which will not only excite them inwardly but will let them *take hold and participate*—actually allow them to fuse with the action on the stage at the peak of cathartic ecstasy.[39]

Moholy also wrote about "the coming theater: Theater of Totality." While his terms owe an obvious debt to Richard Wagner's *Gesamtkunstwerk* (total work of art), Moholy's conception of a total art work is much broader than Wagner's was.[40] Moholy-Nagy expressed his desire to amalgamate the exciting new technologies of the twentieth century; he argued that man should be "employed on an equal footing with the other formative media."[41] In the new Theater of Totality, Moholy-Nagy urged, man will use the spiritual and physical means at his disposal PRODUCTIVELY and from his own INITIATIVE submit to the over-all action process. ... [T]he Theater of Totality with its multifarious complexities of light, space, plane, form, motion, sound, man—and with all the possibilities for varying and combining these elements—must be an ORGANISM.[42]

What this describes is a multimedia spectacle in which actors are part but not the focus of the production. Form and visuals are emphasized rather than sound; neither plot nor narrative plays a major role. The aim is to affect the audience's emotions rather than their intellect. The means that Moholy-Nagy had in mind to achieve these goals are specified in his essay: sound effects created by electric acoustic equipment (machines that were in production as he wrote and which would seem primitive to us today); film projections and "further experiments in space illumination"; "dynamic construction," including "film, automobile, elevator, airplane, and other machinery, as well as optical instruments."[43] Most of all, Moholy was concerned with the shaping of space:

> The next form of the advancing theater ... will probably answer the above demands with suspended bridges and drawbridges running horizontally, diagonally, and vertically within the space of the theater. ... The possibilities for a variation of levels of movable planes on the stage of the future would contribute to a genuine organization of space. Space will then no longer consist of the interconnections of planes in the old meaning, which was able to conceive of architectonic delineation of space only as an enclosure formed by opaque surfaces. The new space originates from free-standing surfaces or from linear definition of planes ... without the need of any direct contact.[44]

For Moholy-Nagy, theater was an art form more aligned with painting and sculpture than with the oral tradition. The dramatic element of theater served, in his view, merely as another means of affecting the watcher's emotions. As Schlemmer explains by way of contrast, "Architecture, sculpture, painting ... are fixed. They are momentary, frozen motion. Their nature is ... the stability of forces in equilibrium. ... The stage as the arena for successive and transient action, however, offers *form and color in motion*."[45]

The fantastic elements in Offenbach's opera provided Moholy-Nagy with the perfect vehicle for experimenting with Bauhaus principles. At the opera's opening, Hoffmann, a poet, believing himself rejected by his beloved diva Stella, relates his fairy stories to a group of students in a tavern while Stella performs next door in *Don Giovanni*. His rival, the wealthy and venal Councillor Lindorf, watches and waits for an advantageous opening. Hoffmann's first tale, based on "The Sandman," is set in the workshop of the eccentric watchmaker Spalanzani, a scientist and inventor with whom Hoffmann is studying. There the youthful Hoffmann artificially "enhances" his eyesight with the rose-colored glasses of Coppelius, another inventor, who specializes in creating aids to eyesight—spectacles, opera glasses, and telescopes—and, as we later find out, realistic eyes for mannequins and automatons. With his new spectacles on, Hoffmann loses his ability to distinguish Spalanzani's watchmakers' craft from the true art of creation. Seeing Spalanzani's masterpiece, his "daughter" Olympia the automaton, through his glasses, Hoffmann perceives her as a beautiful young maiden. He becomes infatuated with her and only realizes that she is an automaton after she is destroyed in a tussle between Spalanzani and Coppelius, the inventor of the eyes that had made Olympia so lifelike. Hoffmann, horrified, finally recognizes the peril in the perfection of artifice and technology.

In another act, set in Venice, Hoffmann cynically dismisses love in favor of sensation and dissipation; yet he loses his heart once again when the courtesan Giulietta, at the instigation of an enchanter, sets out to ensnare Hoffmann by pretending to love him. With her success, she wins his reflection for her mysterious, fiend-like master; Hoffmann is only able to retain his soul, which she also covets, because he tears himself away from her. In yet another tale, that of the young singer Antonia, Antonia's life is endangered by singing—a particularly sad fate because singing is her passion. Prompted by a mysterious doctor-magician who animates a portrait of Antonia's dead mother, Antonia goes against medical advice; the scene comes to a climax with a trio sung by Antonia, the doctor, and the portrait. Antonia collapses and dies; Hoffmann rushes in, horrified at the high price his beloved has had to pay for her art. The final scene returns to the tavern, where Hoffmann, worn out from storytelling and quite drunk, passes out. *Don Giovanni* concludes and Stella enters, eager to reunite with Hoffmann. Finding him unconscious, she accepts the Councillor Lindorf as her escort instead.[46]

The structure of *The Tales of Hoffmann* manifests possibilities that would have engaged Moholy-Nagy's interest at once. Offenbach and Barbier's opera is episodic in nature, with three fantastical tales framed by more realistic action. The very structure bears a resemblance to the variety show, appealing to the artist who sought "simultaneously interpenetrating sets of contrasting relationships ... such as: the tragicomic, the grotesque-serious, the trivial-monumental" and praised "[t]oday's CIRCUS, OPERETTA, VAUDEVILLE, the CLOWNS of America and elsewhere."[47]

Moholy-Nagy concretely realized his principles for a Theater of Totality in the set design for *Hoffmann*'s prologue, set in "Luther's Tavern," represented in the 1881 premiere of the opera as a German beer hall. In Moholy-Nagy's designs, the tavern becomes a Bauhaus café. Moholy-Nagy's very geometrical colored drawings in mustard, black, red, and white resemble his own Constructivist paintings. In Teo Otto's hands, the set became a striking composition of light and shadow, famously making use of Bauhaus designer Marcel Breuer's chairs. A low, black, geometrical flight of stairs descends from stage right, and a cylindrical stand for a cask of beer balances a tall spiral staircase in metal on the other side, which ascends above a tiny catwalk extended toward the middle of the stage, thereby placing Lindorf's table in the center and over the student chorus. The stand and the spiral of the staircase are the only circles in a very geometric design which was lit from above. Critics were astounded at the effect: Adolf Weißmann commented,

> Every Beer-Philistine will be disappointed because of the absence of a recognizable beer or wine cellar; this set doesn't offer comfortable seats. Mugs gleam, a stairway snakes up to where Lindorf sits and everything stands in the black night of shadows.[48]

Oscar Bie adumbrates Weißmann's description: "Out of the cellar, he makes a vision with ghostly, gleaming tables, with a spiral staircase, and seats the observant Lindorf on a large red bridge, much too central for his participation in the scene."[49]

This design realizes Moholy-Nagy's plans for intersecting planes: Lindorf, Hoffmann's shadowy, yet powerful nemesis, appears above.[50] The presence of the spiral staircase recalls the praise of Oskar Schlemmer, Moholy's Bauhaus colleague, for "the metaphysical forms of expression symbolizing various members of the human body: the star shape of the spread hand, the [eternity] sign of the folded arms, the cross shape of the backbone and shoulders";[51] in

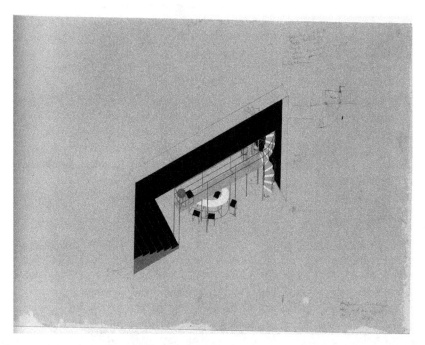

Figure 4.1 Set design by László Moholy-Nagy for the Prologue of Jacques Offenbach's *The Tales of Hoffmann*. Courtesy of the Moholy-Nagy Foundation, Inc.

Figure 4.2 Photograph of the set for the Prologue of the Kroll Opera's production of Jacques Offenbach's *The Tales of Hoffmann.* Courtesy of the Moholy-Nagy Foundation, Inc.

this case, the spiral suggests the Romantic ascent evident in the final address of Hoffmann's Muse in the epilogue. The delicacy of the metal frameworks evokes the unreality of Hoffmann's fantasies, already allied by Barbier with champagne bubbles and smoke rings via the chorus of the Spirits of Wine and the lines from the students' chorus, "Il est doux de boire / Au recit d'une folle histoire, / En suivant le nuage clair / Que la pipe jette dans l'air!" ("It is sweet to drink / During the telling of a crazy tale, / While watching the transparent smoke / That the pipe throws into the air").[52] The fact that Hoffmann and his companion Nicklaus must enter stage right orients the audience to a left-to-right narrative effect appropriate to an opera about story; this effect is reinforced when the stage revolved in full sight of the audience, moving the opening set off stage left to make way for the set of act 1.

Given Moholy-Nagy's desire to minimize the role of plot in the Theater of Totality, it is ironic that his first efforts in the theater were spent on an opera whose basis is the tale—the narrative. One change resulting from Barbier's adaptation of Hoffmann is the shift from Hoffmann's turgid text to a more aphoristic style, set in a much more dreamlike landscape. Comic moments abound, but in all three acts of the opera the plots are much more tightly structured than in Hoffmann's actual stories. Trying to place the predominant aesthetic of the Kroll's production is a challenge; Gerald Köhler links "monochromatic colored strips, hard lineation, rectangles or excessively elongated triangles" with Expressionism, a valid connection given the artist's earlier involvement with *Der Sturm* (a leading Expressionist journal founded in 1910).[53] But from another perspective the Kroll's production seems to have combined Bauhaus theories with a Symbolist aesthetic; what is most vivid are isolated images: Coppelius's collection of eyes; Hoffmann whirled to senselessness by an automaton; the dreadful realization when the puppet is torn apart. These images are strengthened by the flow of the music, something whose importance Oskar Schlemmer realized: he grouped together speech and the

Figure 4.3 Photograph of the Prologue of the Kroll Opera's production of Jacques
Offenbach's *The Tales of Hoffmann* in performance. Courtesy of the
Moholy-Nagy Foundation, Inc.

musical tone (*Sprech- oder Tonbuhne*) as one essential element in the theatrical
event. The very nature of opera lessens the temporal nature of dramatic form;
as Moholy-Nagy suggests should be done in his Theater of Totality, ensemble
singing can permit the simultaneous expression of different, though related,
thoughts.[54]

Like so many theater professionals, Moholy objected to the proscenium
stage: "It is clear that the present peep-show stage is not suitable for such
organized motion."[55] He hoped for a new stage design that would incorporate
elements reminiscent (whether he knew it or not) of medieval pageant platforms:
"The new space originates from free-standing surfaces or from linear definition
of planes ... so that the surfaces stand at times in a very free relationship to one
another, without the need of any direct contact."[56] (This plan is probably the
circus element that the essay's title refers to.)

This element of theater design was not something that could be fully realized
during Moholy's stint with the Kroll Opera House. The Kroll had been renovated in
the early 1920s, and many of the improvements were salutary: both stage and
auditorium had been enlarged, there were new lighting controls, machinery
could lower the stage, and the orchestra pit could similarly be lowered.[57] Nonetheless, the Kroll had red plush curtains, a deep orchestra pit, and the inevitable
proscenium, as well as a broad, deep stage with a narrow apron. While he
could not alter the stage-space, Moholy-Nagy shaped it with light and sculptural
sets. The artist himself comments,

The stage set to "Hoffmann" is an experiment with the problem of creating space from light and shadow. Among other devices, the wings are employed here to create shadows. Everything is transparent, and all the transparent surfaces work together to make an organized and well-perceptible space articulation. It seems that from all this study of material, volume and space, the stage will, first among all the fields of expression, gain the most in the very near future.[58]

Diebold, the *Frankfurter Zeitung* reviewer, notes explicitly that Moholy-Nagy changed the concept of Spalanzani's home from a society salon to a scientist's laboratory: "The Empire Salon of yore has become a laboratory in white. The entire stage lies naked in front of the white horizon upon which vague shadows play."[59] The design was typical of the sculptural geometric designs common in Moholy-Nagy's photography and constructions around this time: at stage right a tall scaffold delineated the workshop, drawing the audience's eyes upward to a height of twenty or thirty feet. The audience saw sets of rectangles and squares, some framed in, others open, the pattern almost resembling a Mondrian painting. As Gerald Köhler observes, the theater functioned as

> a Lichtspiel-Haus, or house for the play of light. The scenic apparatus was, on the one hand, a technoid construct; on the other hand, it was an aesthetic object. ... The revolving stage of the Kroll already transformed each of Moholy's stage constructions into an isotropic spatial sculpture along the lines of a Light-Space-Modulator.[60]

Figure 4.4 Photograph of the set for act 1 of the Kroll Opera's production of Jacques Offenbach's *The Tales of Hoffmann*. Courtesy of the Moholy-Nagy Foundation, Inc.

Lights from the flies cast geometrical shadows on the wall behind the structure. A Breuer armchair, a desk, and a cabinet completed the decor. At stage left a long white wall with a series of closed shutters seemed to conceal who knows what experiments. They suggest wonder-cabinets (*Wunderkammer*), as if inventions needed to be organized, categorized, and confined, while the space overhead, hung with "a flying doll, a gold ball, a [suspended] glass cabinet with an arm, and leg, and head of wax," represents the intellectual ether of theoretical freedom.[61]

In drawing on his own artistic experiments to create the designs for *Hoffmann*, Moholy-Nagy opens up new vistas for theatrical design. But his work on this particular opera is closely tied to the thematic concerns that appear in both the opera libretto and the tales that serve as its foundation. With the publication of his story "The Sandman" in 1817, E. T. A. Hoffmann delineated his view of the artist and presented his interest in technology and its relation to the human body. Hoffmann's mingled fascination with and anxiety about technology were recast by Barbier and Carré as an artist's antipathy toward science. Their ideas were expressed both musically and visually in Offenbach and Barbier's opera. In the hands of Moholy-Nagy, the opera took a new turn, as the poet (already a fictional version of Hoffmann) became a stand-in for the craftsman-designer himself, fascinated by the potential of a marriage between art and technology. In this production Moholy-Nagy, aided by Curjel and Teo Otto (who realized his designs), reframes—and to some extent challenges—Hoffmann's ideas.

The subjects that Hoffmann and Barbier had investigated through plot, description, and dialogue were addressed in semiotic terms by Moholy's designs. While Hoffmann perceived the artist and the scientist as opposed to one another, Moholy viewed science as the rightful, even the necessary, purview of the artist. Hoffmann, an early Romantic, expressed his anxiety about the artist's relation to the natural world by creating magicians who serve in his stories as the nemesis of his protagonists. Moholy celebrates science in his suggestive designs as part of his attempt to usher in a new relation between art and technology. With these designs, Moholy played the role of Modernism's mage, an artist who united within himself the vision of the poet with the technological know-how of the engineer. The sets revise the thrust of the opera's plot: while the artist onstage rejects the temptations of science, the one behind the stage brought art and science together.

Hoffmann's treatment of mechanical marvels in his stories made him a touchstone for members of the Bauhaus. But while the Bauhaus member Oskar Schlemmer perceived Hoffmann's stories as representative of "[t]he endeavor to free man from his physical bondage and to heighten his freedom of movement beyond his native potential [which] resulted in substituting for the organism the mechanical human figure ... the automaton and the marionette,"[62] in fact Hoffmann's work manifests a profound anxiety at the possibility of substituting a mechanical human figure for a living organism.[63] Hoffmann's story "The Sandman," which serves as the basis for act 1 of both Barbier's play and his opera, focuses on the dangers of using science to exalt man to the role of creator. The story concerns an automaton designed by a grotesque inventor. It begins with an epistolary section in which the student Nathanael writes to his fiancée, Clara, telling her that a terrifying figure from his past has resurfaced in his college town of Göttingen: the repulsive Coppelius, a German lawyer and alchemist who, during Nathanael's childhood, had threatened to remove the boy's eyes for use in a scientific experiment. After Clara urges Nathanael to dismiss the past from his mind, he buys a telescope from the peculiar Italian optician Coppola, whom he realizes he has confused with Coppelius. Seeing the mysterious and beautiful Olimpia through the telescope, Nathanael forgets about his fiancée and begins to court Olimpia. When she is destroyed by a tug-of-war between Coppola and her "father," the inventor who had created her, he sees a pair of bloody eyes on the floor and, believing them to be his own, loses his reason. Recovering, he becomes reunited with Clara but inadvertently finds the telescope again. Looking through it, he loses his mind once more and nearly kills Clara before he ends his own life instead.

In Barbier and Offenbach's opera, "The Sandman" may be the basis for just one of the acts, but in a sense all three acts of *Hoffmann* are concerned with the same subject: art (or artificiality) and its creation.[64] Each act characterizes the process of making art as a quest for making or enhancing the soul, but in each case making art destroys the soul instead, thereby threatening the artist's identity. At the end of the opera, Jules Barbier's libretto anticipates Freud by implying in Romantic terms that the poet Hoffmann, unlucky at love, will sublimate his feelings in his art. Having renounced Stella, the opera singer represented in his stories by three fictional heroines, Hoffmann will redirect his passion toward his art, accepting instead the masculine companionship that channels his *eros* toward his Muse, who appears after Hoffmann's ties to the diva have been definitively severed.

Hoffmann's choice of an automaton to represent artistry as well as the artificial is part of a larger orientation toward spirituality and the natural world. This orientation involves the very status of epistemology as well as the place of the individual in the world. According to the cultural scholar Victoria Nelson, the realm of the spiritual was divided from the natural world during the Protestant Reformation:

> Once Protestant Christianity had internalized the influence of the invisible world and restricted it solely to religious experience, the physical world became the only legitimate subject of scientific study and knowledge was balkanized into areas of specialist expertise. ... [By the seventeenth century] the Renaissance man of knowledge had split into three mutually exclusive figures: theologian, philosopher, and scientist. A shadowy fourth figure, the magus ... found his role as manipulator of the forces of nature usurped by the scientist. Some of the magus's fading energy would also transfer to secular artists and writers as they moved to greater cultural prominence during and after the Renaissance.[65]

Such views still affected assumptions about knowledge in the early nineteenth century: Hoffmann's stories manifest the Romanticist's view of the technological innovations of the Industrial Revolution. Most of Hoffmann's villains are characterized as rationalists, at least outwardly: they are scientists, inventors, doctors. Yet they are also diabolical figures that manifest both scientific and apparently supernatural control over the natural world. Nelson offers a perceptive view of such figures: commenting on "the curious way the Western popular imagination chose to assign the roles of good and bad magus after the Renaissance," she suggests that

> the bad magus role, with its supernatural powers linked to the dark grotto of the underworld, was absorbed into the figure of the scientist. ... The figure of the "mad scientist" did not arise, as is commonly believed, from a mistrust of the new empirical science's stupendous achievements, good and bad, but rather from a much older mistrust of those who mediate with the supernatural outside the bounds of organized religion. Now as then, it represents a disguised fear of sorcery.[66]

According to Nelson's interpretation of this aspect of Western civilization's intellectual development, "the good magus role, with its benign demiurgic powers first divorced from divine inspiration, then aestheticized and psychologized, was ultimately absorbed into the figures of the artist and the writer."[67] This framework provides a way of understanding Hoffmann's tales and their variants. Hoffmann occasionally suggests—and Barbier repeatedly reiterates—that the artist is a hero engaged in a cosmic struggle between those who channel the forces of nature for benevolent purposes and those who represent malevolent uses of nature. Barbier's opera embroiders this theme in its conclusion by ceding the world of mere substance to the malevolent force (the villains) and granting the higher world of art to the hero, whose stories have cleansed from him the adulterate nature of carnal love.

The opera's plot manifests two related attitudes that developed in European culture hand in hand: the valorization of the artist, based on the belief that "the act of high artistic creation ... [is] the *summum bonum*," and the denigration of the scientist, "typically shown as a power-mad, misguided tinkerer."[68] The conflict between these types is certainly played out in *Hoffmann*, but the dualism implicit within it is not one that Moholy-Nagy subscribed to. From its inception, the Bauhaus school sought to develop a more holistic approach to design, combining high culture (art) and low culture (crafts and engineering). Moholy-Nagy has even been criticized for his overidealized and utopian vision of technology.[69] Rather than perceiving science and technology as antithetical to or antagonistic toward the arts, he saw technology as a medium for creativity:

> This reality of our century is technology: the invention, construction, and maintenance of machines. To be a user of machines is to be of the spirit of this century. It has replaced the transcendental spiritualism of past eras.

Before the machine, everyone is equal—I can use it, so can you. ... There is no tradition in technology, no class-consciousness.[70]

These words indicate a foundationally anti-Romantic stance: they imply a skepticism about the uniqueness of the artist, about being visited by inspiration, and about the Romantic view of the artist as set apart from his society and yet able to speak for it. Even before becoming a member of the Bauhaus faculty, Moholy-Nagy had written a position statement arguing against "the special interests of the 'individual artist.'"[71] In that document, Moholy-Nagy elaborated a version of the Constructivist ethos—turning art toward social purposes—and though he later left that movement, he retained an almost religious faith in technology as an artistic medium. In 1937, Moholy-Nagy envisioned an alliance between art and technology:

all have to cooperate, the scientists, the technicians and the artists, in order to find which course our designs should take; how they should be controlled, simplified, or enriched in accordance with the needs of the individual today and for future generations. We must be far-sighted enough to visualize the effect of our actions on mankind.[72]

In *Vision in Motion* (1947), he further defined the affiliation between technology and artistry:

It is the artist's duty today ... to search the new dimensions of the industrial society and to translate the new findings into emotional orientation. The artist unconsciously disentangles the most essential strands of existence from the contorted and chaotic complexities of actuality, and weaves them into an emotional fabric of compelling validity, characteristic of himself as well as of his epoch. ... This intuitive power is present in other creative workers, too, in philosophers, poets, scientists, technologists. They pursue the same hopes, seek the same meanings, and—although the content of their work appears to be different—the trends of their approach and the background of their activity are identical. They all must draw from the same source.[73]

The rupture that Nelson asserts was formed during the spread of Christianity is mended in his vision of the intuitive and artistic scientist.

What, then, could have attracted Moholy-Nagy to Offenbach's opera, which seems to present a philosophy directly opposed to his own? According to Hans Curjel, dramaturge of the theater,

Offenbach's opera was to be separated from the traditional concept of a gemütliche petty-bourgeois romantic, to reveal, freed from a period-piece atmosphere, its real substance contained in its music: an interpenetration of automaton mechanics and genuine emotions of the soul.[74]

This explanation makes sense: the Kroll Opera production was not the first artistic work in which Bauhaus members had engaged with elements of "The Sandman." In 1922 and 1923, Oskar Schlemmer had staged a performance piece called "The Figural Cabinet" whose stage directions indicate the odd fascination that E. T. A. Hoffmann held for him. In this piece, "half shooting gallery—half *metaphysicum abstractum*," headless figures process across the stage as they keep a lookout for their heads, "which are moving in opposite direction across the stage. A jerk, a bang, a victory march, whenever there is a union of head and body."[75] After a gigantic hand halts the proceedings, "the Master, E. T. A. Hoffmann's Spalanzani, [appears] spooking around, directing, gesticulating, telephoning, shooting himself in the head, and dying a thousand deaths from worry about the function of the functional."[76] The performance concludes when the Master finally succeeds in shooting himself dead. In an imagistic, almost Symbolist production, Spalanzani seems to represent the specter of the incompetent craftsman, the inorganic scientist—a kind of Sorcerer's Apprentice whose failure to control his medium is both comical and unsettling. In his designs for the Kroll, Moholy-Nagy seems to have been trying to combine Hoffmann's art, the enchanter's magic, and the scientist's technology.[77] Teo Otto, the stage designer, later described Moholy as "a fascinating combination of charm and relentless tenacity," commenting, "One remembers *Tales of Hoffmann* as something special; that production was a sensation at the time and much criticized."[78]

The sets designed by Moholy-Nagy imbued the production with the artist's own perception of the potential in the marriage of art and technology. Adolf Weißmann describes the set for act 1 in his review for the *B. Z. am Mittag*:

> One can grasp the creation of homunculus; limbs on string-thin trapezes swing in the air, a doll without a torso, rods everywhere and to the right, a wall with closed shutters. What's hiding in there? One soon finds out in this grotesque, oddly-lit experimental lab: in walks a person in the shade between living beings and machines.[79]

More details emerge from the review by Oscar Bie (written for the *Berliner Börsen-Courier*), despite his condemnation of the production:

> Moholy-Nagy did not satisfy. His detail is ingenious, his whole effect inorganic. … Out of Spalanzani's cabinet, he makes an amusing variety of structural games, balls, swaying little men, roosters, body parts, rolling light shows, whirling colors and electric moving pictures.[80]

These sets reveal the titular character's alienation. They do form a marked contrast to the lush score, but they also bring out elements of the opera that are certainly unrealized in more standard stagings of the show. What the critics describe indicates a presentation of the wonders of technology. The designer's concept modified the story of the opera and, seemingly, challenged the opera's position in the German cultural tradition.

Most significant, perhaps, was the portrayal of Olympia herself—the mechanical doll with which the hero becomes infatuated. As I have already said, the perception of science is tied to the sense of our place in the world, a sense frequently expressed in art through representations of the human figure. "The Sandman" was one of the first works about the puppet/automaton/robot: human images whose lifeless animation has intrigued many writers. A number of writers, among them Kleist, Craig, and Freud, have theorized about the human through consideration of the automaton. In the changing treatment of Olimpia from 1817 to 1880 to 1929, one can see a changing understanding of the human and its relation to the body, the body and its relation to the self.

Hoffmann himself regarded the potential for confusion of the human and the robotic with revulsion: "I could imagine that it might be possible to enable figures to dance quite graciously by means of a secret mechanism within them. ... Could you watch this for one minute without horror?"[81] This horror seems to stem from an unacknowledged sense of the power inherent in reproductions of the living, as in our popular culture's depiction of voodoo dolls. Human simulacra functioned in their earliest forms as *lares* and *penates*, household gods.[82] The Judeo-Christian stricture against graven images was a response to a longstanding tradition of worshipping idols; iconoclasm reinscribed that stricture during the Reformation. Victoria Nelson observes that Western cultures often "materializ[ed] the spiritual by making human simulacra as physical embodiments of the divine."[83] In fact, she argues, "We can locate our unacknowledged belief in the immortal soul by looking at the ways that human simulacra ... carry on their role as direct descendants of graven images" in literature, play, and performance.[84]

The idea that the divine could be located in physical matter was dismissed after the Protestant Reformation and "the concomitant elevation of human reason as the ultimate arbiter of reality by philosophers such as Bacon and then Descartes."[85] But Nelson asserts that the notion of the divinity of matter, once purged, reemerges during the rise of rationalism in depictions of "that newly valorized human creation the machine, and specifically into mechanical artificial humans as imagined in literary and theatrical works."[86] Descartes originated the idea of God as the Great Watchmaker in his *Discourse on Method*, commenting that the human body resembles a machine "which, having been made by the hand of God, is incomparably better structured than any machine that could be invented by human beings."[87] Since the creation of the automaton, the suggestive parallel between God and the automaton's creator has troubled writers, and E. T. A. Hoffmann is no exception. Stefani Engelstein notes how Hoffmann almost equates the narrator Nathanael's biological parents with Olimpia's inventor-parents, Spalanzani and Coppelius, who create the automaton and pass her off as Spalanzani's daughter in a grotesque myth of masculine origin.[88] The male inventor can be read either as a mother or as an earthly creator, both of them characterizations that could evoke anxiety. In "The Sandman," creator and Creator are linked when Nathanael recounts how old Coppelius examined his joints, finally commenting that they are well designed: "'It's better the way they were! The Old Man knew his business!'"[89]

But Hoffmann's story raises the possibility of closing the gap between inventors and creators by positing the existence of a simulacrum capable of imitating human feeling so well that she cannot be distinguished from human beings. The anxiety raised by this possibility is expressed in the fate of the foolish Nathanael, which results in part from his willful confusion between true womanhood and mechanical imitation. When Nathanael learns that Clara is repulsed by the fantastic tales he has written, he pushes her away, calling her a "'damned, lifeless automaton'."[90] Later in the story, he praises the almost speechless Olimpia: "'It's true that she says little; but the few words she does utter are in a sacred language which expresses an inner world imbued with love, with the higher, spiritual knowledge gathered from a vision of the world beyond'."[91] Yet Nathanael's friend describes Olimpia's singing and dancing as "unpleasantly perfect, being as lifeless as a music box."[92] What is obvious to others is far from clear to Nathanael.

Hoffmann resolves the anxiety produced by Nathanael's failure of perception by imagining a reaction against simulacra once Olimpia is destroyed. "The Sandman" concludes by recounting that in Göttingen,

> a horrible distrust of human figures in general arose. Indeed, many lovers insisted that their mistresses sing and dance unrhythmically ... above all else, they required the mistresses not only to listen, but to speak frequently in such a way that it would prove that they really were capable of thinking and feeling.[93]

The story suggests that the search for an ideal can only too easily be confused with a search for physical perfection, resulting in the worship of mechanization. Imperfection, then, is seen as uniquely human.

By the twentieth century, however, attitudes had undergone a sea change. The positive perception of technology and science in institutions like the Bauhaus resulted from the early twentieth-century conviction that the natural world was becoming increasingly known to man and that new inventions were enabling humankind to control the natural world. With this change came a renewed interest in the puppet/automaton. Like the Romantic writer Heinrich von Kleist, Moholy-Nagy and the other Bauhauslers fed their interest in humans' relation to the mechanistic with marionettes. The designs that ensued became the forerunners of Schlemmer's costumes for the ballets he produced, in which actors were costumed in geometric forms and shapes that represented organic movements such as pirouetting bodies or the vibrations of sound waves. The costumes were intended to depict "*[t]he laws of motion of the human body in space*,"[94] and made the figures look like primitive marionettes. Schlemmer's "abstract stage" correlated geometric divisions of the stage with the Vitruvian geometry of the human body, creating balance "by means of movements ... which by their very nature [were] determined *mechanically and rationally*"—as Schlemmer said, "the geometry of calisthenics, eurhythmics, and gymnastics."[95] Juliet Koss asserts that "technology became the guiding force of Bauhaus creativity, and theater provided an ideal showcase for contending with the body's increasing reification, mechanization, and androgyny."[96] In her view, underlying the creation of these and other ambiguously human artworks was an attempt "to embrace the mounting mechanization of Weimar Germany."[97]

When Moholy-Nagy imagined a new kind of theatrical performance, he wished to incorporate the human figure as a type of mechanism in itself:

> Man, who no longer should be permitted to represent himself as a pheno-
> menon of spirit and mind through his intellectual and spiritual capacities, no
> longer has any place in this concentration of action. For, no matter how
> cultured he may be, his organism permits him at best only a certain range
> of action, dependent entirely on his natural body mechanism. ... The
> inadequacy of "human" *Exzentrik* led to the demand for a precise and fully
> controlled organism of form and motion, intended to be a synthesis of
> dynamically contrasting phenomena. ... This is the Mechanized Eccentric.[98]

Moholy attempts here to define the potential of technology and its relation to the human, just as Hoffmann did in "The Sandman."

The designs that Moholy developed for *The Tales of Hoffmann* manifest the increasing objectification of the human, and particularly the *female*, form evident in the work of other Bauhauslers.[99] As Koss has shown, collaborative projects by Bauhaus students and faculty resulted in images of women as machine-like or as mass-producible forms:

> With the rise of the mass audience, and in conjunction with the emerging
> machine aesthetic, the individual body lost its value as the privileged site of
> human identity. ... The mechanical woman of the late nineteenth century
> had transmogrified into a larger performing machine.[100]

Both their gestures and their evident reproducibility rendered them products of the industrial age. Even the erotic appeal of women could be transferred to the curve and sheen of metal, the dynamic shape of the machine.

Hoffmann's treatment of the automaton was a deeply Romantic one: in his story the desire for perfection is revealed as dangerous. Even more significantly, he links technological perfection to feminine perfection—and both to aesthetic perfection. "The Sandman" emphasizes the seductive nature of the artificial and the way that desires inspired by human design can cause men to forget what is real and, by extension, more wholesome. In contrast, Moholy and Schlemmer primarily saw the potential of science; in fact, in Schlemmer's view the auto-maton's apparent deficiencies become advantages when the automaton is used as an aesthetic object rather than as a substitute for an organic organism:

> The artificial human figure ... permits any kind of movement and any kind
> of position for as long a time as desired. It also permits ... a variable
> relative scale for figures: important ones can be large, unimportant ones

small. An equally significant aspect of this is the possibility of relating the figure of natural "naked" Man to the abstract figure, both of which experience, through this confrontation, an intensification of their peculiar natures. Endless perspectives are opened up: from the supernatural to the nonsensical, from the sublime to the comic.[101]

Schlemmer's description is exactly what is offered in *Tales of Hoffmann*, particularly because the role of Olympia must of course be played by a human being.

In 1881, when Adele Isaac originated the role of Olympia, her characterization as a doll depended entirely on body language, as her clothes gave no indication that she was an automaton. Similarly, in the Kroll production, Moholy-Nagy's Olympia was more human than puppet-like, but she was sharply distinguished from the other women onstage. While the contemporary clothes of the female guests recalled nineteenth-century costume with empire waists and fantail hemlines (causing Oscar Bie to remark that "those accompanying Spalanzani were clothed as grotesque proletariats, which certainly did not complement the Menuett"),[102] Moholy-Nagy's Olympia costume hewed to the Bauhausler valorization of technology. Though not manifestly a robot, this Olympia combined the appeal of the feminine with the brittle charm of intricate machinery. He drew on the trends of the latest women's fashions: shingled hair and a skirt that alludes both to flapper dresses and to the motions of machine shop lathes. Olympia's hair was bobbed; she wore white tights, a white blouse, metal disks on her arms, and a thigh-length wired skirt. She resembled a figure from a Schlemmer ballet, or his diagram of the "technical organism," which was supposed to represent "the various aspects of rotation, direction, and intersection of space: the spinning top, snail, spiral, disk."[103] The objectification of Olympia was extended by the design of the set, which suspended models on wires from the ceiling, including a model of Olympia herself. Olympia appears as a Bauhaus woman: a "New Woman" in the latest style, merging fashion with mechanization. Her silhouette suggests motion and evokes the rotation of machine parts. The *Frankfurter Zeitung* theater critic, Bernhard Diebold, noted the implication with pleasure: "The director Legal asks a fabulous question: is a mechanical doll only a toy or a technical wonder? Hello, technical wonder! How modern! We want that! We need no magician, rather a physicist."[104]

Olympia's costume also corresponds to the aesthetic of the act 1 set, in accordance with the Bauhauslers' stricture that the human body should serve as part of the theater's design, not as an individual with human concerns. The set design recalls Schlemmer's stricture to mark out the stage-space using linear divisions:

> We first divide the square surface of the floor in the middle and then into bisecting axes and diagonals. We shall also delineate a circle. Thus we obtain a geometry of the floor area. ... By means of taut wires which join the corners of this cubical space, we obtain its midpoint, while the diagonal lines divide it stereometrically.[105]

Figure 4.5 Photograph of act 1 of the Kroll Opera's production of Jacques Offenbach's *The Tales of Hoffmann* as Valentine Wischnevskaja sings Olympia's aria (sometimes called "The Doll Song"). Courtesy of the Moholy-Nagy Foundation, Inc.

This careful measurement of space orients the actor, helping him sense his relation to the space:

> Let us now observe the appearance of the human figure as an event and recognize that from the very moment at which it becomes a part of the stage, it also becomes a "space-bewitched" creature, so to speak. Automatically and predictably, each gesture or motion is translated in meaningful terms into a unique sphere of activity.[106]

When only a few characters are onstage, sets and lighting combine to resemble the photo of "spatial delineation with figure" that illustrates Schlemmer's point. The dimensions of the Kroll's stage dwarf the actors, and they become figures in an angular visual composition. In the ensemble scenes, the horizontal curve of the tall scaffold shapes the positioning of the guests as they watch Olympia perform her song at center stage. Her body serves as a theatrical prop in that, as Garner says of props, it serves "both to implement the individual's self-projection through space—that process in which the subject transcends its corporeal boundaries through operations on its environment—and to ground the individual, as body, in its material surroundings."[107] Valentine Wischnevskaja, the soprano who played the part of Olympia, is simultaneously subject and object, woman and machine, singer and prop.

Moholy-Nagy's designs clearly incorporate his admiration for new technologies and the possibilities of spatial design. They alter the thrust of the opera's plot, changing the lessons that the hero learns. Barbier's Hoffmann, like Hoffmann the author, aligns science with magic and fears it. His experience with Olympia causes him to reject artificiality and to seek a beloved who is herself a natural artist, not the product of a mechanic. But Moholy-Nagy's designs reveal the possibilities of technology rather than its dangers. Hoffmann's spectacles become a potent symbol of individual perspective: for the Romantic E. T. A. Hoffmann, the ruthlessness of science threatens to crush the artistic temperament, but for the Modernist, technology opens up new vistas and new opportunities.

In some ways Offenbach's opera may not have been the best vehicle for the artist's beliefs. If Moholy-Nagy expected to produce "cathartic ecstasy" in the Kroll's attendees (as in "Theater, Circus, Variety"), he must have been sadly disappointed. That very Romantic expression bespeaks Moholy's overwhelming enthusiasm for his work. More likely, the artist saw his designs as advancing the Modernist agenda; he must have been aware that his work was part of a program at the Kroll to present contemporary art by composers and artists of all kinds.[108]

The nature of the Kroll's decidedly Modernist program was evident in Moholy-Nagy's designs; the condemnation that emerged from some quarters was based, perhaps, more on nationalistic grounds than aesthetic ones. One wants to ask, in the spirit of Lionel Trilling, "Who shall inherit Deutschland?"[109] Paul Zschorlich, for example, writing for the right-wing extremist newspaper the *Deutsche Zeitung*, was inflamed by his dislike of the program instituted by the Opera House director, Otto Klemperer: "The Klemperer Ensemble, which is largely composed of foreigners to Germany, is eating away at the entire position of opera. They direct the most beloved operas 'in the spirit of the times,' which means from the Jewish spirit."[110] In addition, Zschorlich felt affronted by the Russian Constructivist influence on the set design: "Spalanzani's workshop with childish modern elements was obnoxious. Granted, this is only from the per- spective of German good taste. ... The Misters Klemperer and Legal did well, at least, to bring color and cultural Bolshevism to their trumpeted 'Jewish Opera'."[111] Yet other critics responded more positively to the production— among them, the Marxist thinker Ernst Bloch. Reviewing the opera for *Der Querschnitt*, he commented,

> What could be more truly Hoffmannesque than this power to bring ghosts into *our world*? Without nightgowns, but with machinery? In the cold, phosphorescent world of machines, in the empty chambers of our time, what is suppressed is here liberated in the form of what is to come ... The ghosts that appear are new ... [This] conspiracy in steel is worth seeing.[112]

His positive response may be based on his approval of the liberation of what had been previously suppressed.

Like Zschorlich, the *Berliner Börsen-Courier* critic Oscar Bie responds angrily to Klemperer and Moholy-Nagy's vision:

> I am, in principle, not against using an epoch's visual style on an older work. After all, every epoch has done it. But, these days, it is especially

complicated. ... [I]s this style of construction really the absolute expression of our time? The pure, all-encompassing theater in stage, flats, and buttresses that even in Russia haven't gained popularity, which seems the last remains of the formal direction; a new art for art's sake, a desire for conquest, yes, even tyranny, rather than an inner necessity. There are too many abstractions to which people on stage must react, to force a natural appearance in a system with this technical absolutism.[113]

On the face of it, Bie's complaint is that a realistic setting is an organic part of the performance; the magical elements of Hoffmann's tales must be set off by Ibsenesque sets. But Bie's review also brings to the forefront a more crucial issue that Zschorlich also addresses, though his anti-Semitism obscures it: was Russian-inflected Bauhaus design truly the vision of Germany that the country's inhabitants would endorse? Could Gropius and the other Bauhaus members create a Modernist aesthetic that would be embraced by the German people?

While the negative reviews show that the production alienated a portion of the audience from the action onstage, Zschorlich's scornful disdain for the production cannot override the implication of his informative complaint: "Three-quarters of the audience were Jews, and they were very impressed with their Klemperer Ensemble."[114] Much of the audience evidently responded to the production positively, whether or not they were already members of the Modernist camp. Adolf Weißmann characterized the production as a positive victory for the new aesthetic; his review opens by saying that operagoers came to the theater asking, "'What have you got against sweet opera kitsch?'"[115] The question suggests the operagoers' recognition that the Kroll's production was going to transform the opera on a number of levels. Weißmann describes the change that transpired as the evening progressed: "Most are curious, the others are armed. But even those who were armed held their whistles. They were convinced. The applause buried every hint of ill will, pomposity, and old hat."[116]

In one thing, Zschorlich and Bie were correct: the aesthetic of these conservative critics was fundamentally at variance with the goals of the avant-garde. Moholy-Nagy challenged the audience with more than just his scenography; there were real differences in what members of these camps hoped and expected theater to be.

In "Theater, Circus, Variety" Moholy-Nagy advanced a program that, like Antonin Artaud's, was intended to dispense with what he called "literary encumbrance":

the result of the unjustifiable transfer of intellectualized material from the proper realm of literary effectiveness (novel, short story, etc.) to the stage, where it incorrectly remains a dramatic end in itself. The result is nothing more than literature if a reality or a potential reality, no matter how imaginative, is formulated or visually expressed without the creative forms peculiar only to the stage.[117]

Zschorlich's comment that the production was satisfying to those who were "not interested in Art, rather surprises, thrills and director's gimmicks" shows the degree to which his and Moholy-Nagy's definitions of theater diverge.[118] Moholy-Nagy suggests in his essay that the theater of his time was at a crossroads: after assessing theater of the past according to its performative goals, he treats "Attempts at Theater Form for Today" before advocating for his Theater of Totality and explaining how it ought to be realized. In his view, "sound, light (color), space, form, and motion" were crucial elements of theater, not merely incidental to the plot.[119] The "amusing variety of structural games, balls, swaying little men, roosters, body parts, rolling light shows, whirling colors and electric moving pictures" that Oscar Bie decries is for Moholy-Nagy the very basis of theater.[120] Offenbach's opera offered Moholy-Nagy the chance to engage in theatrical play, and to combine several artistic media in a performance-based work of art.

Another aspect of the controversy created by Moholy's designs rests on the implicit endorsement of Marxism in the exaltation of utilitarian materials in the Bauhaus program. As in many of the Bauhaus products, the sets for the Kroll's production of *Hoffmann* reveal a perception of technology as a tool to improve the quality of life for all, thereby weakening the class system. In the materials used and the way they were showcased, there was little ornament; there was little upholstery in the designs. Instead, space was shaped by scaffolds derived from construction designs. The clean lines of Bauhaus design result in part from use of common industrial materials such as metal tubing. The materials so prominently featured in Moholy-Nagy's sets proclaimed the designer's allegiance to the ideology of a classless society.

This vision posed a decided challenge to a country that had been dominated by the bourgeoisie. The character of Prussia was shaken up during this period; both Gropius and Otto Wilhelm Lange, founder of the Kroll Opera, had hoped to create a new aesthetic that would represent the future of their homeland. In his plans for the Bauhaus school, Gropius complained that "a broad mass of bourgeois philistines are suffocating living art. The intellectual bourgeois ... has demonstrated his inability to support a German culture."[121] Lange had initiated his plan for the opera company by proposing a joint venture to the Prussian Ministry of Culture to partner in the creation of a "Grosse Volksoper" that would produce art at low prices for thousands of spectators at a time.[122] The dramaturge Hans Curjel, characterized as the company's "intellectual and ideological mainspring," and the designers were "contemptuous of the naturalistic approach," though perhaps not the radicals the German press made them out to be.[123] In hiring Moholy-Nagy, Curjel had sought to "put into effect his plans to bring about a renewal of scenic design."[124] He himself may have been dismayed at the result; he commented later that he thought the production had gone "too far."[125]

Reviews of the production, which serve as a reasonably good index of audience perception, break down along party lines. They also intimate the political uses to which art was put at this time. In the volatile world of German politics, warring parties did not hesitate to exploit the Kroll's artistic venture for their own gain: eight days after the premier of *Hoffmann*, the Deutschnationale Volkspartei condemned the Kroll "as a centre of cultural Bolshevist experimentation" and demanded that it be closed.[126] The Kroll survived for two more years, until 1931, but the changing political climate in Germany rendered its eventual fall inevitable. Gropius's Bauhaus school was also closed down by the Nazi government, on April 11, 1933. As the art historian Frank Whitford notes, "The life-span of the Bauhaus [in Germany] was precisely that of the Weimar Republic."[127]

Both the Bauhaus school and the Kroll Opera advanced a Modernist agenda in response to the conditions of their time. The outraged responses to Moholy-Nagy's work are a function of his challenge to received ideas; as a member of an international artistic avant-garde, Moholy-Nagy could not avoid challenging the German bourgeois perspective. If the artist's desire in crafting his designs for the Kroll was to create a "kind of stage activity" which would let the spectators *"take hold and participate*—actually allow them to fuse with the action on the stage," then his attempt was a failure.[128] But if we regard the performance as an assay of Modernism, then the cause was advanced with some success. Even the negative reviews of this production show that, despite their horror, critics could not simply omit discussion of the sets—they were too important to ignore. Moholy-Nagy updated Hoffmann's ideas, presenting a vision of the artist derived from Constructivist ideals, an artist whose art

> has declared the acceptance of the scientific age and its spirit as a basis for its perceptions of the world outside and inside human life. ... [which] rejected the belief that the personality alone and the whim and the mood of the individual artist should be the only value and guide in an artistic creation.[129]

The principles of design with which Moholy was working were far more widely disseminated as a result of the opera, and a wider audience eventually held a referendum on the Modernist aesthetic as a result.

Hoffmann's stories reveal the Romantic rejection of attempts to control the natural world in his depiction of villains as sinister scientists and magicians. In contrast, Moholy demystified science: "Before the machine, everyone is equal. ... There is no tradition in technology, no consciousness of class or standing. Everybody can be the machine's master or its slave."[130] The idea of technology's role in artistic creation may have pulled the artist down from his pedestal but it gave artists powers to which they had not hitherto aspired. Some of those who attended the Kroll's production of *Tales of Hoffmann* may have felt threatened by the designer's vision of the opera as a story of the marriage between science and artistry. Others, however, more open to a new vision of Germany, welcomed the designs and their representation of contemporary society even though—or perhaps *because*—the designs altered the underlying assumptions of Offenbach's opera.

Notes

1 In an article on Moholy-Nagy's stage designs, Gerald Köhler characterizes the Kroll Opera House during Klemperer's tenure with pardonable hyperbole as "the absolute experimental center of music theater" and asserts that the assembled team of artists at the Kroll "sought the destruction of the conventional scenery of opera" (Gerald Köhler, "Here Light Becomes Space: László Moholy-Nagy's Dramatic Theater Cosmos," in *László Moholy-Nagy Retrospective*, eds. Ingrid Pfeiffer and Max Hollein [London: Prestel, 2009], 96).

2 Stanton B. Garner, Jr., *Bodied Spaces: Phenomenology and Performance in Contemporary Drama* (Ithaca: Cornell University Press, 1994), 91.

3 Jules Barbier collaborated with Michel Carré in writing the play *Les Contes fantastiques d'Hoffmann*. Carré was deceased by the time Offenbach approached Barbier about crafting a libretto for an opera.

4 As Richard Kostelanetz observes and contemporary documents bear out, the surname Moholy-Nagy was frequently shortened simply to Moholy by the artist's friends and colleagues (Richard Kostelanetz, Preface, in *Moholy-Nagy*, ed. Richard Kostelanetz [New York: Praeger, 1970], xiii).

5 Marvin Carlson, *Theories of the Theatre: A Historical and Critical Survey, from the Greeks to the Present* (Ithaca: Cornell University Press, 1984; 2nd ed. 1993), 9.

6 Peter Heyworth, *Otto Klemperer, His Life and Times* (Cambridge: Cambridge University Press, 1983), 1: 197.

7 Ibid., 284.

8 Köhler, "Here Light Becomes Space," 96.

9 Heyworth, *Klemperer*, 183.

10 Ibid., 84, 187.

11 Ibid., 249–57.

12 "Klemperer weist in seiner Tätigkeit an der Krolloper einen Weg, der meines Erachtens von der größten Bedeutung nicht bloß für die deutsche Musik, sondern auch für das deutsche Drama ist. Er befreit uns von dem ganzen Muff, mit dem eine spießbürgerliche, hohl-sentimentale Zeit die deutschen Opernbühnen verpestet und für lebendig empfindsame Menschen unerträglich gemacht hat"; Hans Curjel, *Experiment Krolloper, 1927–1931* (Munich: Prestel-Verlag, 1975), 30. Dorothea Trotter, trans.

13 "In wenigen Jahren wird man nicht mehr begreifen, wie es möglich gewesen ist, diese verstaubte Opposition ernst zu nehmen"; ibid., 30.

14 "Das zu drei Vierteln jüdische Publikum des Abends war von seinem Klemperer-Ensemble wieder einmal sehr angetan. Diesem sensationslüsternen Snob kommt es ja nicht auf die Kunst an, sondern auf Überraschungen, Nervenkitzel und Regiespäße"; Paul Zschorlich, *Deutsche Zeitung*, February 13, 1929. Rpt. in Curjel, *Krolloper*, 264. Translations of items from *Experiment Krolloper* throughout the remainder of this chapter are by Melissa Evans unless otherwise noted.

15 One cogent sign of Hoffmann's artistic significance is that Meyerhold took the name of one of Hoffmann's characters, Dapertutto, as his stage name when he engaged in non-State-sponsored theater work (Robert Leach, *Makers of Modern Theatre: An Introduction* [London: Routledge, 2004], 59).

16 James M. McGlathery, *E. T. A. Hoffmann* (New York: Twayne-Simon & Schuster, 1997), 26.

17 Ibid., 28–29.

18 Bernhard Diebold observes that "[t]he bio-mechanical stage of the Russians remains an example" for Moholy-Nagy (Diebold, rpt. in Curjel, *Krolloper*, 266). Adolf Weißmann comments that Moholy-Nagy is "a Bauhaus member, but one with creative fantasy and not without influence from the Russians, with their opera-based constructs" (Weißmann, rpt. in Curjel, *Krolloper*, 260). Paul Zschorlich sees

pure imitation on the designer's part, which he condemns both for the source and for imitativeness: "No original thoughts, rather a mechanical repetition of the stage direction of stupidity imported by Soviet Russians" (Zschorlich, rpt. in Curjel, *Krolloper*, 264).

19 This statement may be a bit misleading for, as the scholar Gillian Naylor points out, Moholy-Nagy's contribution to the Bauhaus school "contributed to the emergence of a recognizable Bauhaus style" in industrial design (Gillian Naylor, *The Bauhaus*, [New York: Dutton, 1968], 109). In other words, Moholy's own Constructivism played a part in defining the Bauhaus style.

There are also legitimate questions about the relation between Constructivism and performance. Elizabeth Souritz argues, "At the very core of the concept of constructivism [sic] was the deaestheticizing of stage design; i.e., the real object had to take the place of the image. Therefore the idea of constructivism contradicted the essence of theater" (Elizabeth Souritz, "Constructivism and Dance," in *Theatre in Revolution: Russian Avant-Garde Stage Design, 1913–1935*, ed. Nancy Van Norman Baer [New York: Thames and Hudson, 1991], 129). Other scholars, however, have no problem with the term "Constructivist theater"; for example, Nancy Van Norman Baer comments that Meyerhold's production of Mayakovsky's *Mystery-Bouffe* in 1921 "provided a link to constructivism in its organization of the stage space and introduction of principles of architectural order. ... It was not until the following year that constructivist principles were fully developed in *The Magnanimous Cuckold*, the production that officially inaugurated 'theatrical constructivism'" (Nancy Van Norman Baer, "Design and Movement in the Theatre of the Russian Avant-Garde," in *Theatre in Revolution*, Baer, 47). (Moholy-Nagy became an instructor at the Bauhaus in 1923, one year after *The Magnanimous Cuckold* was produced.)

20 For example, Richard Kostelanetz asserts that Moholy-Nagy "was among the immigrant influences who helped make the key thrust of 1950s American art decidedly abstract rather than as representational as 1930s realism" (Richard Kostelanetz, "Moholy-Nagy: The Risk and Necessity of Artistic Adventurism," in *Moholy-Nagy*, ed. Richard Kostelanetz, 15).

21 This brainchild of Walter Gropius emerged from the Weimar regime's attempts to conjoin industry and the arts in the hope that good industrial design could prove financially profitable. Lacking an abundance of raw materials, Germany "relied more heavily on the expertise of its skilled labour force and the ability of its industry to export sophisticated and high-quality goods. There was a growing need for designers, which only a new kind of art education could meet" (Frank Whitford, *Bauhaus* [London: Thames and Hudson, 1984], 28).

As Moholy-Nagy explains it, the Bauhaus attempted to establish "that machines can be legitimate 'tools' of the artist and designer. ... At the time the Bauhaus was founded the term 'industrial designer' did not exist and the profession had not yet crystallized. The profession gained its status through the work of the Bauhaus" (László Moholy-Nagy, *Vision in Motion* [Chicago: Paul Theobald and Co., 1961], 63).

22 Walter Gropius, "Program of the Staatliche Bauhaus in Weimar" (Weimar: Staatliche Bauhaus, 1919). Rpt. in *Das Bauhaus*, ed. Hans M. Wingler (Cologne: Verlag Gebr. Rasch & Co., 1962). *Das Bauhaus* republished as *The Bauhaus*, ed. Joseph Stein, trans. Wolfgang Jabs and Basil Gilbert (Cambridge: MIT Press, 1969, rev. 1976 and 1978), 32.

23 Henri Lefebvre, *The Production of Space*, trans. Donald Nicholson-Smith (Oxford: Blackwell, 1991), 123–24.

24 Ibid., 124. David Wiles similarly notes that "[t]he designers/theorists of the Bauhaus explored the intersections of human and architectural space" (David Wiles, *A Short History of Western Performance Space* [Cambridge: Cambridge University Press, 2003], 58).

25 Lefebvre, *Space*, 124.
26 Ibid., 125.
27 Ibid., 125.
28 Jack W. Burnham, *Beyond Modern Sculpture* (New York: George Braziller; London: Allen Lane The Penguin Press, 1968), 290–91. Excerpted in *Moholy-Nagy*, ed. Richard Kostelanetz, 159–60.
29 Burnham, *Beyond*, 291, and in Kostelanetz, *Moholy-Nagy*, 160.
30 "Das Licht ist das willigste Instrument dieser Bauhausbühne. Es erzielt wunderbare Effekte und wird am ehesten musikalisch"; Oscar Bie, *Berliner Börsen-Courier*, February 13, 1929. Rpt. in Curjel, *Krolloper*, 262.
31 "Man kann als Feind solcher gewaltsamen Modernmachung mit Leichtigkeit und bestem Recht behaupten: hier laufen zwei Stile nebeneinander ab: einer von Paris und einer von Dessau. Offenbach drehte sich im Grabe um—aber nicht in erster Linie, weil er den neuen Stil, sondern weil er die Neuzeit nicht verstände, die diesen Stil geschaffen hat. Aber wir geben zu bedenken, daß die Pariser Auffasung von deutscher Romantik schon eine böse Stilverletzung darstellte und daß der musikalische Stil hier zwischen Opéra lyrique und deutschem Hörnerklang eine nicht so ganz harmlose Verbindung eingang. ... Da liegt's! Bleibt diese Musik noch Musik auch für den Menschen 1929? Die Probe heißt Dessau"; Bernhard Diebold, *Frankfurter Zeitung*, February 17, 1929. Rpt. in Curjel, *Krolloper*, 264–65.
32 "Denn mit deutscher Kunstbetätigung hat das, was dort getrieben wird, nichts zu tun. ... Schließlich ist's doch schade um die originelle an hübschen Einfällen reiche Musik. Könnte der alte Offenbach diese Karikatur seines immerhin ernst gemeinten Werkes sehen, so würde er vermutlich sagen, 'Gott schütze mich vor meinen Freunden!'"; Zschorlich, rpt. in Curjel, *Krolloper*, 264.
33 László Moholy-Nagy, "Von Material zu Architektur" (Munich: Albert Langen Verlag, 1928). Published as "The New Vision," trans. Daphne M. Hoffman (New York: Brewer, Warren, and Putnam, 1930). 3rd ed. rpt. in *The New Vision* and *Abstract of an Artist* (New York: George Wittenborn, Inc., 1947), 57.
34 Ibid., 57.
35 Ibid., 63.
36 Walter Gropius, Introduction, in *The Theater of the Bauhaus*, eds. Walter Gropius and Arthur S. Wensinger, trans. Arthur S. Wensinger (Middletown, CT: Wesleyan University Press, 1961), 10.
37 Oskar Schlemmer, "Theater (Bühne)," in *The Theater of the Bauhaus*, eds. Walter Gropius and Arthur S. Wensinger, 85.
38 Among these are Marvin Carlson, Edward S. Casey, Hollis Huston, Gay McAuley, and Stanton B. Garner.
39 László Moholy-Nagy, "Theater, Circus, Variety," in *The Theater of the Bauhaus*, eds. Walter Gropius and Arthur S. Wensinger, 67–68. Moholy-Nagy also makes this point in his essay "Why Bauhaus Education," where he refers to the stage as "an active principle, including and giving form to all human expression" ("Why Bauhaus Education," *Shelter* 3 [March 1938], 17).
40 Wagner's sense of totality in art as he described it in 1849 was limited to a combination of poetry, music, and dance; in fact, Wagner saw music and dance as supplemental to dramatic narrative (Juliet Koss, *Modernism after Wagner* [Minneapolis: University of Minnesota Press, 2010], xiii). For more information on Moholy's theories in relation to Wagner's, see Matthew Wilson Smith's chapter "Total Machine: The Bauhaus Theatre" in his book *The Total Work of Art: From Bayreuth to Cyberspace* (New York: Routledge, 2007), 48–70.
41 Moholy-Nagy, "Theater, Circus, Variety," 57.
42 Ibid., 58–60.
43 Ibid., 67. As we can see, most artists involved in the theater at this time imagined use of the same technologies; Brecht, and later Artaud, name some of the same

elements, even though the uses to which they plan to put these elements are quite different.

44 Ibid., 68–70.
45 Schlemmer, "Man and Art Figure," in *The Theater of the Bauhaus*, eds. Walter Gropius and Arthur S. Wensinger, trans. Arthur S. Wensinger (Middletown, CT: Wesleyan University Press, 1961), 22.
46 Because Offenbach died before completing the opera, it was completed from his notes by Ernest Guiraud. A number of versions have since been created, all intended to realize Offenbach's original intentions better than Guiraud's version does. It seems likely that the Kroll production used the 1907 Editions Choudens score rather than the 1887 Editions Choudens version. In different versions, dialogue has been spoken or sung; arias have been added or cut; and the order of the acts has been changed, though the story with Olympia has always come first (Cf. Mary Dibbern, "Introduction: A Short History of the Versions," in Mary Dibbern, ed. *The Tales of Hoffmann: A Performance Guide* [Hillsdale, NY: Pendragon Press, 2002], xvii–xxiii). In one version, after Stella has left with Lindorf, Hoffmann's Muse appears to him in a vision and promises to stay with him forever, as she is his true love. He wakes and reprises the love aria that he sang to Giulietta, addressing it now more fervently to the Muse, before collapsing again.
47 Moholy-Nagy, "Theater, Circus, Variety," 64.
48 "Zunächst wird jeder Bierphilister enttäuscht durch die Abwesenheit dessen, was man einem Bier- oder Wein-keller nennt: die Konstruktion zeigt nicht bequeme Sitz-gelegenheiten. Becher blinken. Eine Treppe schlängelt sich hinauf, wo Lindorf sitzt. Dies alles steht in der schwartzen Nacht des Schattens"; Adolf Weißmann, *Berliner Zeitung am Mittag*, February 13, 1929. Rpt. in Curjel, *Krolloper*, 260.
49 "Er macht aus dem Keller eine Vision geisterhaft blinkender Tische mit Wendeltreppe, setzt aber den beobachtenden Lindorf auf eine große rote Brücke, viel zu zentral für seine Beteiligung an der Szene"; Bie, rpt. in Curjel, *Krolloper*, 262.
50 In this production, all four antagonists—Councillor Lindorf, Coppelius, Dapertutto, and Doctor Miracle—were performed by the same singer, as is common practice.
51 Schlemmer, "Man and Art Figure," 27.
52 Jules Barbier, *Les Contes d'Hoffmann*, trans. Mary Dibbern, in Dibbern, ed. *The Tales of Hoffmann: A Performance Guide*, 39.
53 Köhler, "Here Light Becomes Space," 100.
54 Moholy-Nagy, "Theater, Circus, Variety," 62.
55 Ibid., 68. For a brief overview of the ways that designers attempted to challenge the framing effect of the proscenium, see Stephen Kern, *The Culture of Time and Space, 1880–1918* (Cambridge, MA: Harvard University Press, 1983), 199–203. For an analysis of the unifying capacity of the frame for a work of art, see Georg Simmel, "The Picture Frame," *Theory, Culture, and Society* 11, no. 1 (February 1994): 11–17.
56 Moholy-Nagy, "Theater, Circus, Variety," 68.
57 Cf. Heyworth, *Klemperer*, 234, and Georg Linnebach, *Blätter der Staatsoper*, January 1924, rpt. in Curjel, *Krolloper*, 162–63.
58 Moholy-Nagy, "The New Vision," 63.
59 "Der Empire-Salon von einst ist zum Laboratorium in weiß geworden. Der ganze Bühnenraum liegt nackt vor dem weißen Horizont, auf dem vage Schatten spielen"; Diebold, rpt. in Curjel, *Krolloper*, 265.
60 Köhler, "Here Light Becomes Space," 97.
61 Diebold, rpt. in Curjel, *Krolloper*, 265.
62 Schlemmer, "Man and Art Figure," 28.
63 Schlemmer's view was part of the Bauhaus agenda, which Matthew Wilson Smith summarizes effectively: "What Gropius advocated was an artwork that sought to

expose the mechanical rather than burying it beneath the veneer of organicism, and thus sought to expose artists, too, as workers. Or, more precisely, as unabashedly industrialized members of a working collective" (Smith, *Total Work*, 49). This point is related to one of the key principles of Constructivism, "the worship of the industrial process and technology" (Souritz, "Constructivism and Dance," 136).

64 This point is debatable, of course. Gerald Köhler asserts that *The Tales of Hoffmann* is "the paradigmatic musical drama about the stimulation of the optic nerve" and adds, "There is no other opera in which the seductions and catastrophes of the ocular are brought into the plot in similar manner. The story of *Hoffmanns Erzählungen* is the paradigm of the inability to communicate truly by means of the visual: Some medium of stimulation is constantly being interjected" (Köhler, "Here Light Becomes Space," 96). Birgit Röder extensively discusses the significance of eyesight and optical instruments in Hoffmann's tale "The Sandman" (Birgit Röder, *A Study of the Major Novellas of E. T. A. Hoffmann* [Rochester, NY: Boydell and Brewer, Inc., 2003], 57–75); although the theme is arguably less significant in the remaining tales of the opera, this issue was one that certainly would have engaged Moholy-Nagy.

65 Victoria Nelson, *The Secret Life of Puppets* (Cambridge, MA: Harvard University Press, 2001), 7.

66 Ibid., 8.

67 Ibid., 8.

68 Ibid., 8.

69 Smith, *Total Work*, 66–67.

70 László Moholy-Nagy, "Constructivism and the Proletariat," *MA* (May 1922); rpt. in Kostelanetz, *Moholy-Nagy*, 185.

71 László Moholy-Nagy, "Position Statement of the Group MA in Vienna to the First Congress of Progressive Artists in Düsseldorf, Germany." Rpt. in Kostelanetz, *Moholy-Nagy*, 186.

72 László Moholy-Nagy, "The New Bauhaus and Space Relationships," *American Architect and Architecture* 151 (December 1927); rpt. in Kostelanetz, *Moholy-Nagy*, 106.

73 Moholy-Nagy, *Vision in Motion*, 11.

74 Hans Curjel, "Moholy-Nagy and the Theater," *Du* 24 (November 1964), 11. Rpt. in Kostelanetz, *Moholy-Nagy*, 95. Interestingly, Otto Klemperer's biographer Peter Heyworth comments that Curjel

> had the wit to perceive that behind [Moholy-Nagy's] preoccupation with technological innovations lay a romanticism that could be used to illuminate the macabre visions of E. T. A. Hoffmann and Offenbach. A dream world would be evoked with modern materials. Machinery and human emotion would interact so as to reflect the ambivalence that gives the opera its special flavor.
>
> (Heyworth, *Klemperer*, 284–85)

Without more documentation than Heyworth provides, it is difficult to see whether it is Curjel or Heyworth who misread Moholy-Nagy.

75 Schlemmer, "Man and Art Figure," 40.

76 Ibid., 40.

77 Moholy-Nagy's second wife quotes the director, Ernst Legal, as having said of her husband, "I'm supposed to believe I'm walking a dog … when it's actually a lion" (Sibyl Moholy-Nagy, *Moholy-Nagy: Experiment in Totality* [New York: Harper, 1950; 2nd ed. Cambridge, MA: MIT Press, 1969], 49).

78 "Sie erinnern sich an eine besondere Weise—'Hoffmanns Erzählungen'—in der damalig doch sensationellen Aufführung—viel kritisiert"; Curjel, *Krolloper*, 51.

79 "Die Herstellung des Homunculus wird greifbar. Gliedmaßen, an fadendünnen Trapezen, scheben in der Luft. Ein Püppchen, zunächst ohne Unterleib. Gestänge über-all. Doch rechts eine Wand mit geschlossen Läden. Was steckt darin? Man soll es bald erfahren. In diesem grotesken, verschiedenartig erhellten Experimentierkabinett tritt der Mensch in den Abstufungen zwischen Lebewesen und Maschine auf"; Weißmann, rpt. in Curjel, *Krolloper*, 260.

80 "Moholy-Nagy hat das nicht erfüllt. Er ist im einzelnen geistreich, im ganzen unorganisch. … Er macht aus dem Kabinett des Spalanzani ein amüsantes Varieté struktiver Spielereien, Kugeln, schaukelnde Männchen, Hähne, Körperglieder, rollende Lichtbilder, drehende Farben und elektrische Bewegungsbilder"; Bie, rpt. in Curjel, *Krolloper*, 262.

81 E. T. A. Hoffmann, *Die Serapions-Bruder*, ed. Walter Muller-Seidel (Darmstadt: Wissenschaftliche Buchgesellschaft, 1966), 346. Qtd. in Horst Daemmrich, *The Shattered Self: E. T. A. Hoffmann's Tragic Vision* (Detroit: Wayne State University Press, 1973), 75.

82 Nelson, *Puppets*, 31–44.

83 Ibid., 30.

84 Ibid., viii.

85 Ibid., 56.

86 Ibid., 57.

87 René Descartes, *Discourse on Method* in *Discourse on Method and Related Writings*, trans. Desmond M. Clarke (Harmondsworth, UK: Penguin, 1999), 40. Cited in Nelson, *Puppets*, 64.

88 Stefani Engelstein, *Anxious Anatomy: The Conception of the Human Form in Literary and Naturalist Discourse* (Albany: State University of New York Press, 2008), 160–61.

89 E. T. A. Hoffmann, *Tales of E. T. A. Hoffmann*, ed. and trans. Leonard J. Kent and Elizabeth C. Knight (Chicago: University of Chicago Press, 1972), 98.
As Engelstein points out, in many of his stories Hoffmann uses the names of actual scientists of the recent past; the scientist with whom Nathanael is studying in "The Sandman" is named Spalanzani, a name almost identical with that of Lazzaro Spallanzani, an eighteenth-century biologist and physiologist. Engelstein links a story about Spallanzani's gratification of his curiosity about insects by coldheartedly pulling them apart with Coppelius's examination of the young boy Nathanael (Engelstein, *Anatomy*, 157–58).

90 Hoffmann, *Tales*, 110.

91 Ibid., 117.

92 Ibid., 117. Hal Foster suggests that "as soon as [these mechanical figures] are coded as demonic, they are also gendered as female. In this way a social ambivalence regarding machines, a dream of mastery versus an anxiety about loss of control, becomes bound up with a psychic ambivalence, of desire mixed with dread, regarding women" (Hal Foster, *Compulsive Beauty* [Cambridge, MA: MIT Press, 1993], 134).

93 Hoffmann, *Tales*, 123.

94 Schlemmer, "Man and Art Figure," 27.

95 Ibid., 23.

96 Juliet Koss, "Bauhaus Theater of Human Dolls," *The Art Bulletin* 85, no. 4 (December 2003), 728.

97 Ibid., 726.

98 Moholy-Nagy, "Theater, Circus, Variety," 52–54.

99 This argument is informed by Koss's work on the depiction of women in Bauhaus artifacts.

100   Koss, "Dolls," 732.

101   Schlemmer, "Man and Art Figure," 29.

102   "[D]ie Gesellschaft Spalanzanis ist grotesk-proletarisch gekleidet, was gewiß nicht zu einem Menuett paßt"; Bie, rpt. in Curjel, *Krolloper*, 262.

103   Schlemmer, "Man and Art Figure," 27.

104   "Der Regisseur Legal fragt sich mit einem fabelhaften Einfall: Ist eine mechanische Menschenpuppe nur ein Spielzeug oder ein Wunder der Technik? Hallo, Wunder der Technik! Wie modern! Das wollen wir ja! Wir brauchen keinen Zauberer, sondern einen Physiker"; Diebold, rpt. in Curjel, *Krolloper*, 265.

105   Schlemmer, "Theater (Bühne)," 92.

106   Ibid., 92.

107   Garner, *Bodied Spaces*, 90.

108   The first few seasons of the "new" Kroll included operas by Brecht, Krenek, and Hindemith, and a later production featured sets by Schlemmer.

109   The question "Who shall inherit England?" is the one Trilling famously raises with reference to the themes of E. M. Forster's novel *Howard's End*.

110   "Das Klemperer-Ensemble, das zum größten Teil aus Deutschfremden besteht, frißt nach und nach den ganzen Opernbestand an. Es inszeniert die beliebtesten Opern 'aus dem Geist der Zeit,' das heißt: aus dem jüdischen Geist"; Zschorlich, rpt. in Curjel, *Krolloper*, 263. The newspaper is characterized as such by Hans Curjel (Curjel, *Krolloper*, 216).

111   "[D]as Atelier Spalanzanis wirkte mit seinen kindischen Attributen und in seiner 'modernen' Ausstattung geradezu abstoßend. Freilich: das gilt nur für den deutschen Geschmack. … Die Herren Klemperer und Legal täten gut daran, wenigstens Farbe zu bekennen und ihr kulturbolschewistisches Unternehmen als 'Jüdische Oper'"; ibid., 263–64.

112   Qtd. in Heyworth, *Klemperer*, 285; Heyworth, trans.

113   "Ich bin im Prinzip nicht dagegen, daß eine Epoche ihren Anschauungsstil im Theater auf ältere Werke verwendet. Schließlich hat das jede Epoche getan. Es ist nur heute besonders kompliziert. … [I]st dieser konstruktive Stil wirklich der absolute Ausdruck unserer Zeit? Die reine Raumauffassung der Bühne in Gerüsten, Flächen, Baugliedern, die selbst in Rußland nicht wirklich populär geworden ist, scheint eher ein letzter Ausläufer der formalen Richtung, eine neue l'art pour l'art, ein Eroberungsgelüst, ja eine Tyrannei, als eine innere Notwendigkeit. Es gehört sehr viel Absträktion dazu, da nun einmal Menschen auf der Bühne agieren, deren natürlich Erscheinung in ein System mit dieser technischen Absolutheit zu bringen"; Bie, rpt. in Curjel, *Krolloper*, 262.

114   Zschorlich, rpt. in Curjel, *Krolloper*, 264. Previously quoted.

115   "'[W]as hat man gegen den süßen Opernkitsch vor?'"; Weißmann, rpt. in Curjel, *Krolloper*, 260.

116   "Die meisten sind gespannt; die anderen sind gewappnet. Aber auch den Gewappneten ist offenbar die Triller-pfeife eingefroren. Sie sind überstimmt worden. Der Beifall begräbt alles, was an Verrostetheit, Mißmut, Besserwisserei vorhanden ist"; ibid., rpt. in Curjel, *Krolloper*, 260.

117   Moholy-Nagy, "Theater, Circus, Variety," 50.

118   Zschorlich, rpt. in Curjel, *Krolloper*, 263. Zschorlich reveals his nationalistic bent when he offers a blanket condemnation of Klemperer: "Waging his personal, unmoved by the German spirit, unshakeable artistic will against Wagner's work, we recognize the folly of his preoccupation, as two great Wagner Societies have already risen up to protest the soiling of the German culture, warning against Klemperer's *Flying Dutchman*" (Zschorlich, rpt. in Curjel, *Krolloper*, 256). Curjel later recounted, "Because of the reproduction of *Dutchman* in its original presentation by the Dresden revolutionary, the dramaturge was called in front of the Prussian Parliament for an embarrassing interrogation. But what was the actual

sacrilege? That the Hollander didn't wear a beard or that the girl didn't wear braids? Or that rather than threading cotton through a spinning wheel, she had fishnets gliding through her fingers?" (Curjel, *Krolloper*, 58. Trotter, trans.).

119 Moholy-Nagy, "Theater, Circus, Variety," 60.
120 Bie, rpt. in Curjel, *Krolloper*, 262. Evans, trans.
121 Letter to Ernest Hardt, qtd. in Whitford, *Bauhaus*, 37.
122 Heyworth, *Klemperer*, 183.
123 Ibid., 251, 256–57.
124 Ibid., 284.
125 Ibid., 285.
126 Ibid., 287.
127 Whitford, *Bauhaus*, 9.
128 Moholy-Nagy, "Theater, Circus, Variety," 67–68.
129 Naum Gabo, "Art and Science," in *Gabo: Constructions, Sculpture, Paintings, Drawings, Engravings*, ed. Naum Gabo (Cambridge, MA: Harvard University Press, 1957), 180.
130 Moholy-Nagy, "Constructivism and the Proletariat," 185.

5 Box set to the infinite power

Metatheatricality and set design in Albee's *Tiny Alice*

In his volume on the history of environmental scenography, Arnold Aronson follows Richard Schechner's model, using a continuum to characterize stagings that range from purely frontal performance (in which the spectator "rarely has to look more than forty-five degrees to the right or left in order to view the whole production") to entirely environmental stages that incorporate the spectator kinesthetically, enabling the spectator "to experience the stage space physically, much as the performer does."[1] Among the intermediate points within this continuum are the "implied environment," in which "the spectators share the same space (and time) as the performers"; use of a theater in which the stage and auditorium are unified by architectural elements; the "experienced environment," in which some audience members will feel that their space is part of the performance while others will still have an experience of frontal staging; and "surrounding space," a truly environmental theater in which the spectator is surrounded by performance.[2] These distinctions are significant for Aronson because he, like Schechner, sees in them the degree to which the spectator is included within the circle ("frame") of performance or excluded from it, remaining in "a different reality" from that of the stage-space. My previous analysis of the claque should show that even for *théâtre à l'italienne*, as David Wiles puts it, or purely "frontal performance," as Aronson puts it, the auditorium may serve as an environment continuous with the stage, where both actors and spectators play a role in the production. As Marvin Carlson has pointed out,

> [E]very element of the spectator's environment during an operatic performance—the singing, the scenery, the orchestra, the lobbies and bars at intermission, the programs, the ushers, the other audience members—contributes to the way in which that spectator "makes sense" of the event.[3]

Once we challenge the idea that environmental theater must necessarily be "non-frontal," Aronson's characterization of environmental theater may provide a useful way to reassess the audience's experience in proscenium theaters in postwar America.

While some productions on the proscenium stage may indeed entertain passive viewers, others may be staged in such a way that the spectators become part of the performance, included within the mimetic frame that theatrical performance creates. When that situation occurs, the nature of the performance is altered. Once the spectator "is somehow incorporated within the frame," the audience's experience is part of the meaning-making of the production.[4] Aronson cites Luca Ronconi's production of *Orlando Furioso* as an example of environmental scenography because, unless spectators chose to move to a corner of the space, they were surrounded by the action, which occurred "around and among the centrally placed spectators."[5] But the audience does not need to be in the midst of the action to be part of the production. Several of Aronson's categories are combined at the close of Jean Genet's *The Balcony*. Throughout the play, Genet details sets for a proscenium stage and an illusionist theater, and the initial four different sets are soon revealed as different rooms in a fetishist brothel. At the conclusion, however, when the madam, Irma, breaks the fourth wall and addresses the spectators, she creates an implied environment. She suggests that the characters and the audience share the same place and time:

> Prepare yours ... judges, generals, bishops, chamberlains, rebels who allow the revolt to congeal, I'm going to prepare my costumes and studios for tomorrow. ... You must now go home, where everything—you can be quite sure—will be falser than here. ... You must go now. You'll leave by the right, through the alley.[6]

Watchers are implicated as participants in the brothel's rituals, presumably as voyeurs or potential clients; the rooms into which audiences have seen Irma peep at will are the same rooms that audience members have been watching throughout the play. At the same time, however, Irma restructures the theater as a surrounding space: Irma's fictive space is no longer merely The Grand Balcony but a world in which performance can replace reality; the theater in which the watchers are seated replaces the forum in which she operates. Thus, audience members themselves are implicated as actors, and the walls of the theater mark the boundary of Irma's domain. This spatial shift in *The Balcony*, which alters both the space of the stage and the audience's relation to the performance, occurs in the last five minutes of the play. It abruptly broadens the space of performance crucially close to the end of the play.

While *The Balcony* played in coterie theaters for a number of years after its premiere, other Absurdist dramas did not.[7] When the proscenium theater is used in ways similar to that which Genet dictated for his coterie theater, the production's manipulation of the space challenges our basic understanding of the structure's control of its parameters. If set design, dialogue and action can reshape a proscenium theater so that the audience is included within the mimetic frame, the set manifests a powerful ability to redefine the larger space of the theater. We can see this redefinition occur in Edward Albee's *Tiny Alice*, an Absurdist play that premiered in 1964 at the Billy Rose Theatre in New York City. As I shall show, in *Tiny Alice* the space of performance is indicated early on as vastly larger than the theater. The set does not dictate the spectators' role to them as it does in *The Balcony*; instead, it merely designates their role in the drama in order to permit them to act as they choose. The apparently frontal staging, which Aronson believes creates a boundary between performer and spectator, is absolutely necessary in this case in order for the extended space of action to exist.

Edward Albee's plays have consistently been grouped with those of Beckett, Ionesco, and Genet ever since Martin Esslin coined the term "Theater of the Absurd," but *Tiny Alice* is in many ways realistic. Esslin links Albee's early plays, *Zoo Story* and *The American Dream*, with Pinteresque Absurdity but rightly characterizes the mid-period *Tiny Alice* in terms that recall the spinning perspectives of Jean Genet.[8] Genet's dramas, however, most obviously undermine illusionism through costume and dialogue. The audience's position is primarily that of watcher. We may be obliquely challenged to recognize our own culture's power structures in the battles for dominance in *Deathwatch* or the layers of artifice in *The Blacks*, but we are seldom implicated until the close, if then. Genet's best-known drama, *The Maids*, concludes with the fourth wall intact; it is only in *The Balcony* that a character's final speech unquestionably *addresses* the spectators and makes it clear that they are part of the negotiation about what is real that has taken place onstage.

Tiny Alice, in contrast, never presents a character who addresses the audience— unless obliquely. This play is, for the most part, realistic. John Fiske uses the term "modality" to allude to "the measure of the closeness of the representation of the real,"[9] and the modality of *Tiny Alice* is decidedly different from Genet's poetic dramas about members of the underclass and their relation to hegemonic social institutions. While the dialogue of *Tiny Alice* eventually presents a fantastic circumstance that makes it possible to categorize the play as Absurd, it is the space of the stage—its design and the references it provokes from the characters— that challenges the audience to reconsider its position. Moreover, this play about religious faith challenges the audience far more radically if they follow the implications of the staging, which gives the audience not only one but two roles regarding the status of illusionism onstage.

Most critics have focused on the religious implications of *Tiny Alice*, though there have also been many biographical readings, perhaps beginning with Philip Roth's pan of the original production.[10] Despite the insightful recognition that this play, unlike *Who's Afraid of Virginia Woolf*, should be grouped with Albee's early Absurdist work, Esslin fails to note how the audience is implicated in the drama's staging and dialogue, and how that implication translates to a role for the audience itself. The play's self-referential elements, unlike those of Genet, place the audience in two positions: they must take on the role of godlike judges and yet simultaneously submit themselves for judgment, mirroring the role of the character Brother Julian.

In this chapter I draw on theories of proxemics and the phenomenology of space to consider possible roles of the spectator and to examine how the onlookers are manipulated into taking a specific role in the production of *Tiny Alice* that debuted at the Billy Rose Theatre on December 29, 1964, despite the theater's design, which might more readily elicit audience passivity. I begin with the assumption that the proscenium stage for which the production was designed was likely to evoke one kind of audience experience, but that design elements in the set, combined with plot and textual elements, could short-circuit or alter that initial effect.

***

Many critics have noted that the staging of medieval morality plays actively solicited the audience to play a role in judging the proceedings. In her discussion of the stage plan of *The Castle of Perseverance*, Catherine Belsey points out that the stage plan resembles medieval maps of the world, arguing that "[t]he inhabitants of this world include, of course, the audience within the circle, who are implicated in the progress of their representative, Mankind."[11] Belsey suggests that onlookers were called on to empathize with the protagonist and that they implicitly understood the philosophical position presented by the morality play structure:

> The spectators are here offered an image of Mankind's condition and their own, and invited to identify in his perplexity a mirror of their own being. ... The spectators participate in his choices; they are enlisted in the debate between good and evil ... but at the same time, to the extent that they are able to see the visual network of meanings established by the stage plan, as Mankind evidently is not, they are offered a single, stable position from which to understand the nature of human life.[12]

Belsey links the stage design to the assumption that the audience will be able to perceive the allegory as a whole; only the fact of multiple perspectives makes the understanding of the allegorical structure possible.

In contrast to the stage plan of the morality play, Belsey cites Sir William Davenant's playhouse, which opened in 1661. Its design included both perspective backdrops and a proscenium arch and created the sense of a theatrical microcosm without any necessary correspondence to the playgoer's own experience. As Belsey (among others) suggests, the scenic theater

> close[d] the gap the moralities had opened between protagonist and spectator precisely by drawing a clear demarcation line between them. Classic realist theatre isolates the world of the fiction from the world of the audience, and shows the first as an empirical replica rather than an emblematic representation of the second.[13]

The play is no longer a psychomachia but a fiction concerning "concrete individuals who interact with each other as unified subjects."[14] Belsey goes on to argue that the perspective sets, whose design was influenced by Italian painters' use of monocular perspective, imagine an ideal spot "outside of the autonomous world of the fiction" for viewing the picture, a spot in the audience occupied by the royal box.[15] In the scenic theater, there is only one spot perfect for viewing the spectacle, only one spot ideal for mapping the space laid out by the

perspective backdrops. The receding perspective "offers the spectator an absolute and illusory transcendence" of the microcosm onstage, and of the action
enacted there.[16] The necessities imposed by monocular perspective also neces-
sitated that the spectator was aware of the world outside of that microcosm,
for the extent to which the perspective backdrop made visual sense to him
depended on how close he was to the royal box. The existence of the royal box
also set up a contrasting focus, the monarch, who might provide as great a
show as the staged performance. Thus, the world of the play and the world of
the theater were clearly distinguished and brought into at least potential conflict. The spectator transcended the mimetic world and saw the world of the
theater as an entity separate from both the performance and the larger world
outside the playhouse, though the theater maintained a partial correspondence
to both. These conventions are manipulated in twentieth-century dramas,
which call upon the spectators to reevaluate their role and challenge the transcendence brought in by perspective backdrops.

The Broadway theater shares a number of features with Davenant's playhouse, among them balconies and boxes, ornate decor, a proscenium arch, a
curtain that is raised and dropped, and a flat background against which the
actors perform, sometimes even involving the formation of tableaux that evoke
two-dimensional artwork. Other, later conventions still in use are the lighted
stage, the darkened theater, and raked seating; a common element whose use
long predates Davenant's theater is the stage apron, which can function as the
medieval *platea* does for improvisatory action or can simply provide the actor
with a greater opportunity for intimacy with the audience. Though perspective
flats are seldom used today, cycloramas are more common. Instead of painted
scenery, a substantial interior may be built, creating the impression of an invisible
"fourth wall" between the actors and the audience. Today, a set will seldom
correspond to reality in every detail; instead, emblematic stage properties may
be used to suggest a specific place. Sometimes a realistic nineteenth-century style
set may be used as an ironic allusion to the style or the period when such sets
were in vogue; these sets are likely to be used with decidedly non-realistic plays
as an intentionally uncanny element.

The set of Edward Albee's *Tiny Alice* is one such case. After the initial scene,
the play is a one-set drama. Albee's stage directions are quite specific:

> *The library of a mansion—a castle. Pillared walls, floor-to-ceiling leather-
> bound books. … To stage right, jutting out of the wings, a huge doll's house
> model of the building of which the present room is a part. It is as tall as a
> man, and a good deal of it must be visible from all parts of the audience.*[17]

In the original production designed by William Ritman, the one that I discuss
here, the model was in fact a broad Georgian mansion on a plinth, placed
center stage so that it served as a background for much of the action. In every
other way, the library decor was traditional and opulent, with large, vertical
carved-wood panels, damask wallpaper, chairs upholstered in damask and leather.

Figure 5.1 Photograph by Alix Jeffry of Irene Worth and John Gielgud in *Tiny Alice*.
(Ritman's model may be seen behind Gielgud)
Alix Jeffry Photograph, MS Thr 416.1 [472].
© Harvard Theatre Collection, Houghton Library, Harvard University.

The model (which I shall call the doll's house for reasons that will eventually become clear) becomes the center of the play. It is the first thing discussed in the play's second scene, and we later learn that the mansion it seems to represent was actually a replica of the doll's house, which was created prior to the mansion itself. The ensuing debate in the play on the terms "model" and "replica" seems to raise the issue of Platonic forms and their relation to the world we live in.[18] It is emphasized from the beginning that the doll's house, which is sealed and dustless, corresponds in every particular to the house the characters move about in, inside as well as outside: "there's a great ... baronial dining room, even with tiny candlesticks on the tables" (24). Two questions are raised at the outset: first, the question of simulacra, dolls:

JULIAN: It seems to be quite ... empty.
BUTLER: One feels one should see one's self ... almost.

(25)

Second, Butler takes pains to point out that the doll's house should not be seen as a model *or* a replica, but as one of an infinitely receding series:

> Did you notice that there is a model within that room in the castle? A
> model of the model? ... You don't suppose that within that tiny model in
> the model there, there is ... another room like this, with yet a tinier model
> within it, and within ... .

> (25)

His point makes the audience naturally aware of the implications of the set
design. Martin Esslin suggests that the play "clearly tried to evolve a complex
image of man's search for truth and certainty in a constantly shifting world,
without ever wanting to construct a complete allegory."[19] Esslin asserts that

> [i]t is futile to search for the philosophical meaning of such an image. What
> it communicates is a mood, a sense of the mystery, the impenetrable com-
> plexity of the universe. And that is precisely what a dramatic poet is
> after.[20]

Other critics, however, have not been slow to look beyond the play's sense of
mystery, which many alienated theatergoers deemed "obscurity." For the critic
Richard E. Amacher, the passage suggests that

> if we look for deity in the macrocosm, which we ourselves inhabit, why
> should we not also go prospecting for it in the microcosm, which we don't
> inhabit—the world within the model, where, as we discover later in the
> play, *Tiny* Alice, as distinct from *Miss* Alice, the inordinately wealthy
> owner of the mansion, lives?[21]

His is a valid point, and one consistent with the action of the play, but it is not
mine. I suggest that, because *Tiny Alice* is a play rather than a narrative, the
location of the audience within the system described necessitates a significant
question: if the doll's house and its relation to the set implies the existence of an
infinitely receding series, shouldn't the set and its relation to the doll's house
model be seen as part of an infinitely *expanding* series as well? The existence of the
audience supports this theory through inductive reasoning: while the characters
are unaware that there is any world larger than their own, performances of the
play provide an audience existing in a frame of reference altogether outside of
that of the characters (unless one characterizes their references to God as an
oblique allusion to the world of the spectators). For audience members watching
the play, the smallest visible frame of reference is the doll's house while the
next is the set of the play. The largest frame of reference for the audience is
defined either by the walls of the theater or by the space of our entire world.

If the next largest "box," or frame of reference, is the world of the theater
building, what does that mean for the audience? What role is granted to the
silent watchers in the darkened theater? The insoluble questions of metaphysics
are present before the curtain falls on act 1. Audience members can choose
either to see themselves as part of a Seussian Horton-Hears-a-Who universe,

never confident of their place in the cosmos, or to treat the play's concept as a fiction that goes only as far as the theater's walls.

As Amacher implies, the mansion—or the possibly imaginary figure within it—does come to represent a deity (several critics have pointed out that the name "Alice" means "truth" in Old German).[22] The lay brother Julian, who has come to assist Miss Alice in arranging her multimillion dollar donation to the Catholic Church, has gradually become a member of the household and has been seduced by Miss Alice. Her purported employees, the Lawyer and the Butler, agree that it "would be a lovely touch" to marry Julian to Alice (the model) through a marriage with Miss Alice the character (104). In planning their strategy, the Lawyer imagines the conversation:

> There is Alice, Julian. That can be understood. Only the mouse in the model. Just that. ... Believe it. Don't personify the abstraction, Julian, limit it, demean it. Only the mouse, the toy. And that does not exist ... but is all that can be worshiped.
>
> (107)

At the end of the play, the lay brother is united with God, but God in the form of an imaginary doll (or, alternately, a doll's house), to which he must pledge his faith before he dies.

Once again, where does that leave the audience? If, as I have suggested, the audience applies the theory of the regressive series to their own physical forms, they must acknowledge that the model of the whole implies that they are dolls themselves, manipulated by some larger deity as surely as Julian is manipulated by these sardonic puppeteers. Audience members—in fact, all human beings—are the dolls of some unknown and unknowable God according to this model. But if the play's spectators distinguish themselves from Julian by their role as watchers, then the role of the larger box outside the theater is the same as that of the smaller one, the model: the role of God. The audience is thrust away from identification with Julian and pushed toward judging him instead. And the doll's house, which faces the audience from across the stage for most of *Tiny Alice*, especially as it shows odd signs of animation, must be perceived as a sapient entity, looking across at its *semblable*, its macrocosmic equivalent out past the footlights. The audience comes to mirror the mansion in its role as deity.

Yet, far from serving unproblematically as a deity, the doll's house becomes the site of the play's central controversy. Julian refuses to accept it as a symbolic surrogate of either the woman he has married or the God he worships. "There is nothing there!" he insists, rather understandably. And when the Butler and the Lawyer urge him to accept the deity of the house on faith, Julian refuses. The spectators, aware of their own sentience rather more than they know of the doll's house inhabitants', may feel rocked on their comfortable thrones or simply smile in their acceptance of the convention that, to the characters onstage, they are as invisible as God himself. But as Julian is pressed between the house at the back of the stage and the apron of the stage, the audience must see its identity both in the mysterious structure and in Julian, the man judged—if not by the actual house then by the servants of Miss Alice who seem to be following the mandate of a mysterious, rather menacing entity: a Pinterian backstage force.

To understand both dimensions of the audience's role, we must consider why Albee would require something as cumbersome, as laughable, as a doll's house, which his stage directions specify. Like the theater, the house provides a model of mimesis, though on a smaller scale. To understand what the choice means for the audience, however, we must explore the extra-dramatic meanings of the house, including its literary and cultural—even its biographical—connotations. We shall begin by following Albee's lead and examining the link between *Tiny Alice* and the morality tradition.

Albee said shortly before the play opened that *Tiny Alice* should be viewed as "a mystery play, a double mystery, and also a morality play, about truth and illusion, the substitute images we create, that we substitute for the real thing."[23] The connection between *Tiny Alice* and medieval drama is strong enough that Mary E. Campbell has argued that "strands in *Tiny Alice* do indeed echo the intent and certain distinct sections of the medieval guild cycles" and suggested that the play could be read as a morality play in which the world, the flesh, and the devil are represented by the Butler, Miss Alice, and the Lawyer respectively.[24] While I do not regard *Tiny Alice* as schematized to that degree, the parallels are present and quite resonant. What interests me is the significance of the house in *Tiny Alice* and its correspondence to buildings used—and staged—in the morality. As Belsey explains in her discussion of *The Castle of Perseverance*,

> virtue is possible only through withdrawal into the castle, a stronghold which represents a wall against the three adversaries who command the seven sins. The castle is within the world of the play, on earth, but presumably raised above the level of the ground, since it must be supported on posts. ... No escape from the earth is possible until death. ... But the castle represents a way of life which is nearer to perfection than any available in the world.[25]

Albee's house is not a castle, though the stage directions do refer to it as such. But in contrast to the medieval Castle of Perseverance, Alice's doll's house is a symbol of ambiguity. At times, the house itself seems to be a deity. Miss Alice prays to it:

> Let the fire be put out. Let the chapel be saved; let the fire not spread; let us not be consumed. ... I have tried to obey what I have not understood, understanding that I must obey. Don't destroy! I have tried! **Tried.**
>
> (91–92)

At other times, the characters who seem most knowledgeable refer to "the mouse in the model" (107) and later urge, "Her rooms are lighted. It is warm, there is enough. ... *She* is there ... we believe" (162–63). Miss Alice tells Julian, "You have felt her warmth through me, touched her lips through my lips, held hands, through mine" (163). Some critics following Albee's cue, notably Mardi Valgemae, regard the house much as if the drama were a medieval morality in which the structure represents Julian's soul. Valgemae asserts that the fire

> serves as an objectification of Julian's physical passion for Miss Alice, which threatens to destroy the tenuous order he has established for himself as a lay brother. ... When the actual fire breaks out in the chapel, it guts the altar area, just as Brother Julian's sexual fantasies destroy his attempts to come to grips with religious experience.[26]

The doll's house, as we learn early on, is sealed, dustless. What, then, turns lights on and off inside it? What starts the fire in its chapel, a fire that corresponds to the fire in the mansion that Julian inhabits with Miss Alice and her cohort? Julian, as a realistic character, insists nonetheless, "There is no one there! ... There is nothing there!" (164). Yet at the end, he accepts the tiny "Alice," the doll's house or its inhabitant, as his deity. The ambiguity of the doll's house is one of many elements that seem to place this play in the category of Theater of the Absurd, both because it is bizarre and ambiguous and because the use of the house in the play suggests the nihilistic position that there is no Alice, no God, but that it is impossible to be certain.

Albee's doll's house in *Tiny Alice* both attracts and repels. Characters seem instinctively to recognize it as a simulacrum, a way of worshipping Miss Alice's ancestors (whom the Butler refers to) and, by its nature, a structure that does imply inhabitants. The scholar Victoria Nelson comments on the apotheosis of material objects, placing the primitive worship of objects in the context of Platonic theory:

> If all things in the material world are simulacra, copies, of the true World of Forms, then statues and people alike ... acted not just as passive vessels but as magnets to the energies of the higher world, drawing down the gods' powers and materially embodying them.[27]

This link to a higher power seems to be what Albee suggests in *Tiny Alice*, but with this caveat: that Albee wanted his audience to question whether such a structure could be any more than a hollow shell in this modern age. The doll's house onstage embodies either the deepest ·essence of life or its antithesis, a parody of its own expressiveness. The question of "the mouse in the model" is the question of the model's life, its animation. Can it function like the Romans' *lares* and *penates* or has the time passed for such objects of worship? The question is raised by the action and, seemingly, intentionally left unresolved.

If one assumes no randomness in Albee's conception, the house's correspondence with the castle of the medieval morality might resonate; otherwise, one might ask why Albee represents the deity in a house. Clearly, Tiny Alice is not a cozy habitation. Bachelard quotes Michelet on homes:

"In reality," he writes, "a bird's tool is its own body, that is, its breast, with which it presses and tightens its materials until they have become absolutely pliant, well-blended, and adapted to the general plan." And Michelet suggests a house built by and for the body, taking form from the inside, like a shell, in an intimacy that works physically.[28]

This castle-like house, according to Noel Farrand, Albee's childhood friend and the dedicatee of the play, was strongly reminiscent of the Albee family's home. "In common," says Mel Gussow, "they were large and dark and mysterious, places to hide secrets. Imagine that inside the model are miniature versions of two small boys, Edward and Noel, moving from room to room to basement to attic."[29] Albee rejected that home and the suburban narrow-mindedness it represented, walking out when he was twenty-one.[30] During his boyhood, however, when he and Farrand wandered freely through the house together, the family mansion was a place of fantasy and adventure where domestic exploration served as a physical representation of self-exploration and self-discovery. As boys, he and Farrand experienced the mansion as a place where they could lose themselves—even if it was ultimately alienating. In contrast to Michelet's bird's nest, this place would not take the mark of its inhabitants but would remain a family property, used for social display. Albee and Farrand could only make it their own by seeing themselves as outsiders: explorers, buccaneers searching for spoil or an opportunity for transformation. The mansion's social significance for the Albee parents eventually became burdensome to Edward—it was a showplace that never could belong fully to the rebellious and iconoclastic young man. It provided his parents with an appropriate façade with which to present their family to their community, but it apparently felt to Albee like a museum rather than a refuge—in Farrand's words, "uninhabitable."

***

The imagery of enclosure and embrace that pervades the play is commonly used to characterize the welcome and comfort provided by a home: terms of enclosure and penetration are basic linguistic building blocks for defining dwellings.[31] The significance of the house as home is suggested initially by the Lawyer's phrase "the mouse in the model," and later brought out by the play's images of enclosure, of penetration and envelopment, which appear both in the staging and in the imagery described by the characters (107). Most notably, Julian recounts how in childhood he imagined himself as an early Christian martyr:

> I could ... see the gladiator on me, his trident fork against my neck, and hear, even hear, as much as feel, the prongs as they entered me; the ... the beast's saliva dripping from the yellow teeth, the slack sides of the mouth, the ... sweet, warm breath of the lion; great paws on my spread arms.
>
> (124)

At the end of act 2, when Miss Alice seduces Julian, stage directions indicate clearly that she envelops Julian, much as he imagined the lion simultaneously embracing and penetrating him:

> *Miss Alice has her back to the audience, Julian facing her, but at a distance; she takes her gown and, spreading her arms slowly, opens the gown wide; it is the unfurling of great wings.*

(126)

> *Julian utters a sort of dying cry and moves, his arms in front of him, to Miss Alice; when he reaches her, she enfolds him in her great wings.*

(127)

Julian's language suggests that he has long imagined a masochistic consummation in which he experiences something like the embrace of the lion's jaws. The initial embrace of Miss Alice seems to provide the realization of his fantasy. Yet, as Butler and the Lawyer explain, Miss Alice is merely the proxy for the Alice inside the house, the Alice who is also represented by the proxy of the doll's house. At the play's conclusion, Butler brings out sheets to drape all the furniture as he closes up the mansion, draping and wrapping each of the opulent props that indicate the worldly value of Miss Alice. This draping represents a kind of *en*closure that involves both closing and closure, a chilly—perhaps empty—embrace of the elements of the home. Terms of enclosure, embrace, and attack have also been used to characterize the individual's relation to God for centuries. When Butler asks Julian, "You loathe sham, don't you? ... You are dedicated to the reality of things, rather than their appearance, are you not?", the imagery links dwelling to religious faith (138). As Butler is draping the furniture, he attempts to smooth the way to Julian's acquiescence by talking about Julian's spiritual dilemmas.

Julian's preference for reification rather than the symbols of God at first appears to be mocked by the proposition that the other characters offer him. The suggestion that he acknowledge God in the model is ridiculous and seems to demean his faith. But the imagery of the home helps Julian eventually to see the home itself as a covering—first as a concealment of sham but later as a concealment of something real. Miss Alice has concealed her relation to the model; she has concealed the true power relation between her and the Lawyer, and Julian's preference for "the reality of things" triumphs when he "throws off" the trappings of reality and accepts the model as a deity, an "Alice" that controls the actions of both him and the other characters. The true "Alice"—the intangible "mouse in the model" Alice—appears initially only in the form of a series of lights in the model that come to rest in the library. This room in the doll's house represents a room in Miss Alice's mansion; on the stage of the theater, this same room is represented by the theatrical set: it is the room where the action occurs, and where, finally, Julian lies dying, shot by the Lawyer. "Alice" then manifests herself by a heartbeat audible to the audience and then "[*a*] *great shadow, or darkening, fills the stage; it is the shadow of a great presence filling the room*" (189). The lights in the doll's house, visible to the audience, indicate that these larger signs of Alice occur in reality and do not originate within Julian or his perceptions (as the heartbeat, or even the darkening of the room might). But the heartbeat and the shadow indicate that the magnitude of Alice is substantially beyond that of "the mouse in the model"; Alice is bigger than the set, bigger than the theater—a presence, as Albee suggests, that cannot be measured. Alice the deity is both within the model and in a recursively expanding series.

The audience's role in the schema provided by the play becomes evident when we consider the blocking of the conclusion. Throughout the play, Julian has been forced by the stage directions to retreat until he reaches the rear of the stage. During the seduction of Julian, for example, Miss Alice turns her back to the audience and opens her robe, facing the appalled Julian, whose face must be seen by the audience. Julian, then, must be upstage, facing both Miss Alice and the spectators, and as she approaches him, he must initially retreat backward. His position onstage distanced the audience both literally and figuratively; at the same time, it enabled watchers to see him as a mirror of themselves, with Miss Alice as the fulcrum that balanced watchers both behind and in front of her. In the third act, Julian turns to exit from the upstage door to escape the Lawyer, but when he is shot, he "*clutches his belly, stumbles forward a few steps, sinks to the floor in front of the model*" (170). When Miss Alice and Butler attempt to move him, saying, "We can't leave Julian just ... ," implying that they cannot leave him to die on the floor, his pain is such that he urges them, "Leave me ... be," as "[h]e *slides along the floor, backing up against the model*" (183, 184). Throughout his final speech, Julian faces the audience from the very back of the set, looking at the spectators looking at him, both sides wondering if God/Alice will manifest herself by some supernatural feat before the end of the play. The point that the staging makes is that what can be seen is inadequate in conveying meaning. Viewers can only make sense of the action by accepting the unseen, recognizing the house as a visual substitute for the backstage forces that threaten or manipulate characters in Absurdist dramas from *Godot* to *The Dumb Waiter* and *The Birthday Party*. This implicit mandate simultaneously challenges the spectators to share in Julian's fear and to fear their own nascent power.

Julian's final monologue at the conclusion effectively challenges the dominance of the visual; as Bert O. States says, "poetry triumphs over neutral space."[32] As Julian wonders whether the other characters might be lingering just behind the door to see how he responds to his plight, his musings reinforce the fact that, like him, the audience cannot know what is behind the door. The early modern theater scholar Henry S. Turner has noted that "[a]s an architectonic element of the theatre building, the backstage wall formed the boundary that served as the most basic structuring principle of drama as a 'performative form' ... the opposition between onstage and offstage space."[33] As Turner points out, "The actual staging invites the audience to complete the new topographic sequence imaginatively by projecting the route of the [characters] backstage. ... The new theatrical syntagm ... is both topographic and scenic, both discursive and structural."[34] In the first production of *Tiny Alice*, Alice manifests herself when her false representatives, Miss Alice, the Lawyer, and Butler, leave Julian bleeding in the library after mocking his beliefs. He cries out but then stops, inhibited by his recognition that the other characters may be listening, unseen by him:

> Unless you have left me, tiptoed off some, stood whispering, smothered giggles, and ... silently returned, your ears pressed against, or ... of one eye into the crack so that the air smarts it sifting through. HAVE YOU COME BACK? HAVE YOU NOT LEFT ME? (*Pause*) No. No one.
>
> (187)

What is behind the door is, by definition in the theater, offstage. An unmoving set remains open to interpretation, to the potential implied by the offstage area. Within the larger framework, "behind the door" may represent the unknowability of the cosmos and the deity who may or may not be watching all of us.

As Julian suggests, what is unseen may be imagined, may even be imagined into existence. But what must be unseen must be accepted as unknowable. In imagining the other characters as watchers, he raises the possibility that in fact they may be there, and this possibility, even if false (which we cannot tell) raises the possibility of other watchers. In fact, the actor who first played Julian was *not* alone, since the audiences at the Billy Rose Theatre watched him enact Julian's death. For the character Julian himself, were audience members not playing a role as watchers, deities, figures outside of Julian's world whose companionship prevented him from being entirely alone? Though the framework of Albee's play does not admit of audience members, the framework of the drama certainly does; the audience, easy enough to elide when reading the play, is embodied and full of presence so long as the seats in the theater are filled with bodies.

For the audience, seeing Julian against the wall with the model behind him made him a potential mirror once again. If they were the watchers who kept him company, his crisis of faith may have mirrored theirs. The watchers at the Billy Rose should have recognized that, just as their presence provided Julian with companionship and gave them the role of judging his response, the cosmos outside of human understanding could produce a deity for them—a large-scale Alice, if you will, who sees us inside our houses and knows that the lights we keep on show our fear of the dark. While the watchers of *Tiny Alice* were scripted into a godlike position vis-à-vis Julian, the inner logic of the trope of the mansion implies a larger world outside our own, a god to oversee our Godlikeness, a judge to look over our shoulders and shrink us to Julian size (if not actually to doll size).

Audiences at the theater may not have followed the implications of the model through to this extent. They may not have felt themselves to be part of that ever-expanding series implied by the receding series that the Butler describes to Julian. However, Julian's final relation to the model would certainly have challenged them to look across the stage at the lay priest and consider the possibility of kinship. With that accomplished, the performance challenged the stability of the onlooker's position. I do not suggest that reality itself was necessarily undermined but that the passive onlooker became active on two levels. He or she occupied two positions: one of Godlike viewing and another of human empathy with Julian's powerlessness. The stability of the spectator was challenged by the dual role that the staging and the use of the model forced upon the watchers. To characterize their position in another way, the performance of *Tiny Alice* challenged spectators to reexamine the knowledge that theatergoers assume they possess because of their spatial position within the theater, and because of the privileged position suggested by darkness, theater design, and their own visual orientation.

Theater design in itself may not dictate a specific audience experience. The directives from Albee that shaped the audience's experience and their role in the original production of *Tiny Alice* included plot elements, specifics of the set design, and strictures about the actors' interaction with scenic elements. Albee's use of the doll's house sets up the proscenium stage as a transverse stage, with the audience encouraged to see the house as another entity with whom they have a relationship. Their relationship with the house, moreover, restructures their relationship with both the protagonist, Julian, and the world outside the theater. The mimetic possibilities of the play expand its referents beyond the theater itself: conceptually, the stage-space has been expanded to the size of the world, partly by the play's topoi and partly by Albee's exploitation of the possibilities of the house as a prop. The design of the theater is reconfigured by the mimetic nature of the Tiny Alice house. This production exemplifies one way that a theater's physical space may be refigured by the drama's manipulation of fictional place, particularly in self-conscious or self-referential dramas.

As David Wiles points out in his history of performance space, "The basic western device to create a theatre of dreams is the curtain which reveals and conceals, effecting a gap between the embodied human being in the here-and-now and the 'heart' which has its place elsewhere."[35] He notes that Russian Constructivists "opened up the aristocratic *théâtre à l'italienne* in order to expose the proletariat working the mechanisms behind the trickery."[36] But this attempt reproduced theatrical illusion on another level: "Attempts to destroy illusion only recreated it."[37] Wiles cites both the Polish director and set designer Tadeusz Kantor and the Czech scenographer Josef Svoboda as theater professionals who address this problem in their work, quoting Svoboda as saying, "I've always been an advocate of the proscenium stage because it is the most theatrical space available; moreover, the routine transformation of theatre into mere spectacle isn't readily possible in it."[38] Albee's play is only one example of an experimental drama that has challenged assumptions about the limitations of the proscenium theater. Albee and Ritman's design for *Tiny Alice* demonstrates one of many uses to which that theater can be put—one in which the audience members become much more than silent witnesses, and in which the auditorium is merely an intermediate level in an infinitely expanding series.

Notes

1 Arnold Aronson, *The History and Theory of Environmental Scenography* (Ann Arbor: UMI Research Press, 1981), 1, 2.

2 Ibid., 4–7.

3 Carlson, *Places of Performance: The Semiotics of Theatre Architecture* (Ithaca: Cornell University Press, 1989), 5.

4 Aronson, *Scenography*, 2.

5 Ibid., 6. According to my own recollection of that production, the actors moved on small wheeled platforms through a crowd of audience members who, by their very location, also played the role of the crowd in the action of the play.

6 Jean Genet, *The Balcony*, trans. Bernard Frechtman (New York: Grove, 1958), 96.

7 *The Balcony* premiered in London at the Arts Theatre Club, a "private theater club." Subsequent productions occurred in Berlin; in New York at the Circle in the Square, a renowned off-Broadway theater; in Paris at the Théâtre du Gymnase, a theater devoted to experimental drama; and in Vienna. Eventually (in 1985), the play was performed at the Théâtre-Français—the first play by Genet that the Comédie-Française staged.

8 Martin Esslin, *The Theatre of the Absurd* (Garden City, NY: Anchor Books, 1969, rev. ed.), 266–69.

9 John Fiske, *Understanding Popular Culture* (Boston: Unwin Hyman, 1989), 156.

10 Philip Roth, "The Play That Dare Not Speak Its Name," *New York Review of Books* 4 (February 25, 1965), 4.

11 Catherine Belsey, *The Subject of Tragedy: Identity and Difference in Renaissance Drama* (London: Methuen, 1985), 20.

12 Ibid., 22.

13 Ibid., 23.

14 Ibid., 24–25.

15 Ibid., 25.

16 Ibid., 25–26. See also Stephen Orgel and Roy Strong, *Inigo Jones: The Theatre of the Stuart Court* (London: Sotheby Parke Bernet, 1973), 1: 7, which Belsey quotes, and Stephen Orgel, *The Illusion of Power: Political Theater in the English Renaissance* (Berkeley: University of California Press, 1975), 8–21.

17 Edward Albee, *Tiny Alice* (New York: Atheneum, 1965), 23. All further references will be given in-text and to this edition.

18 Cf. Albee, *Tiny Alice*, 85–87.

19 Esslin, *Absurd*, 269.

20 Ibid., 269.

21 Richard E. Amacher, *Edward Albee* (Boston: Twayne, 1982, rev. ed.), 123.

22 Cf. C. W. E. Bigsby, "Curiouser and Curiouser: A Study of Edward Albee's *Tiny Alice*," *Modern Drama* 10, no. 3 (December 1967), 261; and Mardi Valgemae, "Albee's Great God Alice," *Modern Drama* 10, no. 3 (December 1967), 268.

23 Mel Gussow, *Edward Albee: A Singular Journey* (New York: Simon and Schuster, 1999), 218 (from an interview of Albee on December 8, 1964).

24 Mary E. Campbell, "The Tempters in Albee's *Tiny Alice*," *Modern Drama* 13, no. 1 (May 1970), 24, 27–33.

25 Belsey, *Tragedy*, 21.

26 Valgemae, "Alice," 270.

27 Victoria Nelson, *The Secret Life of Puppets* (Cambridge, MA: Harvard University Press, 2001), 32–33.

28 Gaston Bachelard, *The Poetics of Space*, trans. Maria Jolas (Boston: Beacon Press, 1969; 2nd ed. 1994), 100–101.

29 Gussow, *Edward Albee*, 214.

30 "'I'd learned to hate their politics, their morality, their bigotry. I was really very very unhappy in that whole environment'" (Albee, qtd. in Gussow, *Edward Albee*, 70).

31 The term "enter," for example, is used to indicate both sexual penetration and physical movement of a body into an enclosed area. This point is made much of in Judith Haber's analyses of early modern English dramas in her book *Desire and Dramatic Form in Early Modern England* (Cambridge: Cambridge University Press, 2009).
32 Bert O. States, *Great Reckonings in Little Rooms: On the Phenomenology of Theater* (Berkeley: University of California Press, 1985), 56.
33 Henry S. Turner, *The English Renaissance Stage: Geometry, Poetics, and the Practical Spatial Arts, 1580–1630* (Oxford: Oxford University Press, 2006), 196.
34 Ibid., 201.
35 David Wiles, *A Short History of Western Performance Space* (Cambridge: Cambridge University Press, 2003), 209.
36 Ibid., 237.
37 Ibid., 237.
38 Josef Svoboda, *The Secret of Theatrical Space*, ed. and trans. J. M. Burian (New York: Applause, 1993), 19. Qtd. in Wiles, *History*, 238.

6 Design and double vision

Spectatorial experience and *M. Butterfly*

For many New Yorkers in 1988, the experience of David Henry Hwang's play *M. Butterfly* began with hearing the show's radio ads, which mysteriously began, "M. Butterfly! ... M. Butterfly ... How could he not have known?" The ads encouraged listeners to misunderstand the story—to assume that the play was a new version of Puccini's *Madame Butterfly* plot, and that the crucial lack of knowledge was Pinkerton's failure to guess that he had become a father. The radio spot transferred the French diplomat Gallimard's ignorance to the listener. As they were set right by the first playgoers, listeners flocked to the Eugene O'Neill Theatre to see the full story.

Listening to a snippet from *M. Butterfly*, a play about bodies, is paradoxical: on the radio, the body of the actor is absent and the audience member is present in a defamiliarized context—defamiliarized, at least, as long as the auditor assumes that the proper context for this play is a theater. This initial experience of the play resonates with the lacks at the center of the play: the lack of an Asian female body as the focus of the action, the lack of a "Butterfly" figure (a submissive and self-sacrificing "Oriental" woman) in Gallimard's 1960s Beijing. These lacks—and that confusion—were, I believe, intentional on the author's part: for Hwang, the actual plot of Puccini's opera was less important than the slang meaning of the term "pulling a Butterfly" within the Asian-American community.[1] Hwang's play also uses continual displacement as a feature of its plot—a feature used quite consciously, just as the ads attempted to instantiate the displacement that listeners experienced. The displacement of the play's setting occurs in three contexts: though *M. Butterfly* is set largely in 1960s Beijing, its shadow location is Viet Nam, where US military buildup was occurring during that period; despite a plot about a Frenchman and a Chinese man, the play repeatedly reverts to snippets of an Italian opera about a Yankee sailor and a geisha girl in Yokohama; and finally, the framing sequences set in France seem, to anyone with some knowledge of the playwright's biography, to substitute France for its true cultural referent, the United States.

Those involved in creating the original production of *M. Butterfly*—playwright David Henry Hwang, producer Stuart Ostrow, director John Dexter, and designer Eiko Ishioka—had no particular revolutionary program. The play was presented in the Eugene O'Neill Theatre, part of the Shubert group, built in 1925 and designed by Herbert J. Krapp, one of the premier theater architects of the time. (Previews were performed in Washington, DC's National Theater, a nineteenth-century structure that had undergone extensive renovation in the 1920s.) Such sites as these might create the expectation that theater attendees merely look on the drama passively: the prosceniums are elaborate; the theaters vast (holding 1,000 and 1,700 spectators respectively). Audience members at the Eugene O'Neill sit in an auditorium curved in a gentle fan-shape; two aisles divide the orchestra, with three boxes on each side. There is a mezzanine, divided into front and rear sections; this structure overhangs about the last ten rows of the orchestra section. The Eugene O'Neill typifies standard Broadway theaters, designed in the Adamesque style that might be characterized as pala-tial. Designed by Krapp with excellent acoustics and sightlines, the theater sports elaborate painted plasterwork with arches, egg-and-dart moldings, and rope-patterned pillars.

Even in this setting, however, the audience members are far from passive. In the case of this production, the seating location altered the experience of the spectator. *M. Butterfly* can be either a classic memory play in the tradition of Tennessee Williams or Brechtian epic theater, depending on where one's seat is located—or both at once, if one can hold two mutually exclusive possibilities in mind simultaneously. Seating location is crucial, for the set designs and staging manipulated audience perceptions with a constant play of visuals that directed the audience to "read" the stage either as two-dimensional—painterly—representation or as three-dimensional—dramatic—representation.[2] What Dexter, Ishioka, and Hwang produced was a scenography of whirligigs—of incompatible images, in the terminology of Jean-Paul Sartre.[3] In the case of *M. Butterfly*, an audience member seated close to the stage was more likely to see the stage in three dimensions presenting Gallimard's memory play. Within this vision of the action is contained another whirligig, in which the stage represents the body of the title character—initially Song Liling, but eventually the European, Rene Gallimard. But for the audience member seated toward the back of the theater, *M. Butterfly* was more likely to be Brechtian theater in which changing political and cultural tides carried hapless characters back and forth as Western power was challenged in Asia and western Orientalism began to be scrutinized and sometimes repudiated. Thus, where you sat, and perhaps what you were already inclined to see, affected how you perceived the actors—whether they represented individuals or economic and political forces—and, accordingly, how you perceived the stage as well.

In saying this, I do not wish to imply that gender and sexuality were not part of the text of *M. Butterfly*—far from it—but that the play's concern with bodies and meaning was presented in two different frameworks: one, the frame-work of Marxist challenges to capitalist assumptions about economics and class; the other, the framework of individualism that makes the assumptions of Freudian psychology possible. These ideological frameworks were brought into *M. Butterfly* through the use of staging and set design that encouraged these interpretive approaches with the manipulation of representations and visual cues.

***

Surprisingly few of the numerous critical responses to *M. Butterfly* discuss the staging at any length. In fact, the most popular scholarly approach to the play has involved various forms of gender theory, frequently applied to reach the conclusion that Rene Gallimard is a closeted homosexual, even though Frank Rich, theater critic of *The New York Times*, asserted shortly after the play's opening that Hwang "refuses to explain away Gallimard by making him a closeted, self-denying homosexual."[4] Other critics review the relation between *M. Butterfly* and Puccini's (or librettists Illica and Giacosa's) *Madama Butterfly*.[5] Gabrielle Cody and Kathryn Remen are among the few who talk about staging at length. Cody discusses staging in making her argument that the play's "most lyrically compelling moments" offer an ideology that undermines Hwang's stated intentions; Remen talks about staging in the course of arguing that Hwang's "Foucauldian understanding of power. ... transform[s] our theater from one of a traditional, observational arrangement into a spectacular theater of punishment that both involves and implicates the audience."[6]

The scenographer of *M. Butterfly*, Eiko Ishioka, has commented that the play "takes full advantage of how fantasy can be a source of both joy and danger," and said, "I knew I had to take this double-edged nature of fantasy and translate it to the stage somehow."[7] Ishioka, herself a Japanese woman, provides the Western audience of *M. Butterfly* with the same sense of disorientation and vertigo that the Frenchman Gallimard experiences until he can place Song, his "authentic" embassage of Asian culture, within familiar Orientalist tropes. Gallimard's difficulty in placing Song is part of his difficulty with locating himself within Western culture, and both are represented onstage by his difficulty in locating himself physically in the bustling streets of Beijing. Gallimard has difficulty finding out where he wants to go when he ventures beyond the diplomatic circle of Western ambassadors and European expatriates in Beijing to search out the site of the Peking opera. Ishioka does not reproduce that experience, but she reproduced its effect for the original production's spectators.

Ishioka's design for *M. Butterfly* was dramatic: it featured a Chinese red backdrop bisected by a white ramp spiraling out from between two wing flats, passing diagonally from upstage left across the stage to descend past the second set of wing flats, down into the empty orchestra pit. The area of the stage underneath the ramp was concealed sometimes by a framework of Chinese Chippendale-style screens and at other times by a scrim. The initial impact of the set provided a strong impression of color and geometry: a rounded rectangle bisected diagonally by the white line, the top half a very bright red, the bottom half black. Because, as Ishioka said herself, "a strong color like red on a minimalistic set tends to dominate the view," the set seemed to offer a two-dimensional representation of color: an abstract painting in three shades.[8] Lighting and the presence of actors could change that, of course. When the set was fully visible, lighting could

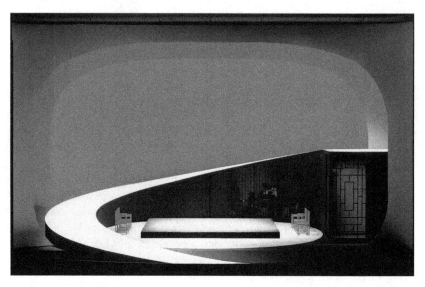

Figure 6.1 Photograph by Kuni Shinohara of the set for the Broadway production of
M. Butterfly. Courtesy Eiko Design, Inc. and Stuart Ostrow. © M. Butterfly Co.

"flip" the observer's sense of the stage-space, changing the perception of it from
a flat artwork to a three-dimensional set. The design still invoked geometry,
however, because of Dexter and Ishioka's desire "to create a continuous flow of
movement from the highest point on the set to the lowest point."[9]

To frame the set, Ishioka emphasized the proscenium arch, ensuring that the
frame of the action was a part of the audience's subliminal experience. Two pairs
of wing flats, painted the same red as the cyclorama in the background, curved
upwards into false prosceniums and were rounded as they met the floor. The
effect was a soaring, yet womb-like, somewhat rounded stage-space, resembling
in shape the rounded television screens of the 1960s.[10] The design both invited
the gaze of the audience and encouraged the audience to be conscious of their
watching, perhaps provoking in them a voyeuristic combination of guilt and
excitement. The audience experience was thereby linked to the voyeurism that
Gallimard gestures toward in 1.2, when he imagines a cocktail party in which
his sex life is the subject of current gossip, and in 1.5, when he imagines or
recollects looking through a window and watching a woman undress.

Audience members sitting well back in the auditorium would have been likely
to feel more detached from the action, more likely to perceive the set as an
abstract design. This perception, though dispersed by the presence of actors,
would be likely to leave behind some ambiguity about depth perception. Such
ambiguity would have been considerably enhanced by the use of three banners
created for the production: the enormous butterfly curtain (with the butterfly
formed out of birds and peonies), which fell at the end of act 1 and remained
for part of the second act; the vertical poster banner representing typical

workers drawn in a Communist propaganda style, used as a backdrop for the scene of Song's "rehabilitation"; and the similarly used poster banner featuring a raised fist holding a flower, representing the political unrest brewing in France when Gallimard returned in 1968. These three fabric hangings confuse the observer's sense of scale and reinforce the sense that the stage was meant to be perceived as flat, two-dimensional art. When the banners were in use, the production took on a Brechtian feel, as tiny figures moved and acted at the base of these huge icons of culture and history. Yet the curtains also functioned as propaganda posters, as commentaries on the action of the small, personal drama, and as graphic art.

Ishioka has said in print, "Theater sets should be powerfully expressive. ... I did not want [the set] to be just the humble underling of the script or the acting, or to be mere visual wallpaper."[11] Accordingly, perhaps, each curtain confirms one of the themes of the play and encourages the spectators to see the action as exemplifying the social conflicts of the time. The butterfly curtain represents the seductiveness of pure fantasy: the enormous outline of a butterfly at least twenty feet high appears on a golden background framed by a blue border patterned with Chinese dragons; the wings of the butterfly are formed by enormous pink and red camellias and their leaves; the body and the antennae of the butterfly are formed by three beautiful long-tailed birds. The image evokes the romance and the cruelty of Gallimard's fantasies (and Song's gratification of them). As Ishioka comments, Puccini's *Madama Butterfly* "provides the fantasy that binds together Gallimard's many mispresumptions. As the play unfolds, we find that this very need for fantasy is both sexist and racist."[12] Ishioka also comments on the importance of using silk and rich embroidery for Song Liling's costumes: "From a distance you couldn't tell that the gown was actually embroidered, but you could definitely sense the sumptuousness that only embroidery conveys."[13] Similarly, the sensuousness of the curtain was evident even at a distance.

Seeing a photograph of the curtain, one might assume that its purpose was to represent the allure of the Orient that so powerfully affects Rene Gallimard. But in production, that effect did not occur. The bold graphic design and its very strangeness both enticed the audience and held it at arm's length. The delicacy of the design recalls a line from *Madama Butterfly*: "Dicon che ... se cade in man dell'uom ogni farfalla d'uno spillo è trafitta ed in tavola infitta" ("They say that if it should fall into the hands of man a butterfly is stuck through with a pin and fixed to a board!").[14] Yet the sheer size of the image recalls Mothra (the Japanese monster-moth), and the way it seems to represent a butterfly on display rather than in flight made it difficult for audiences to see its delicacy. It is used after the first act, which concludes with Gallimard and Song's first night together, moving toward the bed as they softly sing the conclusion of Madame Butterfly's duet with her new "husband," Pinkerton. The curtain remains for the opening of the second act, in which Gallimard asserts that few men would pass up the chance to share the experiences of the selfish and opportunistic Pinkerton.[15] What would the spectators have seen?

Figure 6.2 Photograph by Kuni Shinohara of the butterfly curtain designed by Eiko Ishioka. Courtesy Eiko Design, Inc. and Stuart Ostrow. © M. Butterfly Co.

At first, perhaps, that the butterfly is fixed, unmoving—that for it to signify, they need to read some meaning into it themselves. Perhaps, as a curtain, it might suggest that the key to understanding the banner is to imagine what is behind it. But as the start of act 2 begins with Gallimard's comment that "while we men may all want to kick Pinkerton, very few of us would pass up the opportunity to *be* Pinkerton" (42), the sheer size of the image may become ominous—a gigantic butterfly, coming to wreak its revenge on the wimpy Gallimard, who so clearly craves the power to hurt women. Even the very tall actor who debuted the role of Gallimard, John Lithgow, was dwarfed by the butterfly, which was almost three times his size. Or perhaps the image represents the inauthenticity of the Oriental ideal that Gallimard craved to possess—a butterfly in the style of Archimboldo done in Asian flowers, the kind of kitschy Oriental art popular in Western countries when cheap Asian imports flooded our markets. In a photograph of the Broadway production, Gallimard stands under the butterfly's wing, reading from a leaflet. Ishioka's suggestions here are oblique, but surely the tableau intimates that Gallimard is in the thrall of the Butterfly.

The two political banners, though they appear more briefly, are crucial to contextualizing Gallimard's relation with Song: they contrast the ideals of Communist China with the practice, embodied in the actions of Song Liling; more broadly, they illuminate the themes of the play. The first banner is used in 2.9 for the scene of Song's trial; it represents the workers of Communist China. In front of a red background, three Chinese revolutionaries are pictured: an

officer in olive drab waves a red banner with a single star across the red background; on the left are two workers, a handsome woman wearing a kerchief on
her head, and a young, brawny man in a white shirt and a yellow neckerchief.
Both male figures have their arms bared to the elbow. Brawny, muscled arms
are much in evidence, and all three figures extend their fists, creating a complex
pattern of diagonals. Since both men extend their arms forward, the arms are
somewhat foreshortened, so that their fists look abnormally large, exaggerated
by the hyperrealistic art style as well as the sheer size of the banner. At the
bottom are white block letters spelling out "PEKING 1966–68." This image of
the worker glorifies labor, recalling the economic program of Mao's Great Leap
Forward, which took place from 1958 to 1961. The program's faith in manu-
facture and production was eventually succeeded by the Great Proletarian
Cultural Revolution of 1966–76, during which individuals perceived as Westernized or as in sympathy with Western culture were sent to re-education centers
to be cleansed of their errors through manual labor. Hwang's Gallimard briefly
summarizes the movement, explaining,

> Mao became very old, and his cult became very strong. And, like many old
> men, he entered his second childhood. So he handed over the reins of state
> to those with minds like his own. And children ruled the Middle Kingdom
> with complete caprice.

(68)

Figure 6.3 Photograph by Kuni Shinohara of Song Liling's trial, with Eiko Ishioka's
          "PEKING 1966–1968" banner as a transparent scrim.
          Courtesy Eiko Design, Inc. and Stuart Ostrow. © M. Butterfly Co.

Part of the strategy for cultural change during this period was to indoctrinate the young, and fanatical teens were mobilized as members of a "Red Guard" who proselytized the doctrine of Mao and sought to root out elements of Western corruption. The banner typifies the Communist propaganda poster in its idealization of the worker and the worker's body: the men are handsome, the women good looking; bulging muscle groups indicate physical strength and hint at the worker's determination and resolve. The fact that all the figures on this banner are in the prime of life reminds us how the PRC had left behind the veneration of the aged so central to Confucian tradition: the young couple in the foreground are working together as a unit for the betterment of China. The image manifests an assumption that a normal family unit is a two-person heterosexual pair; the ideology of normative heterosexual formation also underlies this representation of the new China.

At the same time, however, graphic elements of the banner undermine the heteronormative assumptions it presents. Notably, the exposed arms and clenched fists rising up, across, and out of the backgrounds resemble erect phalluses forcefully asserting their aggressive masculinity. The Communist salute with the raised fist parallels and parodies the aggressive sexual act, as fisting (in the popular straight imagination) exaggerates the violent penetration of anal sex so often read as a humiliation and unmanning of the recipient. The image works against the aggressive heterosexuality of the workers pictured, suggesting that concealed homoeroticism may lie beneath the overt heterosexuality of Chinese Communist culture. This implication adds an additional layer to the initial contrast between the aggression of the poster's heterosexual salutes and the passive, often non-penetrative sex that Gallimard recounts he has had with Song: "ever so delicately, and only if I agreed, she would start to pleasure me. With her hands, her mouth ... too many ways to explain" (49). Yet it is in front of this poster that Song performs her exaggerated, crude confession: "I engaged in the lowest perversions with China's enemies! ... I let him put it up my ass! ... My language ... is only as foul as the crimes I committed" (70). In an earlier scene, Song has brusquely dismissed Comrade Chin's concern that she is "not gathering information in any way that violates Communist Party principles": in response to Comrade Chin's urging, "Remember: when working for the Great Proletarian State, you represent our Chairman Mau in every position you take," Song dryly answers, "I'll try to imagine the Chairman taking my positions" (48). Song seems to imagine that despite her spying and despite the substantial network of Party affiliates throughout China, society will overlook indiscretions like her affair with Gallimard indefinitely. She fails to anticipate the dangers as her culture changes abruptly, almost from one month to the next.

At the same time, the poster comments on the play's challenge to essential definitions of gender that results from including not only a male-to-female cross-dresser, Song Liling, but also another spy, the female Comrade Chin, whose Mao suit and chunky build give the impression of a female-to-male cross-dresser. For gender studies scholar Marjorie Garber, the play is "intermittently antifeminist and homophobic, ridiculing the *female* cross-dresser, Miss Chin, while it elevates Gallimard's plight to the plane of high drama."[16] Melinda Boyd takes issue with Garber: she sees Chin as evidence not of "a clash between East and West [but of] a significant gap between the old order and the new within Chinese culture itself."[17] Boyd points out that Chin will later shore up her self-confidence by aggressively asserting her new status as wife and mother: "From Chin's perspective, it is she, not Song, who epitomizes not just the 'successful Communist,' but, more importantly, 'successful' femininity, for bachelors and spinsters were equally outcasts in Communist China."[18] The poster calls our attention specifically to the question of gender in Chinese Communist propaganda: can sexual difference be acknowledged when the prevailing ideology demands the elimination of class difference?

Most of all, the banner draws our attention to the shaping power of clothing and costume. Though the woman bears a striking resemblance to her male counterpart, her glossy lips, her modest bosom under the shirt, and her kerchief, which wraps her hair rather than being draped around her neck, all provide an alternative Communist model—the female comrade. Can Song serve the Chairman in positions that she cannot imagine him taking?

The banner challenges the audience to recognize Song's clothes as signifying markers and to see how Song uses these markers to manipulate Gallimard, a naïve reader who fails fully to recognize Song's control over her signifiers. Song wears many different costumes throughout the play. She first appears in traditional Chinese garb, then in Madame Butterfly costumes; she appears in one scene wearing a slinky black outfit that makes her look *"like Anna May Wong"* (Hwang, 27). Later, she wears a dressing gown, a cheong sam, a Mao suit, and finally a man's Armani suit. Some of these outfits may be common clothing for Asian women, but for Westerners they are unusual enough to be perceived as costumes—and as easily readable costumes. They represent, variously, traditional Chinese culture, Japanese culture, Westernized Japanese culture, Communist Chinese culture, and contemporary European fashion. We can interpret the changes either as a suggestion that Song's identity is totally fluid, entirely dependent on circumstances, or as an intimation that the actor is a *tabula rasa* upon which others project their expectations or their fantasies.

The final banner designed by Ishioka was more abstract: red with black patterning in a woodcut style, it imitates the silk-screened posters of many late twentieth-century student movements and the poster art of the May 1968 student protests in particular. This banner pictures a huge, upraised fist holding a rose aloft; enormous letters above proclaim "AURORE"; smaller black letters run behind the arm, commenting, "LE TEMPS VIEILLE." Other phrases appear in various blocks in graffiti style: "Front Populaire," "Le Mao Seul Revolutionnaire," "la culture est l'inversion," "Non à l'amour-mort, oui à l'amour-libre." Block letters at the bottom in a very different style spell out "PARIS 1968–70." The banner provides visual context for the events in 2.11, which directly reference the events of May 1968. May 1968 was the brief period of political upheaval in France when, sparked by student protests, demonstrations, riots, and strikes

Figure 6.4 Photograph by Kuni Shinohara of Ishioka's set with the "PARIS 1968–1970" banner. Courtesy Eiko Design, Inc. and Stuart Ostrow. © M. Butterfly Co.

brought life to a standstill. France's president, Charles de Gaulle, fled the country temporarily; France teetered on the brink of a revolution somewhat akin to that of China. The protests occurred in response to the government's closing of the University of Paris at Nanterre.

Though the events of May 1968 began with student protests at the University of Paris, the administrators' unwise decision to call in the police resulted in a march; organized by the national student union and the union of university professors, it involved 20,000 students. Further police violence against protesters backfired: more students occupied university buildings, eventually joined by nearly eleven million workers, who not only participated in a general strike but also occupied their own factories. Both students and workers refused the government's offer of leniency for the arrested students and a wage increase for workers—even a twenty-five percent increase in the minimum wage; instead, they held out for a major change in workers' rights and a broader, more radical agenda of restructuring the social system. After de Gaulle capitulated by calling for new elections, however, the protests died away, and initially the only result was actually to strengthen the President's party. But more arguable change came in the years that followed, and the events of May 1968 are still remembered internationally as one of the more successful popular movements of a turbulent decade.

The scene in *M. Butterfly* for which the banner is a backdrop, 2.11, is a crucial scene for understanding Gallimard in Brechtian terms. The scene is comic, as the student riots bring an end to Gallimard's marriage, which has been a sham for some years. The scene initially deflects attention from Gallimard's failure to comprehend the political theater by scapegoating his wife, Helga, instead. Her inability to grasp the larger political situation that prompts student unrest cannot, however, entirely paper over Gallimard's own refusal to understand the political dimension to his life.

Helga enters soaking wet, having been caught up outside in a tide of student protesters and then doused by water cannons wielded by the police. Recounting what has just happened, Helga concludes her explanation with an oblique plea for sympathy from Gallimard: "Rene, what's happening to France?" (74). Gallimard refuses to engage with her distress or her outrage, responding, "Nothing! ... that I care to think about" (74). Helga attempts to draw a parallel between the political situations in France and China, pointing out, "When we left, this exact same thing, the riots ... [s]tudents screaming slogans, smashing down doors ... It was all going on in China, too. Don't you remember?" (74). Helga expresses a desire to comprehend the political situation, asking her husband to look at the events outside his window and develop a hypothesis that explains the correlation of events in the two countries. Gallimard, however, is now obsessed with his image of Song as the Perfect Woman, a concept that he laboriously explains to the audience later in this scene after he finds his friend Marc, a Don Juan, less than fascinated by his stories of Song. Gallimard conflates his notion of Song as the Perfect Woman with his perception of Song as typically Asian (typically Oriental, to be precise). And, seeing the Song he knows as the emblem of China, Gallimard summarily dismisses Helga's version of events: "You walk in here with these ridiculous ideas, that the West is falling apart, that China was spitting in our faces. You come in, dripping of the streets, and you leave water all over my floor" (74). When Helga urges, "But it's the truth!" he asks for a divorce (74–75).

Gallimard's withdrawal from public life in favor of seclusion with his fantasies and his memories of Song becomes evident in this scene; this aspect of his life in France *must* be staged, as Gallimard lacks the self-knowledge to recount it. More significantly, however, the scene also contrasts Gallimard with Helga; though interested primarily in the students' effects upon her own life, Helga attempts to gain perspective on what has just happened to her. She is able to look outside herself enough to guess that the rioting in China and in France signifies political upheaval—and may herald political change. To ask "What is happening?" may simply be Helga's plea for sympathy along the lines of "They're all crazy!" but her query could also indicate an interest in understanding the underlying causes of the protest movements. Gallimard, however, has come to see political institutions in terms of cultural clichés based on Occidental/Oriental gender constructs. Gallimard sees political change primarily in terms of how it affects his ability to see Song: "The doctrine of the Cultural Revolution implied continuous anarchy. Contact between Chinese and foreigners became impossible. Our flat was confiscated. Her fame and my money now counted against us" (68). When the reunion between Song and Gallimard occurs onstage, Gallimard fails to ask a single question about what Song has done since they parted four years earlier or how she escaped from Communist China. It is not until Song takes over the narrative in act 3 that we learn that Gallimard actively betrays his country after that point:

SONG: [F]inally, at my urging, Rene got a job as a courier, handling sensitive documents. He'd photograph them for me, and I'd pass them on to the Chinese embassy.
JUDGE: Did he understand the extent of his activity?
SONG: He didn't ask. He knew I needed those documents, and that was enough.

(81)

The banner nudged the audience to recognize the larger conditions that make Song a spy and Gallimard her prey. It also helped spectators to see the connection between popular power in the two countries that Gallimard was unwilling or unable to examine. The French banner, like the Chinese one, features a raised fist, frequently an emblem of the left; this symbol reminds us, if not the Gallimards, that France's politics were moving in the same direction as China's. Both banners also recall a period when popular movements prompted amateurs to design and paste up posters like these because groups of civilians believed they had the power to effect political change. History tells us that they *were* correct, and the fact that they could have such far-reaching effects is a potent reminder that personal actions are political, that they support or undermine government policies. For Gallimard's affair with Song to continue, he had to maintain his ignorance of that idea. And in doing so, Gallimard made himself a pawn that political institutions could move for their own advantage.

***

For these backdrops to force their meanings upon the audience, they had to be visually overwhelming—and they were. Given their size, ten or more paces across and almost as high as the proscenium arch, how could they have failed to make an impression? The answer is simple. The spectators sitting close to the stage of the Eugene O'Neill did not see the banners in their entirety as they watched the action: their visual field could not encompass the entire image. Those audience members who had to tilt their heads to see the entire banner were much more likely to accept them as backdrops and focus on the actors, who were closer to them and larger—larger, in perspective, than they were for those sitting in the mezzanine or the back of the orchestra. I contend that these members of the audience are, in essence, seeing a different play, a play in three dimensions, so to speak—one much more focused on the characters (as represented by the actors onstage) and their personal motivations. Though this *M. Butterfly* shares the other version's concern with bodies, this version differs in genre: it is in essence a memory play, in which the stage-space represents the consciousness of the narrator from the beginning.

As a memory play in the classic American tradition, *M. Butterfly* offers the audience the opportunity to enter the narrator's consciousness. Since such landmark works as *The Glass Menagerie*, however, the whole status of memory has changed. Tennessee Williams insisted in 1944 that *The Glass Menagerie* should draw on experimental staging techniques only in order to convey a stronger sense of "truth":

> Expressionism and all other unconventional techniques in drama have only one valid aim, and that is a closer approach to truth. When a play employs unconventional techniques, it is not, or certainly shouldn't be, trying to escape its responsibility of dealing with reality.[19]

There is no such "reality" in Hwang's play, the basis of which is the misconceptions, stereotypes, generalizations, and fantasies of Westerners about Asia and its inhabitants. Hwang succinctly crystallizes the absurdity that is the basis of the play when he explains in the afterword to the printed text, "I ... asked myself, 'What did Bouriscot think he was getting in this Chinese actress?' The answer came to me clearly: 'He probably thought he had found Madame Butterfly'" (Afterword, 95).

The fluidity of identity in the play that Hwang's comment implies is paralleled by the fluidity of the play's settings. *M. Butterfly* is a subjective representation of the past—a dream play as well as a memory play. The stage largely represents Gallimard's consciousness, though, as we have seen, history literally becomes a backdrop at times, and Gallimard's consciousness is posed against the fabric of his time. Gallimard's memory theater is history as Walter Benjamin characterizes it: seizing hold of a memory as it "flashes up at a moment of danger."[20] As Benjamin asserts,

> The true picture of the past flits by. The past can be seized only as an image which flashes up at the instant when it can be recognized and is never seen again. ... For every image of the past that is not recognized by the present as one of its own concerns threatens to disappear irretrievably.[21]

For our purposes, Benjamin's lyrical comment conveys this suggestion: Gallimard's drama, which seems at first to be his recollection, must be recognized as a retrospective creation of his own—one based in large part on what he imagines his reputation must be throughout France. *M. Butterfly* enacts the partial nature of memory, reshaping the conventions of the memory play.

Hwang presents events, then, but not "truth," and in some scenes he offers the audience no way to tell whether the events are pure fantasy or productions of Gallimard's memory. Nor can we tell whether these memories are accurate or have been distorted by time and desire. *M. Butterfly*, though a type of memory theater, stages memory rather less than it does the self: Gallimard's self. And that self is multiform: the self of 1986, explaining himself to an ideal audience and evaluating himself with the perspective he has gained from the trial; the self who overhears (or imagines) himself as the subject of cocktail party gossip; the fantasy self-as-Pinkerton; the adolescent self; and past adult selves from 1960 to the play's present.

While the perspective of the play is that of Rene Gallimard, the subject could be characterized equally as "the body," "gender roles," or "the force of fantasy." For spectators close enough to the stage, these subjects were embodied physically in the play's staging of the spectators' own desire for the sight of Butterfly's body. Spectators could not ignore the physical aspect of the play's subject matter: sexual anatomy and the presence or absence of the phallus. As interpreters, however, they were unlikely to have noticed that the play's concern with these issues is contained within the ambiguity of the play's title. Throughout most of the play, watchers assume that the name "M. Butterfly" refers to Song: the play makes no secret of Song Liling's true biological identity, and Gallimard explicitly states in 2.2 that his pet name for Song is "Butterfly." So the play's conclusion, when Gallimard claims the name "M. Butterfly" for himself, is a complete surprise; the *coup de théâtre* recalls the titular ambiguity of *The Merchant of Venice*. (Antonio becomes a much more significant figure once we remember that he, not Shylock, is the title character.) The play's focus on "the body" should not obscure the interest it arouses in specific bodies: those of Song Liling and, eventually, of Gallimard. Staging the play, Eiko Ishioka and the director John Dexter staged Gallimard's obsession with the body, eventually transferring it to the audience itself. The stage they created represents the body of Song Liling but represents it through absence, through lack and flickering presence, as seems only appropriate for a play about a body that both possesses and lacks a phallus.

For many onlookers, then, *M. Butterfly* focused obsessively on Song's body, heightening their voyeuristic interest by emphasizing both Gallimard's experience of Song's body and his failure to see what should have been obvious. In contrast to Gallimard, who chooses more than once not to part his Butterfly's robes to reveal the body underneath, the audience cannot help but long to penetrate Song's mystery—Song's clothing, Song's thoughts, Song's identity as male or female, straight or gay. The partial penetration of Song's spaces—her culture, her home, and her body—is staged, particularly in acts 1 and 2: partly with lighting that showcases Song as a fantasy element in various places on the stage structure; partly with the repeated references to Song's false femaleness; and occasionally with invasive entrances that may be read as penetrations into Song's personal territory. At the climax, when Song's body is revealed, the audience shares with Gallimard the chance to see for the first time the phallic body of the male actor who forces his naked masculinity upon Gallimard's consciousness.[22] Rape—forcible penetration of an unwilling victim—is emblematized by these aggressive intrusions, though there is never overt physical violence.

M. Butterfly complicates the progression of self-revelation that we saw in Ford's *'Tis Pity She's a Whore* by featuring two protagonists whose trajectories of revelation cross during the course of the play. In *'Tis Pity*, the spectacle urged the audience toward a prurient interest in Annabella's body; access to the character's inwardness was metaphorized as the sight of Annabella in the act of sex (ironically, the fact that a boy actor played the role renders the situation somewhat akin to that of *M. Butterfly*); yet what that play first offers is access to Annabella's private thoughts and, at the end, to her biological interior (her heart on a dagger). The dramatic arc of *M. Butterfly* offers two progressions that move in inverse relation to one another. As the audience gains greater access to Rene Gallimard's thoughts, they become increasingly eager to gain access to the sight of Song Liling's body, which is revealed in act 3; once Song begins to speak out and offers his own view as the dominant perspective in act 3, the body of Gallimard is substituted for that of Song as the object of the audience's gaze, and the play concludes with the same biological revelation as that offered in *'Tis Pity*.

The first two acts of *M. Butterfly* focus through both plot and staging on the physical penetration of Song's various spaces. This misdirection occurs in conjunction with the presentation of the story as a memory play narrated by Gallimard. But the play's final scene turns its tables on the audience: the revelation is not that Song is a man (stale!) but that Gallimard is the true Monsieur Butterfly. *M. Butterfly* stages Gallimard's thoughts and memories throughout the first two-thirds of the play, but the concluding act suddenly and violently draws the spectator's attention to the Frenchman's body when he presents himself as Monsieur Butterfly. His secret is revealed as his own metamorphosis into the feminized Oriental body, and the revelation of his consciousness throughout the play is succeeded by the revelation of his body at its conclusion.

The staging of *M. Butterfly* is particularly important to this drama's personal dimension because of the play's emphasis on lies, misperceptions, and surfaces. In his afterword to the play, Hwang comments that cultural stereotypes, "myths" as he calls them, so thoroughly "saturate our consciousness that truthful contact between nations and lovers can only be the result of heroic effort. Those who prefer to bypass the work involved will remain in a world of surfaces" (100). While it could truthfully be said that surfaces are drama's stock-in-trade, it is equally true that surfaces are an element that countless dramas try to shatter. Appropriately, then, *M. Butterfly* stages penetration of space as a metonymy for the penetration of surfaces, appearances, stereotypes or, in Hwang's term, myths. As in *'Tis Pity She's a Whore*, the stage of *M. Butterfly* is a space penetrated both by actors' entrances and by the spectators' watching eyes, the playgoers' active attempts to penetrate the concealment and opacity of Gallimard's self-interested explanations. Interest in Song's body is represented onstage by the progressive penetration of her personal spaces onstage. This penetration should be viewed, however, in conjunction with the staging of proxemics and penetration in *M. Butterfly*'s parent text, *Madama Butterfly*.

Hwang's reference to "a world of surfaces" surely alludes, among other things, to Gallimard's rampant Orientalism, which the play suggests originated in the libretto of Puccini's opera. Recent interpretations of *Madama Butterfly*, however, reveal that there is more than one way to read the story. Gallimard's one-dimensional interpretation of *Madama Butterfly* is limited by his European perspective; equally, Song's scornful comments fail to take into account Japanese values. With sympathy, feminism, or a culturally Asian perspective, it is possible to see Illica and Giacosa's Butterfly as strong, not weak; motivated by honor, not passion; true to Japanese values, not her American love. These possibilities are evident not only in the libretto but also in the way the opera is commonly staged. A brief examination of the traditional staging of Puccini's *Madama Butterfly* will demonstrate that the possibility of depth, of three-dimensionality, is inherent in the very *sine qua non* with which Gallimard begins.

Essentially, the typical staging of Puccini's *Madama Butterfly* can be taken either as a visual correlative to Cio-cio-san's statement, "Noi siamo gente avvezza alle piccole cose, umili e silenziose" ("We are a people used to small, modest, quiet things"), or a subversion of that statement.[23] There is only one set, generally a proscenium stage with a Japanese house set upon a plinth. The plinth suggests the hilltop location of the house mentioned several times (the American consul Sharpless, for example, is heard offstage commenting, "You sweat and climb, puff and stumble!").[24] Shoji screens and minimal furniture offer great flexibility; as a result, lighting takes center stage.[25] The tableau emphasized by the proscenium arch almost invariably offers a series of strong horizontals formed by the long plinth and the sliding rectangles of the screens, sometimes topped by a quaint pagoda roof. As a typical Japanese structure, the design recalls Frank Lloyd Wright's dictum, "No house should ever be on a hill. It should be of the hill. Belonging to it."[26]

This set is dictated by comments in the opening scene in which the marriage broker, Goro, is showing Lieutenant Pinkerton, an American naval officer stationed in Nagasaki, the house that Pinkerton has just leased to live in with his temporary wife. Pinkerton's first words reveal his amusement at what he sees as the quaintness of shoji screens and multipurpose room areas. Goro explains that the walls "go back and forth at will, so that you can enjoy from the same spot different views to the usual ones."[27] Despite Goro's insistence that the house is "solid as a tower, from floor to ceiling," Pinkerton comments that "this ridiculous little place. ... is a concertina house."[28] Whether or not the house is structurally sound, what Pinkerton has failed to note is the screens' ability to conceal and to restructure the space they enclose.

The flexibility of the architectural design is emblematic, I think, of Cio-cio-san herself: both of her concealed strength and her ability to reconceive herself in relation to Japan. Thus, the opera stages Butterfly analogically. What is most evident in the opera initially is Butterfly's desire to reconfigure herself as Madame B. F. Pinkerton rather than Madame Butterfly. This desire, evident in her decision to convert to Christianity and adopt Western customs, seems at first to be a sign of her submissiveness—the kind of action that Asians today call "pulling a Butterfly." From this point of view, Butterfly's attempts to Americanize herself or adapt to Pinkerton's presumed preferences may seem distasteful or even grotesque. But those attempts can be read very differently: as a strategy learned by geishas to adapt themselves to their customers' tastes, for example. The musicologist Vera Micznik argues that Butterfly's submissiveness is actually a manifestation of her training as a geisha. In Micznik's view, after Pinkerton's desertion, the geisha subservience seems to disappear. As she grows throughout the opera, as she gradually has to accept reality, Butterfly gives up both the hopes and strength—the façade of the geisha in her and the fetishistic borrowing of the language, customs, and music of the foreigner—that served as her life support. Her language matures, the music becomes more and more her own, filled with anxiety and dissolution, and that of her ancestors, thus signalling the danger that once she lets go of her fetish, she can no longer live.[29]

One can also perceive Butterfly's desire to become Americanized as evidence of her resilience, or flexibility, perhaps: an ability to reimagine herself. Certainly, neither Japan nor Butterfly is portrayed as entirely soft and yielding, and in staging the drama, the softness and insubstantiality of set, lighting, and costumes are contrasted with a few hard unyielding principles and their staged representations. Most notably, among the few possessions concealed in the soft "wings" of Butterfly's capacious kimono is one long, rigid object: the sword with which Butterfly's father committed hara-kiri at the order of the Mikado. Her concealment of this phallic object suggests that Butterfly may conceal a masculine strength beneath her submissiveness. As she produces the sword on her wedding day, Puccini's scoring shifts from the rising and falling pentatonic motif that accompanies the appearance of Butterfly's other possessions to a violent stroke of strings in a descending chromatic arpeggio, followed by a brief melody in a minor key. Butterfly refuses to answer Pinkerton's inquiry about the nature of this object and puts it away carefully. Later in the opera, the honorable actions of Butterfly's father will be contrasted with those of Pinkerton, who relies on Sharpless, the consul, to tell Butterfly that he has broken his troth and married an American woman. Even at the opening, Butterfly's regard for this sword, for which she makes a place of honor visible throughout the rest of the opera, suggests that she too would be able to act in a similarly honorable manner, even though she tries to adapt to Western culture upon her marriage. Her eventual use of the sword shows her willingness to follow her father's example. Exhibiting what Japanese people would have considered masculine courage, Butterfly's suicide also suggests a reversion to Japanese culture.

Much of the opera does feature the title character fluttering around the stage like a butterfly—not least because act 1 presents Butterfly's wedding, and part of act 2 shows her joyous preparation for Pinkerton's return. Act 1 closes, in fact, with the first embrace of Pinkerton and Butterfly: the guests have departed, Butterfly has donned her nightclothes, and Pinkerton himself states that he "is consumed by a fever / of sudden desire."[30] To Butterfly's fear of being pierced like an insect on a pin, Pinkerton replies, as he wraps his arms around her, that he will catch her and keep her safe. But act 2 emphasizes Pinkerton's absence; entrances and exits show Butterfly acting both as Pinkerton's representative and as a phallic—or perhaps genital—representation of sexuality on her own behalf. In act 2, Butterfly asserts to Suzuki that Pinkerton had the house fitted with locks "to keep mosquitos, / relations and troubles outside."[31] In accordance with what she believes to be her husband's wishes, Butterfly tells her Japanese suitor to leave and shoves the marriage broker off the stage.

Butterfly herself leaves the stage only once before the twilight interlude of the "Humming Chorus": upon the consul's urging that she should forget Pinkerton. To blaring trumpets repeating rising arpeggios in a major key, she exits and then returns to the stage carrying a child. Butterfly's confidence in the effect that her fecundity will have upon Pinkerton is reinforced by the music, which reaches its climax upon the appearance of mother and child; the dramatic moment is heightened because there has been no sign or mention of her son until that moment. Butterfly's reentrance with the boy held aloft represents sexual penetration and more. The fanfare motif, the clash of cymbals, and the eager, galloping—even, perhaps, "horny"—motif played by trumpets and strings suggest sexual climax[32] and its result. The staging, the music, and her words link sex, motherhood, and triumph as Butterfly's faith in the child's power to transform her situation is revealed. Butterfly's revelation of the child pierces Sharpless's embarrassed obfuscation and, recalling the desire that inspired Pinkerton to marry Butterfly, demonstrates that their union has had results that cannot be denied.

Butterfly's heroic stature does not rest on her fecundity alone, of course, but on her transformation from an avowedly non-heroic stature ("Noi siamo gente avvezza alle piccole cose, umili e silenziose") to a greater one. Gallimard's reading of the opera is unusually thick-headed; he calls Butterfly's death "a pure sacrifice": "He's unworthy, but what can she do? She loves him ... so much" (17). Butterfly offers two motives for her suicide: in her rereading of the sword's inscription—"He dies with honor who cannot live with honor"—and her explanation to her unknowing child: "Butterfly is about to die ... so that you may go away beyond the sea without being subject to remorse in later years for your mother's desertion."[33] Though Vera Micznik asserts that, according to Puccini's music, Butterfly dies "because death was the natural outcome inscribed in her condition," she also alludes to "the pentatonic 'Japanese' hymn of the closing measures, often thought of as representing Butterfly's redemption by having finally returned to her original faith."[34] Butterfly does not sacrifice herself *for* Pinkerton; she commits suicide, following her father's example, to retain the honorable position that she would lose if she continued to live as Pinkerton's cast-off rental. His considerable remorse is not the point, though it gratifies the heart of every female watcher I have known. The point is Butterfly's self-assertion, her refusal to take herself at Pinkerton's valuation, and her decision to engage in what her culture characterized as a traditionally masculine act of courage on her own initiative.[35] As I said earlier, the strong horizontal lines of the traditional set for this opera, which stay low, hugging the ground, are also changing throughout the opera to enclose or expand the interior, restructuring the domestic space according to Cio-cio-san's needs. The humble, girlish bride surprises us by manifesting psychological complexity that belies easy East-West, masculine-feminine dichotomies.

A superficial consideration of Ishioka's set for *M. Butterfly* may find no similarities to the sets commonly designed for *Madama Butterfly*. The colors are bold, the set minimal and non-representational; it seems designed as a framework for the fluid shifts in scene appropriate to a complex plot with multiple scene-changes. Nonetheless, in the use of stark geometry, sliding screens, and the emphasis on light as an integral part of the set, Dexter and Ishioka echo the traditional stage set of *Madama Butterfly*. While *Madama Butterfly* sets generally draw on Japanese architecture, Ishioka's set for *M. Butterfly* drew on the conventions of Kabuki, one of several types of traditional theater in Japan.

Eiko Ishioka explains that the initial interest in Kabuki elements came from the play's director:

> [Dexter] hated the way technology was used on Broadway—the flashing laser beams and motor-driven revolving stages. "To me," he explained, "the *kurogo* idea of Kabuki theater [stagehands dressed in black to make them 'invisible'] is the most sophisticated technology I've seen on stage. Keep that in mind." ... In fact, Dexter ended up reinterpreting *kurogo* for *M. Butterfly*; it was probably the first time anyone on Broadway had done it.[36]

Equally, however, other Kabuki elements were incorporated into the Chinese setting in order to represent the *Japonisme* of Gallimard's obsession, as well as his Orientalist confusion of East Asian cultures. The very fiber of *M. Butterfly* derives from the use of the traditions of transvestite theater in the characterization of Song Liling. Just as the Peking opera uses all-male casts, Kabuki theater has, since 1629, used *onnagata*, specially trained male actors, to enact female roles. The *onnagata* tradition seems to adumbrate the vexed question of Song's true relation to Gallimard. Yoseharu Ozaki explains that the term *onnagata* can mean both "one in charge of a woman part" and "the female shape or form ... i.e. the ideal feminine form, and also one who embodies that ideal, i.e. not simply an imitator of a living woman but a creator of the woman in ideal form both physically and spiritually."[37] Gallimard's reiterated insistence that Song is "the Perfect Woman" may be less a sign of enormous gender confusion than of his submission to the ideology upon which the *onnagata* in Kabuki was based.

The most notable Kabuki element of Ishioka's set is the ramp, whose design resembles that of the Kabuki theater's *hanamichi*.[38] The *hanamichi* is a platform walkway, about five feet wide, running from the back of the theater to the stage, joining it about fifteen feet from the wings to stage right. The term means "flower way," and refers metaphorically to "the unique appeal of the individual actor's performance."[39] Though in basic terms the *hanamichi* functions as an aisle actors use in entering and exiting, these entrances and exits assume such an importance in Kabuki that an actor can take twenty minutes to traverse the *hanamichi*. Actors often pause in their progress to enact *mie*, static poses and "display sequences" occurring during the course of a performance. As John Wesley Harris points out, the *hanamichi* is "ideally placed to achieve an aesthetic 'isolation' from the stage while still preserving a strong diagonal relationship to any actors who are occupying a central position."[40] It allows an actor to "warm himself gradually into his role with the audience all around him from the moment that he enters the auditorium" and enables the actors, by allowing them to come "into the audience from the stage, [to] arouse a strong sense of affinity with the audience."[41] Ishioka comments on how the ramp she designed functioned within the production:

> Made entirely of wood, with small interlocking panels creating the curve, the ramp was only six feet wide and without edges. It was quite dangerous for the actors. ... With practice, all of the actors became adept at running up and down, but I imagine it was especially scary for someone as tall as John Lithgow, who played Gallimard, the French diplomat. There was one scene that required a lot from him in particular: when he discovers the true identity of his lover, in a state of shock he falls down and rolls all the way to the bottom of the ramp.[42]

As should be evident, while the design of the Eugene O'Neill Theatre aligns it solidly with a nineteenth-century European theatrical tradition, incorporation of Japanese elements on the stage created a promiscuous visual mix that reinforced the play's concern with culture clashes and cultural misreadings.

In planning the stage design, John Dexter specified that the set "should have three levels of interplay (top, middle, and bottom) [and] that the mechanics should be kept simple."[43] In response, Eiko Ishioka created flexible staging that could easily be altered to achieve different effects. Within the space formed by the spiraling ramp was an oval platform of blond wood and, on top of that, a

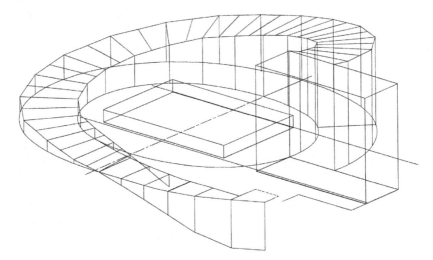

Figure 6.5 3-D computer simulation by Duke Durfee of Eiko Ishioka's design for the ramp of M. *Butterfly.*
Courtesy Eiko Design, Inc. and Stuart Ostrow. © M. Butterfly Co.

black, rectangular plinth. The bright overhead lighting suggested a sterile environment (used to great advantage in both the prison scenes and the court scene). Red lacquered chairs were placed at each side of the platform, and a matching bench sat at the center. Though the ramp's support system was concealed by black velvet hangings during parts of the play, for others, Ishioka installed "a gauzy scrim covering the space at the bottom of [underneath] the ramp. When lit from behind, any action on the other side would be visible. When lit from the front, however, the scrim would become completely opaque, a true wall."[44] A rolling set of bars and two sets of Chippendale lattice screens could be used to suggest a specific location. Ishioka's design ensured that the locales of the visual tableaux could shift fluidly from world to consciousness to embodiment and back. In the opening, for example, "*Lights fade up to reveal Rene Gallimard, 65, in a prison cell. … Upstage Song, who appears as a beautiful woman in traditional Chinese garb, dances a traditional piece from the Peking opera, surrounded by the percussive clatter of Chinese music*" (1). Song's dance, which began at stage left at the top of the spiral ramp, is clearly Gallimard's fantasy, fragmented recollections of many performances. As Song moved back and forth, staying high up and well upstage, her long sleeves, which swooped as she gestured, seemed to weave a spell. Later in the play, the Chippendale screens are lit, the area behind them darkened, to suggest a scene at an ambassadorial

Figure 6.6 Photograph of the opening scene of *M. Butterfly*, the prison where Gallimard recalls the past. Photographer unknown.
Courtesy Eiko Design, Inc. and Stuart Ostrow. © M. Butterfly Co.

function; still later, the screen is shadowed, the area behind it uplit in red to represent Song Liling's apartment. At one point, *kurogo* help Song Liling change kimonos as she squats halfway up the ramp on the far stage right.

Dexter's blocking used Ishioka's set to stage Gallimard's and Song's attempts to penetrate each other both sexually and metaphorically. Each character tries to penetrate the façade of cultural behaviors and gendered behaviors in order to read the other's feelings. I shall begin this section by showing how penetration of Song is staged by Gallimard's intrusions into the spaces she owns or controls, and then examining what these stagings suggest about Song.

Song is a performer, first and foremost. He identifies himself as such to the judge in act 3. As an actor, Song draws tremendous power from his place: the stage, which functions as a representational space, a space which embodies "complex symbolisms, sometimes coded, sometimes not, linked to the clandestine or underground side of social life, as also to art."[45] Yet the stage also renders Song vulnerable to the audience's gaze, and Gallimard, an accomplished voyeur, draws strength from watching Song as one member of a multitude in an anonymous throng. Song's identities and the position of power over Gallimard that each identity attains may be traced by charting the progression of Gallimard's attempts to penetrate Song's personal space at the pinnacle of the ramp. After he becomes familiar with the Chinese opera, the place where she performs publicly, Gallimard goes to that part of the stage and enters her private apartment. This place becomes the site where he attempts to explore her body, disrobe her, and penetrate her body through sexual intercourse. Later, after he has moved her to an apartment he owns, where she is technically "under his protection," he attempts to disrobe her once again. It is only in act 3, when Song is no longer cross-dressed, that Gallimard begins to consider what he might find if he penetrated Song's heart or her mind.

As the action moves through the period of their liaison, stage entrances—and the lack of them—reinforce Gallimard's anxious desire for dominance. He tries to torment Song, but characteristically uses physical absence as his weapon. To test her affection, he ceases coming to her performances. As Song tries to lure him back with a series of rhetorical ploys, he becomes increasingly complacent at the success of his passive-aggressive strategy. Gallimard demonstrates his increased sexual confidence at his office, conversing in fantasy with his friend Marc while he energetically fulfills his responsibilities sorting papers, cleaning out files, writing a position paper on trade, attending a diplomatic reception. Then, greeted at another ambassadorial party by his intimidating boss, Gallimard learns that he has been promoted. When Ambassador Toulon, his superior, praises the "new aggressive confident … thing" that Gallimard has become, as well as Gallimard's ability to "get along with the Chinese," Gallimard's egotism expands further. His cruel treatment of Song seems to have been justified, and he feels able to meet her on a new footing. He climbs the ramp to bang at her door late at night, almost forcing his way in, and challenges her: "I've come tonight for an answer: are you my Butterfly?" (38, 39). Only after she shamefacedly gives him an affirmation does he proclaim his love for her and move to the next step: "*He starts to caress her; her gown begins to open*" (40). Their love (as he sees it) is consummated that night, shortly after he accedes to Song's request to darken the room in order to respect her "modesty." Gallimard now fails to recognize that it is passivity—the refusal to visit—that has won him his success with Song; he sees himself as the aggressive Pinkerton who proclaims his desire to "take ... his pleasure and his profit, indifferent to all risks" in *Madama Butterfly*.[46] Though Gallimard and Song conclude act 1 by initiating sexual involvement that presumably includes his climax, he respects her wish and does not try to remove her clothes. This paradoxical aggression, which both penetrates and fails to penetrate, is consistent with his hesitance in entering the stage area that designates Song's apartment.

The trope of penetration in *M. Butterfly* is reiterated—at first obliquely in Gallimard's repeatedly stated assumption (fostered by Song Liling) that, just as Song submitted to his phallic masculinity, Viet Nam will yield to US military penetration. In conversation with his superior, Monsieur Toulon, Gallimard plays the man of the world: "If the Americans demonstrate the will to win, the Vietnamese will welcome them into a mutually beneficial union. ... Orientals will always submit to a greater force" (46). Later Song will explain to the judge at his trial that he has actively fostered this impression: "The West has sort of an international rape mentality toward the East. ... Her mouth says no, but her eyes say yes. The West believes the East, deep down, *wants* to be dominated" (82–83). The repetition of subtle (and less-than-subtle) double-entendres invokes, in Judith Haber's words, "the logistics of penetration."[47] The logistics of penetration recur when Gallimard is humiliated by his senior colleague's high-handedness: feeling shamed and emasculated, Gallimard compensates by bursting into Song's apartment and penetrating her domestic space. The staging enacts in social terms his desire to "reappropriate ... her body/room/stage and define ... it as his container—the empty, passive receptacle that is the ground of his existence."[48] Gallimard's intentions involve both literal and figurative penetration as well: his older self freely admits that he had come to find "a vessel to contain [his] humiliation"—specifically, Song's body (58). However, instead of merely sheathing himself in her body (a violation he has already achieved with Song's consent), he now insists upon penetrating her visually—opening up her clothes and seeing the body beneath. Gallimard's request asserts his ownership of this body, his right to invade it—see it, expose it, enter it—when he pleases. As his words intimate, he also seeks to conceal his own shame, sheathing himself within Song at the same time as he humiliates her by leaving her entirely open, as he has been psychologically open with Toulon. Just as Toulon has betrayed Gallimard's trust, forcing Gallimard to play the fall guy and cover his superior, Gallimard wants to betray Song's trust, invading her like the Viet Nam that he hopes will "always submit to a greater force" like a submissive Oriental woman (46).

As audiences knew what the Gallimard of 1963 did not—that Song's doubleness would be evident were Gallimard to see his lover's male genitalia—its members almost certainly indulged their own prurience at this juncture. Is it

Song's body or Gallimard's surprise that watchers were more eager to see? The confounding of their own eyes or the response of the diplomat who is even more invested in Song's femaleness than they were? Hwang plays on both aspects of the voyeur's pleasure.

Of course, Hwang does not reveal the phallic body of Song at this point. Yet in this scene the subordinate Oriental in the relationship turns the tables on the Westerner. Song's response to Gallimard's attempt at both literal and symbolic penetration is unforgettable: she challenges him to strip her himself. Song's capitulation ironically reverses the power relations between her and her lover. Because she submits despite his caddish aggression, Gallimard unexpectedly gives the power over to her, embracing her and apologizing on his knees rather than removing her clothes. The power exchange is complete when Song interrupts his apology to announce (clearly, to us, on the spur of the moment), "I'm pregnant." After a beat, Gallimard exclaims, "I want to marry you!" and the stage goes black (61). The scene is particularly notable because the dramatic action itself seems to mimic the sexual act: a long buildup of the rising action, an almost painful moment of suspense, and then a crashing, very satisfying climax—the pinnacle of Gallimard's relationship with Song. This dramatic pattern is achieved through one of the many techniques that the playwright and the director borrowed from the Kabuki tradition—in this case, the use of *mie*, static poses that distend the drama's tension and give the audience a chance to detach from the action and recognize the drama's artifice. Audience members absorbed in the action expected the scene to conclude with either the stripping or with Song's evasion of it; what they did not expect was for Song to extend the suspense with what purports to be a revelation:

SONG: I'm pregnant. (*Beat*) I'm pregnant. (*Beat*) I'm pregnant. (*Beat*)
GALLIMARD: I want to marry you!

(61)

The stage blacked out momentarily, and when the lights came up again, Gallimard remained in a frozen pose on his knees while Song engaged in a conversation with Comrade Chin, recounting, in her position as informer, what had happened and analyzing the event. "I need a baby," Song insists. She tells Chin,

> He told me to strip, and I took a chance. Oh, we Chinese, we know how to gamble. ... Suddenly, it hit me—"All he wants is for her to submit. Once a woman submits, a man is always ready to become 'generous.'" ... And it worked! He gave in!

(62)

Upon his capitulation, Song explains, she gambled again, disorienting Gallimard by offering something even more important than the sight of her naked body and engaging in a psychological bait-and-switch.

Until this point, Song's body has been presented as an erotic object. Upon her statement, it transforms into the other identity of the female body—a fertile receptacle for childbearing. The transformation resembles that of Puccini's Butterfly, who similarly changes from girl to mother. The body's meaning also changes: from a receptive body capable of holding or sheathing the male member to a productive body, able to carry a child within and to succor that child. Now more than ever, having Song as a mistress enhances Gallimard's masculinity, particularly since his union with his wife, Helga, has produced no children. While Song's news changes Gallimard's perception of her, the audience's perception is also changed. For while the play's dramatic structure ensures that the audience cannot forget Song's true sex, the performer, B. D. Wong, seemed entirely believable. Song's news affected their picture of "her" body, just as it changed Gallimard's.

Once Chin exits, Gallimard unfreezes and, after responding from the vantage point of 1986, returns to the position he was in at the end of the previous scene. In an effort to revise the *Madama Butterfly* plot, Gallimard immediately offers to divorce Helga and marry Song. But this is not Song's goal; Puccini's opera is a cover for another tale she is writing. She refuses, and the two engage in a new power struggle. To clinch her arguments, Song states, "I'm flattered to decline your offer," and exits (65).

The tension, which had held through the intervening scene with Song and Chin, immediately drains away. The staging affected the spectators almost physically. Hwang ratcheted up the tension between the two actors, promising nudity and revelation; he held the suspense further by pausing in the middle of the scene for Song's conversation with Chin. The debate had twice changed abruptly and did so a third time when Song insisted that she could not marry Gallimard. Her exit in the middle of the discussion leaves both Gallimard and the audience still hanging, reaching out to empty air. The charged space of the narrow area representing their flat is emptied of static without any corresponding shock. Song has demonstrated her confident grasp of her power by walking out on Gallimard's arguments. The sexual tension between them dissipates as the scene detumesces, shifting the scene from high tragedy to comedy.

This deflation of high drama is extended when Song reenters with an infant wrapped in a blanket. The scene, which could be a high point in the action, is played for laughs. In contrast to Butterfly's touching entrance with her child in Puccini's opera, Song presents the child to its "father" sans music. Gallimard's bemused comment that "babies are never very attractive at birth" offers an ironic counterpoint to the beauty of Butterfly's child, and when Song tells her lover that the child's first name will be the Chinese "Peepee," overriding Gallimard's objections because, as she says, "he will never live in the West," the scene becomes a ridiculous parody of Butterfly's revelation in Puccini's opera. Hwang's use of comedic elements entirely deflates the scene's suspense and undercuts the pathos of the plot turn.

Shortly after this point, however, Song changes his self-presentation from female to male, and with the change his position shifts from object to subject. Up until the end of act 2, Song has permitted Gallimard to construct him as "Butterfly."

Gallimard's narrative commentary has also shaped the audience's expectations of Song, and perhaps the audience's desires as well. But Song's address to the audience at the end of act 2 alters his relation to both Gallimard and the audience. With this change in narrator, Hwang upends the conventions of memory theater: Gallimard exits and Song turns directly to the audience: "The change I'm going to make requires about five minutes. So I thought you might want to take this opportunity to stretch your legs. ... I'll be here, when you return, right where you left me" (78–79). The change Song alludes to is the long-awaited transformation from woman to man, enacted, like a circus stunt, "before our very eyes." By breaking the fourth wall, Song usurps Gallimard's role as narrator, and by taking over the story, Song changes its perspective from Gallimard's to his own. As Gallimard has just exited, Song's "change" is performed directly for the spectators; Gallimard no longer serves as the audience's onstage stand-in. Song begins by removing makeup—surely the most prosaic of actions—except that the cosmetics carry a symbolic valence as the false femininity that Song has worn so well.

The staging reverts again to Kabuki tradition: time in Kabuki theater "is extended and contracted as the dramatist requires."[49] Sometimes the principal actors freeze in order

> to draw attention to some action ... so the audience can be given time to appreciate what is involved. ... This is a particularly obvious example of the dislike of the kabuki actor at having any other action on stage happening at the same time as his own. Again he sees this as distracting from his individual performance and much prefers the story to handle one thing at a time.[50]

Use of this technique enabled the actor B. D. Wong to toy with audience expectation, simultaneously increasing the spectators' anticipation and downplaying it. The audience could watch throughout the transformation or follow the cues (stagelights went halfway down, houselights came up) and take Song's advice.

At this point, the audience's expectations are confounded, and the remainder of the play, staged largely by the character Song Liling, plays violent tricks upon the spectator, using the audience's potential arousal to administer a series of disorienting shocks that amount to a scenographic pistol-whipping. Initially the transformation of Song is something of an anticlimax. The rising action of the play leads to this moment (though the progression is not steady, due to the flashbacks and flash-forwards); nonetheless, the buildup is exaggerated and crude, and seems intended to fall flat. There is a long circus drumroll preceding the moment when the transformation is completed, when Song, clear of makeup, removes the woman's wig to reveal his head, his hair slicked back and parted on the side in a male haircut. Strangely, the change is easy to integrate with one's previous perceptions, like the moment when Wittgenstein's doodled duck becomes a bunny; one can no longer see how the drawing could ever have looked like a duck. Once one's mind makes the shift, Song no longer looks anything like a woman.

This is the point when both playwright and director derail audience expectation and redirect it—for what the actor playing Song does after he removes the wig is to open up the kimono and drop it on the floor—revealing himself as an Asian man wearing "*a well-cut suit*" (80). The surprise, the mental scramble of the watchers to make cognitive sense of the spectacle could not have been more dramatic if it had indeed been the actor's nude body that they saw. Because B. D. Wong, the actor playing the role, began to speak as soon as he revealed the men's suit he wore, the audience had no time to process the change in their expectations. This moment exhibits, perhaps, the crux of the play, the moment when the spectators' confusion of sex and gender, of biology and behavior, is revealed to them. Instead of the male genitalia they expected to see, what was revealed was a masculine figure—masculine because clothed. Moreover, the switch from Asian to European clothing occurred at the same time. And with that, another shift—the shift from a Westerner's Other to his brother, so to speak—is achieved.

For Westerners accustomed to seeing Westernized Asians and Asian-Americans, the suit underneath the kimono changes Song from an exotic to "one of us," to just anybody in a suit. Song even forgoes the urbanity of Gallimard's white suit (presumably a concession to the climate of Beijing); Song wears "*a well-cut suit*" that he will soon identify as an Armani. The change renders Song both similar to Gallimard (in that both are men in suits) and different (one wears white, one black). Moreover, what results from Song's transformation is that, no longer an exotic, Song must be located in the class hierarchy of Western society. The Armani suit, in which Song takes great pride, carries other connotations for Gallimard and, perhaps, for audience members. The short stature of the actor playing Song also altered the impression of Song's presence as a male.

With Song's change from female to male as a lead-in, the staging of act 3 lured the onlookers into a trap. Act 2 concluded with Song's promise to "change"—to enact the transformation that the audience has been anticipating; the implied promise that accompanies it—the chance to see Song's body—is eventually made good in the second scene of act 3. But what purports in this scene to be a striptease becomes a goading provocation that threatens to invade the watchers' anonymity and their comfort zones. With the removal of his clothes, Song forces the onlookers to see, not his masculinity, which was no longer in question, but his nudity, challenging both Gallimard and other watchers with an aggressive stare that deflects the objectifying gaze and encourages the spectators to feel shame at their own prurience. In the scene, Song urges both Gallimard and the audience to guess at his feelings:

SONG: [W]hat's the shame? In pride? You think I could have pulled this off if I wasn't already full of pride when we met? No, not just pride. Arrogance. It takes arrogance, really—to believe you can will, with your eyes and your lips, the destiny of another. ... C'mon. Admit it. You still want me. Even in slacks and a button-down collar.

GALLIMARD: I don't see what the point of—
SONG: You don't? Well, maybe, Rene, just maybe—I want you.

(85)

It is the "maybe" that is unknowable—and that "maybe" engenders frustration equally in Gallimard and the audience. Song's sex, male or female, proves not to be as important as his vocation. He is an actor and a female impersonator; in fact, he has been performing the role of female impersonator even when he is not onstage. And in large part because of that vocation *as actor*, Song's degree of volition in his actions, his motivations, even his sexual orientation is unavailable to us. As the fantasy Song says to Gallimard in a 1986 scene, "I'm an artist, Rene. You were my greatest ... acting challenge" (63). When Song turns his back on the audience to face Gallimard and drop his pants, his body provides no one with any answers. *M. Butterfly*'s focus on Song's body turns out to be the greatest trick of all: Song is simultaneously able to conceal his true self from spectators and unable to reveal it. The great revelation, when it comes, is no revelation. Song stares at the watchers and challenges them to comprehend him, but they cannot even tell whether their inability to do so indicates his victory or his loss.

***

If Song's perspective is tantalizingly dangled just outside of the spectator's reach, Gallimard's perspective is so evident that it obscures the presence of his body for much of the play. Gallimard's body is *not* what the audience is look-ing forward to throughout *M. Butterfly*, yet it becomes the final, most shocking signifier. The role reversal in the final scene, when Gallimard dons the wig of Butterfly and leaves Song the role of a *noir*-ish Pinkerton, is a tour-de-force for both playwright and actor. To make sense of it, we must examine the play's other axis, its treatment of Rene Gallimard's experience of the body and its absences.

As the protagonist of *M. Butterfly*, Gallimard is onstage almost throughout the play; the other characters enter as his recollections or his fantasies. The latter in particular are problematic for him, because Gallimard is always fearful of controlling his mind. His fantasies often spiral out of control, leaving him anxious or ashamed. It is, perhaps, his fear of uncontrolled fantasy that leads him to incorporate the apparently submissive Song Liling into his vision of the Perfect Woman. Song's refusal to follow his directives is certainly what drives Gallimard to fulfill his fantasies by enacting the role of Butterfly himself.

Gallimard's own body is initially presented in such a way as to obscure its presence: according to the stage directions,

> *Lights fade up to reveal Rene Gallimard, 65, in a prison cell. He wears a comfortable bathrobe, and looks old and tired. The sparsely furnished cell contains a wooden crate upon which sits a hot plate with a kettle, and a portable tape recorder. Gallimard sits on the crate staring at the recorder, a sad smile on his face.*

A spotlight illuminates the top of the ramp (stage left), where Song stands:

> *Upstage Song, who appears as a beautiful woman in traditional Chinese garb, dances a traditional piece from the Peking Opera, surrounded by the percussive clatter of Chinese music. Then, slowly, lights and sound cross-fade; the Chinese opera music dissolves into a Western opera, the "Love Duet" from Puccini's* Madame Butterfly. *Song continues dancing, now to the Western accompaniment. ... Gallimard rises, and turns upstage towards the figure of Song, who dances without acknowledging him.*
>
> (1)

Thus Gallimard, played by John Lithgow, first appeared seated and immobile, his height dwarfed by the set, while Wong's exotic costume and ritualized movement drew the eyes of the audience. Gallimard calls to his Butterfly; then, as the lights on her fade out, he turns to address the audience. With his first words, he engages in the old trick of asking the watchers to use their imaginations, just as the Chorus does at the opening of Shakespeare's *Henry V*. But whereas Shakespeare's Chorus asks the audience to imagine a real scene of battle outside the theater in the open air, Gallimard asks the audience to shrink the space of the interior. Standing on the broad stage of the Eugene O'Neill, Lithgow, as Gallimard, offered information that the audience's eyes flatly contradicted: "The limits of my cell are as such: four-and-a-half meters by five. There's one window against the far wall; a door, very strong" (1). As a representative of the play, Lithgow asked the audience to enter into the play's fantasy, the fantasy of mimesis, and the fantasy of the Perfect Woman.

Almost immediately, however, Gallimard's fantasy of mimesis is complicated by recording technology that invokes questions of absence, presence, and power. Initially, the audience saw Gallimard fantasizing about Song as a Peking opera performer, while what he was imagining appeared above him. In front of him, however, was the portable tape recorder on which his eyes were fixed (1). This piece of equipment complicates Gallimard's relation to Song and his fantasy of her in much the same way that it complicated Krapp's relation to the past in Samuel Beckett's *Krapp's Last Tape*. If the music was supposed to emanate from his tape recorder, then Gallimard did in some sense possess, if not Butterfly herself, an aural simulacrum of her. The true sign of her presence is not her body (there only in fantasy) or his projection of that fantasy (enacted by the actor playing Song), but the music—the sound of *Madama Butterfly*, the initial site of Gallimard's obsession. Like the reel of tape in Beckett's play, Gallimard's cassette is a representation of time: in the cassette is a specific amount of material which goes to another area and does so in a specific amount of time. Moreover, this segment of time contains the voice of a Butterfly, if not *his* Butterfly—a Butterfly, in fact, who is certainly more reliable or at least more effectively controlled than Song Liling. Gallimard can manipulate the voice of this Butterfly by raising or lowering the volume; he can alter her song or manipulate recorded time by playing selected portions of the tape, excising arias or phrases that he does not wish to hear. Gallimard's control over the tape contrasts with his lack of control over the fantasy women he imagines.

From the start, Gallimard's fantasy women demonstrate his anxiety about dreams that control him and render him powerless. During the introduction, his fears seem to be assuaged, but soon enough Gallimard's mind produces something that alarms him considerably more: Song's precursor. This figure is the initial phallic body, a creation of light and staging, not solely an actor's movement. Crucial to Gallimard's involvement with Song are his early sexual experiences; Hwang describes a sequence that clarifies the relationship:

> [Gallimard] *reaches into his crate, pulls out a stack of girlie magazines, and begins flipping through them. ... The "Love Duet" creeps in over the speakers. Special comes up, revealing, not Song this time, but a pinup girl in a sexy negligee, her back to us. Gallimard turns upstage and looks at her.*
>
> (10)

When Gallimard produces his girlie magazines, the audience takes as an ironic joke his comment that "[f]or three or four dollars, you get seven or eight women" (10). These women, however, are materialized in the figure that appears where Song had stood. Gallimard explains that he first encountered soft-porn magazines when he was twelve: "The first time I saw them ... all lined up—my body shook. Not with lust—no, with power. Here were women—a shelfful—who would do exactly as I wanted" (10). Recollected fantasy from his adolescent past merges with the memory of the girl's seductive pose: onstage, her white back and bare shoulders shone out from the surrounding obscurity as the overhead spot drew the spectators' attention to her upright body. This white, nude body offers a frightening challenge to the adolescent Gallimard, as the girl refuses the role of object, challenging him (and the spectators) with her aggressively sexual gaze. The ensuing dialogue shows her in a dual role as seductress and aggressor. Gallimard loses his sense of power, panicking as the girl demonstrates an awareness of and a pleasure in his gaze, turning the objectification back on him. She begins by turning her head and commenting, "I know you're watching me"; she goes on to remove the negligee and display the front of her naked body, murmuring, "I like it. ... I want you to see. ... I can't see you. You can do whatever you want" (11–13). Though Gallimard at first expresses pleasure and a sense of his own dominance at the opportunity to get women "who would do exactly what I wanted," he is so overcome with fear and shame that his sense of arousal disappears: "My throat ... it's dry. ... I'm shaking. My skin is hot, but my penis is soft. Why? ... I shouldn't be seeing this. It's so dirty. I'm so bad. ... I can't do a thing. Why?" (10–12). Why indeed? How much power can be enough for Gallimard if he can be threatened by his own fantasies, fantasies derived from looking at a pinup girl in a magazine? At this point, the audience may begin to take more seriously his comment that girls in magazines "would do exactly as I wanted" (10). What he wanted was for them to stay still—not to move, to act, to evince autonomy or, most of all, to challenge him with their own subjecthood and their own sexual desires. Not even to show a nude body that might in itself pose a challenge to his masculinity.

Gallimard's narratorial shaping of the story ensures that, with Song's entrance, the audience focuses on the Oriental rather than the European body. It is not until Song is revealed as a man, wearing garb similar to Gallimard's own, that the performance redirects the audience toward Gallimard's body, making the audience note both what can be seen and what can be expected of it. Then, in the penultimate scene, the audience is assaulted both aurally and visually, as music blares and Gallimard appears onstage in a pose that emblematizes his abjection: "*Music from the 'Death Scene' from* Butterfly *blares over the house speakers. It is the loudest thing we've heard in this play. Gallimard enters, crawling towards Song's wig and kimono*" (84). Hwang implicitly alludes to Jean Genet's dramas when Gallimard enters "*crawling.*"[51] The sight evokes the spinning whirligigs of power play that also appear in Genet's work, for here the figure who had seemed to hold the dominant position in the relationship is now abjected, reduced to serving at the pleasure of his former lover. But for Gallimard, seeing Song wearing male clothing in act 3 is a trick of perception—what Sartre, referring to the dramas of Jean Genet, calls "this superimposing of whirligigs which keep sending us back and forth from the true to the fake and from the fake to the true ... an infernal machine."[52] When Gallimard comments on the action, spectators realize that the whirligig he experiences is of changing perceptions, not changing power relations:

> What strikes me especially is how shallow [Song] is, how glib and obsequious ... completely ... without substance! The type that prowls around discos with a gold medallion stinking of garlic. So little like my Butterfly. Yet even in this moment my mind remains agile, flipflopping like a man on a trampoline. Even now, my picture dissolves, and I see that ... witness ... talking to me.
>
> (84)

Evoking this moment as he addresses the audience, Gallimard is less humiliated than he is astonished. His prior framing of Song is utterly shattered by seeing that, as a male, Song behaves very differently than he did when he was performing the role of himself-as-female. Gallimard's mistaken perception of Song's sex is not what he finds worthy of remark; instead, he is floored at recognizing his misperception of Song's character. Now Gallimard characterizes the male Song in explicitly class-based terms, suggesting that on the witness stand Song seems to be tasteless, tacky, and superficial. Song has been playing the role of Butterfly for him for years, and Gallimard cannot tell whether Song is projecting this new image for a reason, demonstrating perhaps his contempt for Western law, or whether this is, in fact, a Song without artifice, Song as he is when he speaks and acts spontaneously.

As the scene proceeds, it is almost impossible not to presume that at least part of the events is Gallimard's fantasy; how else could Song step out of the witness box and engage in a tête-à-tête with Gallimard? Yet this stage direction could equally well be a theatrical convenience used in order to hurry the action from courtroom scene to private confrontation between the two men. Certainly, the degree of reality in this scene is difficult to interpret. Throughout the play, the audience has seen the story of this liaison through the prism of Gallimard's highly personal perspective. When the play reaches its present, 1986, there is no reason to believe that the events transpiring are told through Gallimard's memory; yet it is impossible to be sure that they are not. And without that assurance, the audience cannot be confident that what they see is free from the coloring of the diplomat's perspective. Another element to consider is that Song's change into masculine clothing has brought with it a substantial change in Song's behavior, suggesting that Song himself is finally taking over his own presentation. These implications render it impossible to know whether the action that follows is mimetically "real," or whether a character—or which character!—is imagining the action. Reality falls by the wayside sometime after Song's removal of his woman's wig.

Again the playwright and the director build the scene for maximum suspense, as the action moves toward what the audience has been waiting for: the revelation of Song's naked body. The playtext dictates a change in lighting that heralds the scene's final action. Then, hailing Gallimard with the same salutation she had used at the first Chinese opera performance, an Armani-clad Song steps down from the witness box and asks Gallimard to admit that he desires Song as a man. Exhibiting his desire for power over his partner as nakedly as Gallimard had done in the past, the male Song now teases: "Maybe, Rene, just maybe—I want you. … Then again, maybe I'm just playing with you. How can you tell?" (85–86). Song pushes Gallimard to admit that he is sexually aroused and challenges Gallimard to acknowledge that Song may still be his "little one." Urging Gallimard "to see through my act," Song begins to strip: "Maybe I've become frustrated. Maybe I'm saying 'Look at me, you fool!' Or maybe I'm just feeling … sexy" (87). Gallimard begs Song to stop, but Song complies instead with the request his lover made twenty-five years earlier, in the middle of act 2.

As Dexter staged this scene, Song turns upstage to face Gallimard, removes his suit, and drops his briefs. Against the dark set, his body gleams white. The audience clearly viewed his ass, his masculine musculature, his short dark hair slicked back; Gallimard, presumably, got the full frontal view. For the audience, Song's body appears as shape more than person—an erect phallus challenging the shrinking Gallimard, whom the audience expects to back away. But Gallimard does not back away: he laughs. "Oh god! What an idiot! Of course! … Look at you! You're a man!" (88).

Song's trump card has always been his flesh, he believed; why does it fail to seduce now? He takes Gallimard's hand and puts it against his cheek. Gallimard, *"like a blind man, lets his hands run over Song's face. 'This skin, I remember. The curve of her face, the softness of her cheek'"* (89). But the naked Song has no power over the open-eyed Gallimard, and perhaps would have had none even had Song been female. Gallimard explains, "I've finally learned to tell fantasy from reality" (90). Fantasy, glamour, and the interaction of the tactile sense with imagination have been the basis of Gallimard's physical attraction to Song. The foundation of their relationship has been Gallimard's Butterfly fantasies; the liaison was built up with the glamour inherent in the actor's performance of a woman and topped off with physical sensation. The naked body—fully visible, boldly presented—affects Gallimard like a thumb in the eye; his desire has never been predicated on the naked body, but on its concealment. Song's presentation of his is a violation that Gallimard cannot abide.

Song's naked body is not his trump card but the joker; his attempt to conquer Gallimard with its revelation frees Gallimard from his attachment to Song instead. Recognizing that Song is indeed "just a man," Gallimard can invest his free-floating fantasy in a new way:

> I have a date with my Butterfly and I don't want your body polluting the room! (*He tosses Song's suit at him.*) Look at these—you dress like a pimp. ... You, if anyone, should know—I am pure imagination. And in imagination I will remain. Now get out! (*Gallimard bodily removes Song from the stage, taking his kimono.*)
>
> (90–91)

Like the Madame Butterfly he now aspires to become for his own pleasure, Gallimard expels his unworthy suitor from the room. Gallimard altogether rejects the phallic body that Song proffers, choosing instead to play the role of Butterfly himself, on his own terms.

Gallimard's subsequent actions onstage return the audience to a stark consideration of the body not unlike that offered by the conclusion of '*Tis Pity She's a Whore*: "My name is Rene Gallimard," says the former diplomat, "also known as Madame Butterfly" (93). Gallimard substitutes his European body for Song's Asian one, acknowledging that ethnicity in itself does not make a Butterfly. He completes the process by an act that combines Giovanni's violence and Annabella's victimization. Refusing the possibility of ever permitting Song's phallus to humiliate him, Gallimard commits *seppuku*, ritual suicide, opening up a new orifice with a knife. The gesture itself recalls the schizophrenia of Othello's suicide, which Othello explains as an attempt to save himself from the part of himself that has betrayed him. In becoming M. Butterfly, Gallimard creates both an alternate self to love and an opposite: he is both, like Othello, a male Westerner and a feminized Other. Rather than admit the possibility of serving as Song's passive partner in anal sex, he chooses the phallic violence of the knife wielded by his own hand.

For the audience, the reversal is completely unexpected, and the act of mutilation painful to watch (despite the knowledge that the mutilation is not enacted in reality). The mechanism at work is revelation, of course, both symbolic and literal. *Seppuku* involves cutting open one's own stomach, an operation that frequently permits the small intestine to spill out. Gallimard's act of *seppuku* represents not only a displaced castration but also a displaced sex-change operation, as the knife opens a vagina-like slit in his body. It offers the audience a new view of Gallimard in which he is feminized but retains his integrity. With this attempt to offer us total visibility, Gallimard presents himself unwittingly as a visual emblem for the impossibility of combining dissimilar cultures. While Gallimard's narrative has focused the audience's attention on Song's body, Gallimard's actions at the end dramatically redirect the spectators' gaze, making them look at the European body and see that it, too, can be alien. His means of suicide transforms him from subject to object, from the shaper of the tale to the spectacle itself.

The subject I have been discussing throughout this treatment of Hwang's play is the question of *seeing*: how spectacle in *M. Butterfly* alters the spectator's perception of the play. The nineteenth-century theater design itself emphasizes the importance of spectacularity; Ishioka's designs worked within the framework that the theater provided to create a variety of experiences for the spectators. For those sitting far enough back to see the stage as a whole, the banners could reverberate as context that dwarfed the concerns of the characters, rendering the drama a Brechtian challenge to Gallimard's attempt at universalizing his plight. For those who sat close enough to be pulled in by Gallimard's narrative control, the story may have begun with the vagaries of memory, but it concluded with a revelation about the consequences of the spectator's desire to rip aside the "world of surfaces" that Hwang refers to in his afterword. As a general rule, the body's relation to the self is problematic, but in *M. Butterfly* the body is the text upon which Gallimard insists upon inscribing his identity.

Notes

1 David Henry Hwang, Afterword, in *M. Butterfly* (New York: Plume, 1986), 95. All further quotations from this play will reference this edition.
  In its use of literary allusion to characterize a member of a minority who complies with Anglo stereotypes of his or her race, the name "Butterfly" parallels "Uncle Tom," an expression used primarily within the African-American community.
2 Condee points out that many theater artists hold that "a proscenium theatre results in an illusionistic production, while an open stage results in one that is presentational" (defining "illusionistic" as a style in which spectators are meant to perceive "what they are seeing onstage [as] an illusion of reality" and "presentational" as a style that reminds spectators "that what they are seeing is an artificial, artistic creation") (William Faricy Condee, *Theatrical Space: A Guide for Directors and Designers* [Lanham, MD: Scarecrow, 1995], 58). However, Condee sagely notes that other directors and designers see no necessary correlation between theater design and the presence of theatrical illusion or theatrical self-consciousness (62).
3 Cf. Jean-Paul Sartre, Introduction, in Jean Genet's *The Maids* and *Deathwatch*: "[Genet] has a vision of an infinitely rapid rotation which merges the poles of appearance and reality, just as, when a multi-colored disk is spun quickly enough, the colors of the rainbow interpenetrate and produce white. Genet constructs such whirligigs by the hundred. They become his favorite mode of thinking. He indulges knowingly in false reasoning" (Jean Genet, *The Maids* and *Deathwatch*, trans. Bernard Frechtman [New York: Grove, 1954], 7).
4 For the review by Frank Rich, see http://theater2.nytimes.com/mem/theater/treview. html?html_title=&tols_title=M%20BUTTERFLY%20(PLAY)&pdate=19880321& byline=By%20FRANK%20RICH&id=1077011430660. Critics who assert that

Gallimard is a closeted homosexual include Quentin Lee, "Between the Oriental and the Transvestite," *Found Object* 2 (Fall 1993): 45–59; David L. Eng, "In the Shadows of a Diva: Committing Homosexuality in David Henry Hwang's *M. Butterfly*," *Amerasia Journal* 20, no. 1 (1994): 93–116; and Ilka Saal, "Performance and Perception: Gender, Sexuality, and Culture in David Henry Hwang's *M. Butterfly*," *Amerikastudien* 43, no. 4 (1998): 629–44.

5 Many, but by no means all, of the essays in this category appear in Jonathan Wisenthal, Sherrill Grace, Melinda Boyd, Brian McIlroy, and Vera Micznik, eds., *A Vision of the Orient: Text, Intertexts, and Contexts of Madame Butterfly* (Toronto: University of Toronto Press, 2006). Other critics who treat this matter include Cecilia Hsueh Chen, "Writing Back to the Empire: From *M. Butterfly* to *Madame Butterfly*," in *Reimagining Language and Literature for the Twenty-First Century*, ed. Suthira Duangsamosorn (Amsterdam: Rodopi, 2005), 331–44; and Maria Degabriele, "From *Madama Butterfly* to *Miss Saigon*: One Hundred Years of Popular Orientalism," *Critical Arts* 10, no. 2 (1996): 105–18.

6 See Gabrielle Cody, "David Hwang's *M. Butterfly*: Perpetuating the Misogynist Myth," *Theater* 20, no. 2 (1989): 24–27; and Kathryn Remen, "The Theatre of Punishment: David Henry Hwang's *M. Butterfly* and Michel Foucault's *Discipline and Punish*," *Modern Drama* 37, no. 3 (1994): 393.

7 Eiko Ishioka, *Eiko on Stage* (New York: Callaway, 2000), 54–55.

8 Ibid., 56.

9 Ibid., 55. Ishioka's design also seems to incorporate (perhaps unintentionally) Moholy-Nagy's dictate:

> The possibilities for a VARIATION OF LEVELS OF MOVABLE PLANES on the stage of the future would contribute to a genuine organization of space. Space will then no longer consist of the interconnections of planes in the old meaning, which was able to conceive of architectonic delineation of space only as an enclosure formed by opaque surfaces. The new space originates from free-standing surfaces or from linear definition of planes ... so that the surfaces stand at times in a very free relationship to one another, without the need of any direct contact.
> Laszlo Moholy-Nagy, "Theater, Circus, Variety," in *The Theater of the Bauhaus*, eds. Walter Gropius and Arthur S. Wensinger, trans. Arthur S. Wensinger (Middletown, CT: Wesleyan University Press, 1961), 68.

Whether or not Ishioka shared Moholy-Nagy's aims in designing the structure this way, the result was a set that encouraged the experience of the play as Theater of Totality.

10 Condee comments that set designers must decide whether the performance should "reach out to the edges of the room or sit isolated with empty space around it," conceiving the options as a choice between "sprawl" and "jewel" (Condee, *Theatrical Space*, 16). Ishioka's design is clearly the latter, and it manifests the benefits of this approach. Condee comments that in a large theater it may be best "to keep the set self-contained, creating its own proportions and relating to itself, not to the space." He also quotes the set designer Lowell Detweiler: "'Just isolate this jewel-like little set in all this vast space. You get more focus on a set by placing it in the middle of a vast space. It's wonderful to get as much 'nothing' around a set as possible'" (interview with Detweiler, qtd. in Condee, *Theatrical Space*, 17).

11 Ishioka, *Eiko*, 56.

12 Ibid., 50.

13 Ibid., 61.

14 Giuseppe Giacosa and Luigi Illica, *Madama Butterfly*, trans. Frank Granville Barker (Hayes, UK: EMI Records, 1989), 54.

15 Cf. Ishioka, *Eiko*, 56.
16 Marjorie Garber, *Vested Interests: Cross-Dressing and Cultural Anxiety* (New York: Routledge, 1992), 249.
17 Melinda Boyd, "'Re-Orienting' the Vision: Ethnicity and Authenticity from Suzuki to Comrade Chin," in *A Vision of the Orient: Texts, Intertexts, and Contexts of Madame Butterfly*, eds. Jonathan Wisenthal, Sherrill Grace, Melinda Boyd, Brian McIlroy, and Vera Micznik (Toronto: University of Toronto Press, 2006), 66.
18 Ibid., 66.
19 Tennessee Williams, Production Notes, in *The Glass Menagerie* (New York: New Directions, 1945), 7.
20 Walter Benjamin, *Illuminations*, ed. Hannah Arendt, trans. Harry Zohn (New York: Harcourt, Brace, 1968), 255.
21 Ibid., 255.
22 As Ishioka comments, "The play was controversial in many ways, not least in that for many Western audience members it was the first time they saw an Asian man naked, on stage or off" (*Eiko*, 66).
23 Illica and Giacosa, *Butterfly*, 53.
24 Ibid., 31.
25 Butterfly's relatives, arriving in act 1 for her wedding, comment, "What an expanse of sky! / What an expanse of sea!" (Illica and Giacosa, *Butterfly*, 36).
26 Frank Lloyd Wright, *Frank Lloyd Wright: An Autobiography* (New York: Longmans, Green, and Co., 1932), 168.
27 Illica and Giacosa, *Butterfly*, 28.
28 Ibid., 29.
29 Vera Micznik, "Cio-Cio-San the Geisha," in *A Vision of the Orient: Texts, Intertexts, and Contexts of Madame Butterfly*, eds. Jonathan Wisenthal, Sherrill Grace, Melinda Boyd, Brian McIlroy, and Vera Micznik (Toronto: University of Toronto Press, 2006), 54.
30 Illica and Giacosa, *Butterfly*, 52.
31 Ibid., 56.
32 Strauss uses a similar motif in the opening of *Der Rosenkavalier* to represent the sexual climax of both Octavian and the Marschallin, the climax to which the Marschallin's dreamy line, "How you were!" refers.
33 Illica and Giacosa, *Butterfly*, 86.
34 Micznik, "Cio-Cio-San," 56.
35 As Joshua S. Mostow points out, in the traditional Buddhist society of late nineteenth-century Japan, "Women did not commit *seppuku*, which was an exclusively male practice." See Joshua S. Mostow, "Iron Butterfly: Cio-Cio-San and Japanese Imperialism," in Wisenthal et al., *A Vision of the Orient*, 187.
36 Ishioka, *Eiko*, 54.
37 Yoseharu Ozaki, "Shakespeare and Kabuki," in *Transvestism and the Onnagata Traditions in Shakespeare and Kabuki*, eds. Minoru Fujita and Michael Shapiro (Folkestone, UK: Global Oriental, 2006), 5.
38 Those familiar with Vsevolod Meyerhold's work will recognize his influence as well. Ishioka's ramp recalls the long, curved stairway featured in Meyerhold's designs for *The Second Army Commander* in 1929. Cf. Edward Braun, *Meyerhold: A Revolution in Theatre* (Iowa City: University of Iowa Press, 1995), 253–55.
39 John Wesley Harris, *The Traditional Theatre of Japan: Kyogen, Noh, Kabuki, and Puppetry* (Lewiston, NY: Edwin Mellen, 2006), 157.
40 Ibid., 158.
41 Ibid., 158; Chiaki Yoshida, *Kabuki* (Tokyo: Japan Times, 1971), 104.
42 Ishioka, *Eiko*, 56.
43 Ibid., 54.

44 Ibid., 55.
45 Henri Lefebvre, *The Production of Space*, trans. Donald Nicholson-Smith (Oxford: Blackwell, 1991), 33.
46 Illica and Giacosa, *Butterfly*, 32.
47 Judith Haber, "'My Body Bestow upon My Women': The Space of the Feminine in *The Duchess of Malfi*," *Renaissance Drama* n.s. 28 (1999): 140.
48 Ibid., 144.
49 Harris, *Theatre of Japan*, 190.
50 Ibid., 190.
51 The action vividly recalls 1.2 of Genet's *The Balcony*, which opens with The Judge "*crawling, on his stomach, towards the woman, who shrinks as he approaches*" and holds out her foot, demanding, "Not yet! Lick it! Lick it first" (Jean Genet, *The Balcony*, trans. Bernard Frechtman [New York: Grove, 1958; rev. ed. 1966], 14).
52 Sartre, Introduction, 28.

Bibliography

Adelman, Janet. "'Anger's My Meat': Feeding, Dependency, and Aggression in *Coriolanus*." In *Representing Shakespeare: New Psychoanalytic Essays*, edited by Murray M. Schwartz and Coppelia Kahn, 129–49. Baltimore: Johns Hopkins University Press, 1980.

Albee, Edward. *Tiny Alice*. New York: Atheneum, 1965.

Amacher, Richard E. *Edward Albee*. Boston: Twayne, 1982; revised ed.

Appia, Adolphe. "Eurhythmics and the Theatre." In *Adolphe Appia: Essays, Scenarios, and Designs*. Edited and translated by Walther R. Volbach, 135–39. Ann Arbor: UMI Research Press, 1989.

Aronson, Arnold. *The History and Theory of Environmental Scenography*. Ann Arbor: UMI Research Press, 1981.

Artaud, Antonin. *The Theater and Its Double*. Translated by Mary Caroline Richards. New York: Grove, 1958.

Arvin, Neil Cole. *Eugène Scribe and the French Theatre, 1815–1860*, 2nd ed. New York: Benjamin Blom, 1967.

Astington, John H. *Actors and Acting in Shakespeare's Time: The Art of Stage Playing*. Cambridge: Cambridge University Press, 2010.

Astruc. *Le Droit privé du théâtre ou rapports des directeurs avec les auteurs, les artistes, et le public*. Macon: Protat frères, 1897.

Bachelard, Gaston. *The Poetics of Space*. Translated by Maria Jolas. Boston: Beacon Press, 1969; 2nd ed. 1994.

Baer, Nancy Van Norman. "Design and Movement in the Theatre of the Russian Avant-Garde." In *Theatre in Revolution: Russian Avant-Garde Stage Design, 1913–1935*, edited by Nancy Van Norman Baer, 34–59. New York: Thames and Hudson, 1991.

———, ed. *Theatre in Revolution: Russian Avant-Garde Stage Design, 1913–1935*. New York: Thames and Hudson, 1991.

Barbier, Jules. *Les Contes d'Hoffmann: Opéra fantastique en quatre actes*. Paris: Calmann-Lévy, n.d. The Editiones Choudens 1907 version. In *The Tales of Hoffmann: A Performance Guide*, edited by Mary Dibbern, 12–164. Hillsdale, NY: Pendragon Press, 2002.

Beacham, Richard C. *The Roman Theatre and Its Audience*. Cambridge, MA: Harvard University Press, 1992.

Beckerman, Bernard. *Dynamics of Drama*. New York: Knopf, 1970.

Belsey, Catherine. "Emblem and Antithesis in *The Duchess of Malfi*." *Renaissance Drama* 11 (1980): 115–34.

———. *The Subject of Tragedy: Identity and Difference in Renaissance Drama*. New York: Methuen, 1985.

Benjamin, Walter. *Illuminations*. Edited by Hannah Arendt and translated by Harry Zohn. New York: Harcourt, Brace, 1968.

Bennett, Michael, James Kirkwood, and Nicholas Dante. *A Chorus Line*. New York: Applause, 1975.

Bennett, Susan. *Theatre Audiences: A Theory of Production and Reception*. New York: Routledge, 1990.

Bentley, Eric. *The Life of the Drama*. New York: Atheneum, 1964.

Bergson, Henri. "Laughter." In *Comedy*, edited by Wylie Sypher, 59–190. Baltimore: Johns Hopkins University Press, 1980.

Berry, Ralph. "Casting the Crowd: *Coriolanus* in Performance." *Assaph* C4 (1988): 111–24.

Bevington, David. "*The Comedy of Errors* in the Context of the Late 1580s and Early 1590s." In *The Comedy of Errors: Critical Essays*, edited by Robert S. Miola, 335–53. New York: Garland, 1997.

Bie, Oscar. Review of *Tales of Hoffmann*. In *Berliner Börsen-Courier*. February 13, 1929. Reprinted in *Experiment Krolloper, 1927–1931*, by Hans Curjel, 262–63. Munich: Prestel-Verlag, 1975.

Bigsby, C. W. E. "Curiouser and Curiouser: A Study of Edward Albee's *Tiny Alice*." *Modern Drama* 10, no. 3 (December 1967): 258–66.

Blau, Herbert. *The Audience*. Baltimore: Johns Hopkins University Press, 1990.

Blumenberg, Hans. *The Legitimacy of the Modern Age*. Translated by Robert M. Wallace. Cambridge, MA: MIT Press, 1983.

Boegehold, Alan L. *When a Gesture Was Expected: A Selection of Examples from Archaic and Classical Greek Literature*. Princeton: Princeton University Press, 1999.

Bourdieu, Pierre. *Outline of a Theory of Practice*. Translated by Richard Nice. Cambridge: Cambridge University Press, 1977.

Boyd, Melinda. "'Re-Orienting' the Vision: Ethnicity and Authenticity from Suzuki to Comrade Chin." In *A Vision of the Orient: Texts, Intertexts, and Contexts of Madame Butterfly*, edited by Jonathan Wisenthal, Sherrill Grace, Melinda Boyd, Brian McIlroy, and Vera Micznik, 59–71. Toronto: University of Toronto Press, 2006.

Braun, Edward. *Meyerhold: A Revolution in Theatre*. Iowa City: University of Iowa Press, 1995.

——, trans. and ed. *Meyerhold on Theatre*. New York: Hill and Wang, 1969.

Brockbank, Philip, ed. *Coriolanus*, by William Shakespeare. New York: Arden, 1976; reprinted New York: Routledge, 1988.

Brockett, Oscar. *History of the Theatre*, 7th ed. Needham Heights, MA: Allyn and Bacon, 1995.

Brook, Peter. *The Empty Space: A Book about the Theatre*. New York: Touchstone, 1968.

Brown, John Russell. *Effective Theatre*. New York: Heinemann, 1969.

Brownstein, Rachel. *Tragic Muse: Rachel of the Comédie-Française*. New York: Knopf, 1993.

Burnham, Jack W. *Beyond Modern Sculpture*. New York: George Braziller; London: Allen Lane The Penguin Press, 1968. Excerpted in *Moholy-Nagy*, edited by Richard Kostelanetz, 159–60. New York: Praeger, 1970.

Busnach, William. *La Claque! La Claque! Un Folie-revue en un acte*. Paris: Librairie Theatrale, 1862.

Campbell, Mary E. "The Tempters in Albee's *Tiny Alice*." *Modern Drama* 13, no. 1 (May 1970): 22–33.

Campeanu, Pavel. "Un Role secondaire: le spectateur." In *Sémiologie de la representation*, edited by Andre Helbo, 96–111. Brussels: Complexe, 1975.

Canning, Charlotte, and Thomas Postlewait, eds. *Representing the Past: Essays in Performance Historiography*. Iowa City: University of Iowa Press, 2010.

Carlson, Marvin. *The French Stage in the Nineteenth Century*. Metuchen, NJ: Scarecrow, 1972.

——."*Hernani*'s Revolt from the Tradition of French Stage Composition." *Theatre Survey* 13, no. 1 (May 1972): 1–27.

——. *Places of Performance: The Semiotics of Theatre Architecture*. Ithaca: Cornell University Press, 1989.

——. "Space and Theatre History." In *Representing the Past: Essays in Performance Historiography*, edited by Charlotte M. Canning and Thomas Postlewait, 195–214. Iowa City: University of Iowa Press, 2010.

——. "Theatrical Performance: Illustration, Translation, Fulfillment, or Supplement?" *Theater Journal* 37, no. 1 (1985): 5–11.

——. *Theories of the Theatre: A Historical and Critical Survey, from the Greeks to the Present*. Ithaca: Cornell University Press, 1984; 2nd ed. 1993.

Casey, Edward S. *Getting Back into Place: Toward a Renewed Understanding of the Place-World*. Bloomington: Indiana University Press, 1993.

Casson, Lionel, ed. and trans. *The Menaechmus Twins and Two Other Plays*, by Titus Maccius Plautus. New York: Norton, 1971.

Cavell, Stanley. "'Who does the wolf love?': *Coriolanus* and the Interpretations of Politics." In *Shakespeare and the Question of Theory*, edited by Patricia Parker and Geoffrey Hartman, 245–72. New York: Routledge, 1985.

Chambers, E. K. *The Elizabethan Stage*. 4 vols. Oxford: Clarendon, 1923.

——. *William Shakespeare: A Study of Facts and Problems*. Oxford: Clarendon, 1930.

Chapman, George. *Bussy D'Ambois* (Q2 ed., 1641). Edited by Robert J. Lordi. Lincoln, NE: Nebraska University Press, 1964.

Chaudhuri, Una. *Staging Place: The Geography of Modern Drama*. Ann Arbor: University of Michigan Press, 1997.

Chen, Cecilia Hsueh. "Writing Back to the Empire: From *M. Butterfly* to *Madame Butterfly*." In *Reimagining Language and Literature for the Twenty-First Century*, edited by Suthira Duangsamosorn, 331–44. Amsterdam: Rodopi, 2005.

Cody, Gabrielle. "David Hwang's *M. Butterfly*: Perpetuating the Misogynist Myth." *Theater* 20, no. 2 (1989): 24–27.

Condee, William Faricy. *Theatrical Space: A Guide for Directors and Designers*. Lanham, MD: Scarecrow, 1995.

Corbeill, Anthony. *Nature Embodied: Gesture in Ancient Rome*. Princeton: Princeton University Press, 2004.

Craig, Gordon. *On the Art of the Theatre*. Chicago: Browne's, 1911.

Crane, Mary Thomas. *Shakespeare's Brain: Reading with Cognitive Theory*. Princeton: Princeton University Press, 2001.

Curjel, Hans. *Experiment Krolloper, 1927–1931*. Munich: Prestel-Verlag, 1975.

——. "Moholy-Nagy and the Theater." *Du* 24 (November 1964), 11–15. Reprinted in *Moholy-Nagy*, edited by Richard Kostelanetz, 94–96. New York: Praeger, 1970.

Daemmrich, Horst S. *The Shattered Self: E. T. A. Hoffmann's Tragic Vision*. Detroit: Wayne State University Press, 1973.

Danahy, Michael. "Social, Sexual, and Human Spaces in *La Princesse de Cleves*." *French Forum* 6, no. 9 (1981): 212–24.

Davenport, Alma. *The History of Photography: An Overview*. Boston and London: Focal Press, 1991.

Dawson, Anthony B. and Paul Yachnin. *The Culture of Playgoing in Shakespeare's England: A Collaborative Debate.* Cambridge: Cambridge University Press, 2001.

Defaye, Claudine. "Annabella's Unborn Baby: The Heart in the Womb in *'Tis Pity She's a Whore.*" *Cahiers Élisabéthains* 15 (1979): 35–42.

Degabriele, Maria. "From *Madame Butterfly* to *Miss Saigon*: One Hundred Years of Popular Orientalism." *Critical Arts* 10, no. 2 (1996): 105–18.

Descartes, René. *Discourse on Method.* In *Discourse on Method and Related Writings*, translated by Desmond M. Clarke. Harmondsworth, UK: Penguin, 1999.

Descotes, Maurice. *L'Acteur Joanny et son journal inédit.* Paris: Presses Universitaires de France, 1956.

——. *Le Public de théâtre et son histoire.* Paris: Presses Universitaires de France, 1964.

Dibbern, Mary. "Introduction: A Short History of the Versions." In *The Tales of Hoffmann: A Performance Guide.* Edited by Mary Dibbern, xvii–xxiii. Hillsdale, NY: Pendragon Press, 2002.

——, ed. *The Tales of Hoffmann: A Performance Guide.* Hillsdale, NY: Pendragon Press, 2002.

Diebold, Bernhard. Review of *Tales of Hoffmann.* In *Frankfurter Zeitung*, February 17, 1929. Reprinted in *Experiment Krolloper, 1927–1931*, by Hans Curjel, 264–67. Munich: Prestel-Verlag, 1975.

Diehl, Huston. "The Iconography of Violence in English Renaissance Tragedy." *Renaissance Drama* 11 (1980): 27–44.

Dorsch, T. S. Introduction. In *The Comedy of Errors*, by William Shakespeare, edited by T. S. Dorsch, 1–38. Cambridge: Cambridge University Press (New Cambridge Shakespeare edition), 1988.

Duckworth, George E. *The Nature of Roman Comedy: A Study in Popular Entertainment.* Princeton: Princeton University Press, 1952.

Dupont, Florence. *Daily Life in Ancient Rome.* Translated by Christopher Woodall. Oxford: Blackwell, 1992.

Edmunds, Lowell. *Theatrical Space and Historical Place in Sophocles' Oedipus at Colonus.* New York: Rowman and Littlefield, 1996.

Elam, Keir. *The Semiotics of Theatre and Drama.* London: Routledge, 1988; reprinted 1991.

Eng, David L. "In the Shadows of a Diva: Committing Homosexuality in David Henry Hwang's *M. Butterfly.*" *Amerasia Journal* 20, no. 1 (1994): 93–116.

Engelstein, Stefani. *Anxious Anatomy: The Conception of the Human Form in Literary and Naturalist Discourse.* Albany: State University of New York Press, 2008.

Escolme, Bridget. *Talking to the Audience: Shakespeare, Performance, Self.* Routledge: London, 2005.

Esslin, Martin. *The Theatre of the Absurd.* Garden City, NY: Anchor Books, 1961; revised ed. 1969.

Fiorentino, P. A. *Comédies et comédiens.* 2 vols. Paris: Michel Lévy Frères, 1866.

Fish, Stanley. "Literature in the Reader: Affective Stylistics." *New Literary History* 2, no. 1 (Autumn 1970): 123–62.

——. *Self-Consuming Artifacts: The Experience of Seventeenth-Century Literature.* Berkeley: University of California Press, 1972.

Fiske, John. *Understanding Popular Culture.* Boston: Unwin Hyman, 1989.

Foakes, R. A. Introduction. In *The Comedy of Errors*, by William Shakespeare, edited by R. A. Foakes, xi–lv. London: Methuen (The Arden Shakespeare, 2nd series), 1968.

Ford, John. *'Tis Pity She's a Whore.* Edited by N. W. Bawcutt. Lincoln, NE: Nebraska University Press, 1966.

Foster, Hal. *Compulsive Beauty*. Cambridge, MA: MIT Press, 1993.

Freedman, Barbara. "Egeon's Debt: Self-Division and Self-Redemption in *The Comedy of Errors*." *English Literary Renaissance* 10, no. 3 (1980): 360–83.

———. *Staging the Gaze: Postmodernism, Psychoanalysis, and Shakespearean Comedy*. Ithaca: Cornell University Press, 1991.

Freud, Sigmund. *Introductory Lectures on Psychoanalysis*. Translated and edited by James Strachey. New York: Norton, 1966.

Fujita, Minoru, and Michael Shapiro, eds. *Transvestism and the Onnagata Traditions in Shakespeare and Kabuki*. Folkestone, UK: Global Oriental, 2006.

Fumerton, Patricia. *Cultural Aesthetics: Renaissance Literature and the Practice of Social Ornament*. Chicago: University of Chicago Press, 1991.

Gabo, Naum. "Art and Science." In *Gabo: Constructions, Sculpture, Paintings, Drawings, Engravings*, edited by Naum Gabo, 180–81. Cambridge, MA: Harvard University Press, 1957.

———, ed. *Gabo: Constructions, Sculpture, Paintings, Drawings, Engravings*. Cambridge, MA: Harvard University Press, 1957.

Garber, Marjorie. *Vested Interests: Cross-Dressing and Cultural Anxiety*. New York: Routledge, 1992.

Gardner, Martin, ed. *Alice's Adventures in Wonderland* and *Through the Looking-Glass and What Alice Found There*. In *The Annotated Alice*, by Lewis Carroll (Charles Lutwidge Dodgson). New York: New American Library, 1974.

Garner, Jr., Stanton B. *Bodied Spaces: Phenomenology and Performance in Contemporary Drama*. Ithaca: Cornell University Press, 1994.

Gautier, Théophile. *A History of Romanticism*. In *The Works of Théophile Gautier*. 16 vols. Edited and translated by Frederick C. de Sumichrast. New York: George D. Sproul, 1902.

Genet, Jean. *The Balcony*. Translated by Bernard Frechtman. New York: Grove, 1958; revised ed. 1966.

———. *The Maids* and *Deathwatch*. Translated by Bernard Frechtman. New York: Grove, 1954.

Gernsheim, Helmut. *A Concise History of Photography*. London: Thames & Hudson, 1965. Reprinted New York: Dover, 1986.

Giacosa, Giuseppe, and Luigi Illica. *Madama Butterfly*. Translated by Frank Granville Barker. Hayes, UK: EMI Records, 1989.

Ginisty, Paul. *La Vie d'un théâtre*. Paris: Schleicher Frères, 1898.

Gleason, Maud W. *Making Men: Sophists and Self-Presentation in Ancient Rome*. Princeton: Princeton University Press, 1985.

Goffman, Erving. *The Presentation of Self in Everyday Life*. Garden City, NY: Anchor, 1959.

Gosson, Stephen. *Playes Confuted in Five Actions* (1582). Reprinted New York: Garland, 1972.

Grand Dictionnaire Universel du XIXe Siècle. Paris: Larousse, 1869.

Greenblatt, Stephen. *Shakespearean Negotiations: The Circulation of Social Energy in Renaissance England*. Berkeley: University of California Press, 1988.

Gropius, Walter. Introduction. In *The Theater of the Bauhaus*, edited by Walter Gropius and Arthur S. Wensinger, translated by Arthur S. Wensinger, 7–14. Middletown, CT: Wesleyan University Press, 1961.

———"Program of the Staatliche Bauhaus in Weimar." Weimar: Staatliche Bauhaus, 1919. Reprinted in *Das Bauhaus*, edited by Hans M. Wingler. Cologne: Verlag Gebr.

Rasch & Co., 1962. *Das Bauhaus* republished as *The Bauhaus*, edited by Joseph Stein, translated by Wolfgang Jabs and Basil Gilbert, 31–33. Cambridge: MIT Press, 1969; revised eds. 1976 and 1978.

Gropius, Walter, and Arthur S. Wensinger, eds. *The Theater of the Bauhaus.* Translated by Arthur S. Wensinger. Middletown, CT: Wesleyan University Press, 1961.

Gurr, Andrew. *The Shakespearean Stage, 1574–1642.* Cambridge: Cambridge University Press, 1992.

Gurr, Andrew, and Mariko Ichikawa. *Staging in Shakespeare's Theatres.* Oxford: Oxford University Press, 2000.

Gussow, Mel. *Edward Albee: A Singular Journey.* New York: Simon and Schuster, 1999.

Haber, Judith. "'My Body Bestow upon My Women': The Space of the Feminine in *The Duchess of Malfi.*" *Renaissance Drama* n.s. 28 (1997): 133–59.

Hall, Edward T. *The Hidden Dimension.* Garden City, NY: Doubleday, 1966.

Harris, John Wesley. *The Traditional Theatre of Japan: Kyogen, Noh, Kabuki, and Puppetry.* Lewiston, NY: Edwin Mellen, 2006.

Hattaway, Michael. *Elizabethan Popular Theatre: Plays in Performance.* London: Routledge, 1982.

Heyworth, Peter. *Otto Klemperer, His Life and Times.* Cambridge: Cambridge University Press, 1983.

Hemmings, F. W. J. *The Theatre Industry in Nineteenth-Century France.* Cambridge: Cambridge University Press, 1993.

Hervey, Charles. *The Theatres of Paris.* Paris: Galignani & Co., 1847.

Hoffmann, E. T. A. *Die Serapions-Bruder.* Edited by Walter Muller-Seidel. Darmstadt: Wissenschaftliche Buchgesellschaft, 1966.

——. *Tales of E. T. A. Hoffmann.* Edited and translated by Leonard J. Kent and Elizabeth C. Knight. Chicago: University of Chicago Press, 1972.

Hollander, Martha. *An Entrance for the Eyes: Space and Meaning in Seventeenth-Century Dutch Art.* Berkeley: University of California Press, 2002.

Houssaye, Arsène. *Les Confessions: souvenirs d'un demi-siècle, 1830–1880.* Paris: E. Dentu, 1885.

Huebert, Ronald. *John Ford, Baroque English Dramatist.* Montreal: McGill-Queen's University Press, 1977.

Huston, Hollis. *The Actor's Instrument: Body, Theory, Stage.* Ann Arbor: University of Michigan Press, 1992.

Hwang, David Henry. Afterword. In *M. Butterfly,* by David Henry Hwang, 94–100. New York: Plume, 1986.

——. *M. Butterfly.* New York: Plume, 1986.

Ishioka, Eiko. *Eiko on Stage.* New York: Callaway, 2000.

Issacharoff, Michael. *Discourse as Performance.* Stanford: Stanford University Press, 1989.

Jagendorf, Zvi. "*Coriolanus*: Body Politic and Private Parts." *Shakespeare Quarterly* 41, no. 4 (Winter 1990): 455–69.

Jouslin de la Salle, Armand-François. *Souvenirs sur le Théâtre-Français.* Paris: E. Paul, 1900.

Kelso, Ruth. *Doctrine for the Lady of the Renaissance.* Urbana, IL: University of Illinois Press, 1956.

Kern, Stephen. *The Culture of Time and Space, 1880–1918.* Cambridge, MA: Harvard University Press, 1983.

Kernodle, George R. *From Art to Theatre.* Chicago: University of Chicago Press, 1944.

Kiefer, Frederick. *Shakespeare's Visual Theatre: Staging the Personified Characters.* Cambridge: Cambridge University Press, 2003.

Kiesler, Frederick. "Debacle of the Modern Theatre." *The Little Review* 11 (Winter 1926): 61–72.

Kinney, Arthur F. "Shakespeare's *Comedy of Errors* and the Nature of Kinds." In *The Comedy of Errors: Critical Essays,* edited by Robert S. Miola, 155–81. New York: Garland, 1997.

Knowles, Ric. *Reading the Material Theatre.* Cambridge: Cambridge University Press, 2004.

Köhler, Gerald. "Here Light Becomes Space: László Moholy-Nagy's Dramatic Theater Cosmos." In *László Moholy-Nagy Retrospective,* edited by Ingrid Pfeiffer and Max Hollein, 96–109. London: Prestel, 2009.

Koss, Juliet. "Bauhaus Theater of Human Dolls." *The Art Bulletin* 85, no. 4 (December 2003): 724–45.

———. *Modernism after Wagner.* Minneapolis: University of Minnesota Press, 2010.

Kostelanetz, Richard, ed. *Moholy-Nagy.* New York: Praeger, 1970.

———. "Moholy-Nagy: The Risk and Necessity of Artistic Adventurism." In *Moholy-Nagy,* edited by Richard Kostelanetz, 3–16. New York: Praeger, 1970.

———. Preface. In *Moholy-Nagy,* edited by Richard Kostelanetz, xiii–xiv. New York: Praeger, 1970.

Lalo, Charles. *La Beauté et l'instinct sexuel.* Paris: Flammarion, 1922.

Lan, Jules. *Mémoires d'un chef de claque.* Paris: Librairie Nouvelle, 1883.

Lancashire, Anne. "The Emblematic Castle in Shakespeare and Middleton." In *Mirror Up to Shakespeare: Essays in Honour of G. R. Hibbard,* edited by J. C. Gray, 223–41. Toronto: University of Toronto Press, 1984.

Laurence, Ray. *Roman Pompeii: Space and Society.* London: Routledge, 1994.

Le Breton, André. *Le Théâtre romantique.* Paris: Boivin et Cie, 1928.

Leach, Eleanor Winsor. *The Rhetoric of Space: Literary and Artistic Representations of Landscape in Republican and Augustan Rome.* Princeton: Princeton University Press, 1988.

Leach, Robert. *Makers of Modern Theatre: An Introduction.* London: Routledge, 2004.

Lee, Quentin. "Between the Oriental and the Transvestite." *Found Object* 2 (Fall 1993): 45–59.

Lefebvre, Henri. *The Production of Space.* Translated by Donald Nicholson-Smith. Oxford: Blackwell, 1991.

Les Beaux-Arts. revue nouvelle 3 (1861).

Linnebach, Georg. Review of *Tales of Hoffmann.* In *Blätter der Staatsoper,* January 1924. Reprinted in *Experiment Krolloper, 1927–1931,* by Hans Curjel, 162–63. Munich: Prestel-Verlag, 1975.

Lopez, Jeremy. *Theatrical Convention and Audience Response in Early Modern Drama.* Cambridge: Cambridge University Press, 2003.

Lough, John. *Paris Theatre Audiences in the Seventeenth and Eighteenth Centuries.* Oxford: Oxford University Press, 1957.

Low, Jennifer A. *Manhood and the Duel: Masculinity in Early Modern Drama and Culture.* New York: Palgrave, 2003.

Low, Jennifer A., and Nova Myhill, eds. *Imagining the Audience in Early Modern Drama, 1558–1642.* New York: Palgrave, 2011.

———. "Introduction: Audience and Audiences." In *Imagining the Audience in Early Modern Drama, 1558–1642,* edited by Jennifer A. Low and Nova Myhill, 1–17. New York: Palgrave, 2011.

Malliot, A. L. *La Musique au théâtre*. Paris: Amyot, 1863.

Marrapodi, Michele, ed. *Shakespeare's Italy: Functions of Italian Locations in Renaissance Drama*. Manchester: Manchester University Press, 1993.

Marshall, Cynthia. *The Shattering of the Self: Violence, Subjectivity, and Early Modern Texts*. Baltimore: Johns Hopkins University Press, 2002.

——. "Wound-man: *Coriolanus*, Gender, and the Theatrical Construction of Interiority." In *Feminist Readings of Early Modern Culture*, edited by Valerie Traub, M. Lindsay Kaplan, and Dympna Callaghan, 93–118. Cambridge: Cambridge University Press, 1996.

Matthews, Brander. *French Dramatists of the Nineteenth Century*, 3rd ed. New York: Benjamin Blom, 1968.

Maus, Katharine Eisaman. *Inwardness and Theater in the English Renaissance*. Chicago: University of Chicago Press, 1995.

McAuley, Gay. *Space in Performance: Making Meaning in the Theatre*. Ann Arbor: University of Michigan Press, 1999.

McCarthy, Kathleen. *Slaves, Masters, and the Art of Authority in Plautine Comedy*. Princeton: Princeton University Press, 2000.

McGlathery, James M. *E. T. A. Hoffmann*. New York: Twayne-Simon & Schuster, 1997.

McMullan, Gordon. *Renaissance Configurations: Voices, Bodies, Spaces, 1580–1690*. New York: Palgrave, 1998; revised 2001.

Merleau-Ponty, Maurice. *Phenomenology of Perception*. Translated by Colin Smith. London: Routledge, 1962.

Micznik, Vera. "Cio-Cio-San the Geisha." In *A Vision of the Orient: Texts, Intertexts, and Contexts of Madame Butterfly*, edited by Jonathan Wisenthal, Sherrill Grace, Melinda Boyd, Brian McIlroy, and Vera Micznik, 36–58. Toronto: University of Toronto Press, 2006.

Moholy-Nagy, László. "Constructivism and the Proletariat." *MA* (May 1922); excerpted in *Moholy-Nagy*, edited by Richard Kostelanetz, 185–86. New York: Praeger, 1970.

——. "The New Bauhaus and Space Relationships." *American Architect and Architecture* 151 (December 1927); reprinted in *Moholy-Nagy*, edited by Richard Kostelanetz, 104–10. New York: Praeger, 1970.

——. "Position Statement of the Group MA in Vienna to the First Congress of Progressive Artists in Düsseldorf, Germany." Reprinted in *Moholy-Nagy*, edited by Richard Kostelanetz, 186–87. New York: Praeger, 1970.

——. "Theater, Circus, Variety." In *The Theater of the Bauhaus*, edited by Walter Gropius and Arthur S. Wensinger, translated by Arthur S. Wensinger, 49–70. Middletown, CT: Wesleyan University Press, 1961.

——. *Vision in Motion*. Chicago: Paul Theobald and Co., 1961.

——. "Von Material zu Architektur." Munich: Albert Langen Verlag, 1928. Published in English as "The New Vision." Translated by Daphne M. Hoffman. New York: Brewer, Warren, and Putnam, 1930. 3rd ed. reprinted in *The New Vision* and *Abstract of an Artist*, edited by László Moholy-Nagy, 9–64. New York: George Wittenborn, Inc., 1947.

——. "Why Bauhaus Education." *Shelter* 3 (March 1938): 6–21.

Moholy-Nagy, Sibyl. *Moholy-Nagy: Experiment in Totality*. New York: Harper, 1950; 2nd ed. Cambridge, MA: MIT Press, 1969.

Mostow, Joshua S. "Iron Butterfly: Cio-Cio-San and Japanese Imperialism." In *A Vision of the Orient: Texts, Intertexts, and Contexts of Madame Butterfly*, edited by

Jonathan Wisenthal, Sherrill Grace, Melinda Boyd, Brian McIlroy, and Vera Micznik, 181–95. Toronto: University of Toronto Press, 2006.

Mullaney, Steven. *The Place of the Stage: License, Play, and Power in Renaissance England*. Chicago: University of Chicago Press, 1988.

Naylor, Gillian. *The Bauhaus*. New York: Dutton, 1968.

Neill, Michael. "'What Strange Riddle's This?': Deciphering *'Tis Pity She's a Whore*." In *John Ford: Critical Re-Visions*, edited by Michael Neill, 153–80. Cambridge: Cambridge University Press, 1988.

Nelson, Victoria. *The Secret Life of Puppets*. Cambridge, MA: Harvard University Press, 2001.

Newhall, Beaumont. *The History of Photography from 1839 to the Present*. New York: Museum of Modern Art, 1982.

Nicoll, Allardyce. *The Development of the Theatre*. New York: Harcourt Brace, 1952.

Nixon, Paul, trans. *The Two Menaechmuses*. In *Plautus*, Vol. 2, edited by Paul Nixon, 363–487. Cambridge, MA: Harvard University Press; The Loeb Classical Library, 1925; reprinted 1988.

Orgel, Stephen. *The Illusion of Power: Political Theater in the English Renaissance*. Berkeley: University of California Press, 1975.

Orgel, Stephen, and Roy Strong. *Inigo Jones: The Theatre of the Stuart Court*. London: Sotheby Parke Bernet, 1973.

Oxford English Dictionary. Oxford: Oxford University Press, 1986.

Ozaki, Yoseharu. "Shakespeare and Kabuki." In *Transvestism and the Onnagata Traditions in Shakespeare and Kabuki*, edited by Minoru Fujita and Michael Shapiro, 4–20. Folkestone, UK: Global Oriental, 2006.

Palfrey, Simon, and Tiffany Stern. *Shakespeare in Parts*. Oxford: Oxford University Press, 2007.

Panofsky, Erwin. *Studies in Iconology: Humanistic Themes in the Art of the Renaissance*. New York: Harper, 1962.

Parker, Patricia, and Geoffrey Hartman, eds. *Shakespeare and the Question of Theory*. London: Methuen, 1985; reprinted London: Routledge, 1990.

Paster, Gail Kern. *The Body Embarrassed: Drama and the Disciplines of Shame in Early Modern England*. Ithaca: Cornell University Press, 1993.

Pavis, Patrice. "Pour une esthétique de la réception théâtrale." In *La Relation théâtrale*, edited by Victor Bourgy and Régis Durand, 27–54. Lille, France: Presses Universitaires de Lille, 1980.

Piesse, Amanda. "Space for the Self: Place, Persona and Self-Projection in *The Comedy of Errors* and *Pericles*." In *Renaissance Configurations: Voices, Bodies, Spaces, 1580–1690*, edited by Gordon McMullan, 151–70. New York: Palgrave, 1998; revised 2001.

Plautus, Titus Maccius. *Plautus*. 5 vols. Vol. 2 edited and translated by Paul Nixon. Cambridge, MA: Harvard University Press; The Loeb Classical Library, 1925; reprinted 1988.

Proudfoot, Richard, Introduction to *The Comedy of Errors* by William Shakespeare. In *The Arden Shakespeare Complete Works*, edited by Richard Proudfoot, Ann Thompson, and David Scott Kastan. Walker-on-Thames: Arden, 1998.

Puttenham, George. *The Arte of English Poesie* (1589). Reprinted Kent, OH: Kent State University Press, 1970.

Raman, Shankar. "Marking Time: Memory and Market in *The Comedy of Errors*." *Shakespeare Quarterly* 56, no. 2 (2005): 176–205.

Rancière, Jacques. *The Emancipated Spectator*. Translated by Gregory Elliott. London: Verso, 2009.

Remen, Kathryn. "The Theatre of Punishment: David Henry Hwang's *M. Butterfly* and Michel Foucault's *Discipline and Punish*." *Modern Drama* 37, no. 3 (1994): 391–400.

Rich, Frank. "Theater: 'The Balcony' at Harvard." *The New York Times*. January 23, 1986.

Riss, Arthur. "The Belly Politic: *Coriolanus* and the Revolt of Language." *English Literary History* 59, no. 1 (Spring 1992): 53–75.

Roach, Joseph R. *The Player's Passion: Studies in the Science of Acting*. Cranbury, NJ: Associated University Presses, 1985.

Robert Saisburg. *Mémoires d'un Claqueur*. Paris: Constant-Chantpie, 1829.

Röder, Birgit. *A Study of the Major Novellas of E. T. A. Hoffmann*. Rochester, NY: Boydell and Brewer, 2003.

Roll, Maximin (Jean Raphanel). *Souvenirs d'un claqueur et d'un figurant*. Paris: Aux bureau du magasin pittoresque, 1904.

Roller, Matthew B. *Dining Posture in Ancient Rome: Bodies, Values, and Status*. Princeton: Princeton University Press, 2006.

Roth, Philip. "The Play That Dare Not Speak Its Name." *New York Review of Books* 4 (February 25, 1965).

Saal, Ilka. "Performance and Perception: Gender, Sexuality, and Culture in David Henry Hwang's *M. Butterfly*." *Amerikastudien* 43, no. 4 (1998): 629–44.

Salgado, Gamini. "'Time's Deformed Hand': Sequence, Consequence, and Inconsequence in *The Comedy of Errors*." *Shakespeare Survey* 25 (1972): 81–91.

Salingar, L. G. "Time and Art in Shakespeare's Romances." *Renaissance Drama* 9 (1966): 12–17.

Sartre, Jean-Paul. Introduction. In *The Maids* and *Deathwatch*, by Jean Genet. Translated by Bernard Frechtman, 7–31. New York: Grove, 1954.

Saxon, A. H. "A Brief History of the Claque." *Theatre Survey* 5, no. 1 (May 1964): 10–26.

Schechner, Richard. "6 Axioms for Environmental Theatre." *TDR: The Drama Review* 12, no. 3 (Spring 1968): 41–64.

Schlemmer, Oskar. "Man and Art Figure." In *The Theater of the Bauhaus*, edited by Walter Gropius and Arthur S. Wensinger, translated by Arthur S. Wensinger, 17–46. Middletown, CT: Wesleyan University Press, 1961.

——. "Theater (Bühne)." In *The Theater of the Bauhaus*, edited by Walter Gropius and Arthur S. Wensinger, translated by Arthur S. Wensinger, 81–101. Middletown, CT: Wesleyan University Press, 1961.

Schmitt, Natalie Crohn. *Actors and Onlookers: Theater and Twentieth-Century Views of Nature*. Evanston, IL: Northwestern University Press, 1990.

Schwartz, Murray M., and Coppélia Khan, *Representing Shakespeare: New Psychoanalytic Essays*. Baltimore: Johns Hopkins University Press, 1980.

Scribe, Eugène and Ernest Legouvé. *Adrienne Lecouvreur*. Translator unknown. New York: Baker and Godwin, 1866.

Shakespeare, William. *The Riverside Shakespeare*. Edited by G. Blakemore Evans. Boston: Houghton Mifflin, 1974.

Simmel, Georg. "The Picture Frame." *Theory, Culture, and Society* 11, no. 1 (February 1994): 11–17.

Slater, Niall W. *Plautus in Performance: The Theater of the Mind*. Princeton: Princeton University Press, 1985.

Smith, Bruce R. *The Acoustic World of Early Modern England: Attending to the O-Factor*. Chicago: University of Chicago Press, 1999.

Smith, Matthew Wilson. *The Total Work of Art: From Bayreuth to Cyberspace.* New York: Routledge, 2007.

Sofer, Andrew. *The Stage Life of Props.* Ann Arbor: University of Michigan Press, 2003.

Souritz, Elizabeth. "Constructivism and Dance." In *Theatre in Revolution: Russian Avant-Garde Stage Design, 1913–1935,* edited by Nancy Van Norman Baer, 128–43. New York: Thames and Hudson, 1991.

Southern, Richard. "Unusual Forms of Stage." In *Actor and Architect,* edited by Stephen Joseph, 48–56. Manchester: Manchester University Press, 1964.

States, Bert O. *Great Reckonings in Little Rooms: On the Phenomenology of Theater.* Berkeley: University of California Press, 1985.

Stavig, Mark. Introduction. In *'Tis Pity She's a Whore* by John Ford, edited by Mark Stavig, vii–xix. Arlington Heights, IL: AHM, 1966.

Stone, Lawrence. *The Family, Sex, and Marriage in England, 1500–1800.* New York: Harper, 1977.

Stoppard, Tom. *The Real Inspector Hound.* In *The Real Inspector Hound* and *After Magritte,* 1–59. New York: Grove, 1975.

Stubbes, Phillip. *The Anatomie of Abuses* (1583). Reprinted New York: Garland, 1973.

Styan, J. L. *Shakespeare's Stagecraft.* Cambridge: Cambridge University Press, 1967.

Suetonius. *The Lives of the Twelve Caesars,* edited by J. Eugène Reed and translated by Alexander Thomson. Philadelphia: Gebbie, 1889.

Svoboda, Josef. *The Secret of Theatrical Space,* edited and translated by J. M. Burian. New York: Applause, 1993.

Thomas, Sidney. "The Date of *The Comedy of Errors.*" *Shakespeare Quarterly* 7, no. 4 (1956): 377–84.

Traub, Valerie, M. Lindsay Kaplan, and Dympna Callaghan, eds. *Feminist Readings of Early Modern Culture.* Cambridge: Cambridge University Press, 1996.

Treille, Marguerite. *Le Conflit dramatique en France de 1823 à 1830 d'après les journaux de l'époque et les revues du temps.* Paris: Picart Editeur, 1929.

Tuan, Yi-fu. "Space and Place: Humanistic Perspective." In *Philosophy in Geography,* edited by Stephen Gale and Gunnar Olsson, 387–427. Dordrecht: D. Reidel, 1979.

Turner, Henry S. *The English Renaissance Stage: Geometry, Poetics, and the Practical Spatial Arts, 1580–1630.* Oxford: Oxford University Press, 2006.

Ubersfeld, Anne. *Reading Theatre.* Translated by Frank Collins and edited by Paul Perron and Patrick Debbèche. Toronto: University of Toronto Press, 1999.

Valgemae, Mardi. "Albee's Great God Alice." *Modern Drama* 10, no. 3 (December 1967), 267–73.

Veron, Louis-Desire. *Mémoires d'un bourgeois de Paris.* Paris: G. de Gonet, 1853–55.

Vialaret, Jimi B. *L'Applaudissement: claques et cabales.* Paris: Harmattan, 2008.

Walker, Jarrett. "Voiceless Bodies and Bodiless Voices: The Drama of Human Perception in *Coriolanus.*" *Shakespeare Quarterly* 43, no. 2 (Summer 1992), 170–85.

Warren, Michael. "The Perception of Error: The Editing and the Performance of the Opening of *Coriolanus.*" In *Textual Performances: The Modern Reproduction of Shakespeare's Drama,* edited by Lukas Erne and Margaret Jane Kidnie, 127–42. Cambridge: Cambridge University Press, 2004.

Webster, John. *The Duchess of Malfi.* Edited by Elizabeth Brennan. New York: Norton, 1993.

Weimann, Robert. *Shakespeare and the Popular Tradition in the Theater: Studies in the Social Dimension of Dramatic Form and Function.* Baltimore: Johns Hopkins University Press, 1978.

Weißmann, Adolf. Review of *Tales of Hoffmann*. In *Berliner Zeitung am Mittag*, February 13, 1929. Reprinted in *Experiment Krolloper, 1927–1931* by Hans Curjel, 260–62. Munich: Prestel-Verlag, 1975.

Whitford, Frank. *Bauhaus*. London: Thames and Hudson, 1984.

Whitworth, Charles, Introduction. In *The Comedy of Errors* by William Shakespeare, edited by Charles Whitworth, 1–79. Oxford: Oxford University Press, 2002.

Whorf, Benjamin. "Relation of Thought and Behavior in Language." In *Collected Papers on Metalinguistics*. Washington, DC: Foreign Service Institute, 1952.

Wickham, Glynne. *Early English Stages, 1300–1600*. 3 vols. London: Routledge and Kegan Paul, 1963.

Wiles, David. "Seeing is Believing: The Historian's Use of Images." In *Representing the Past: Essays in Performance Historiography*, edited by Charlotte M. Canning and Thomas Postlewait, 215–39. Iowa City: University of Iowa Press, 2010.

———. *A Short History of Western Performance Space*. Cambridge: Cambridge University Press, 2003.

Williams, Tennessee. Production Notes. In *The Glass Menagerie* by Tennessee Williams, 7–10. New York: New Directions, 1945.

Wiseman, Susan J. "*'Tis Pity She's a Whore*: Representing the Incestuous Body." In *Revenge Tragedy*, edited by Stevie Simkin, 208–28. New York: Palgrave, 2001.

Wisenthal, Jonathan, Sherrill Grace, Melinda Boyd, Brian McIlroy, and Vera Micznik, eds. *A Vision of the Orient: Text, Intertexts, and Contexts of Madame Butterfly*. Toronto: University of Toronto Press, 2006.

Worthen, W. B. *Shakespeare and the Force of Modern Performance*. Cambridge: Cambridge University Press, 2003.

Wright, Frank Lloyd. *Frank Lloyd Wright: An Autobiography*. New York: Longmans, Green, and Co., 1932.

Yates, Frances. *The Art of Memory*. London: Pimlico, 1992.

Yoshida, Chiaki. *Kabuki*. Tokyo: Japan Times, 1971.

Ziegler, Georgianna. "My Lady's Chamber: Female Space, Female Chastity in Shakespeare." *Textual Practice* 4, no. 1 (1990): 73–90.

Zschorlich, Paul. Review of *Tales of Hoffmann*. In *Deutsche Zeitung*, February 13, 1929. Reprinted in *Experiment Krolloper, 1927–1931* by Hans Curjel, 263–64. Munich: Prestel-Verlag, 1975.

Index